This book is a must-read if…

- You like reading real-life inspirational stories
- You like to read short stories that you can dip in and out of as you choose
- You are searching for hope
- You are looking to change your life
- You are on a healing journey
- You are searching for something that is missing
- You are looking to connect with other like-minded women who have experienced what you have
- You are considering writing your own inspirational story
- You have a story to tell
- You want to inspire others

Words of Love

"The New Woman: Stories of Kintsugi Experiences is a truly inspiring and empowering book. The 33 women who share their stories are survivors in the fullest sense of the word. It is a privilege to read about their lives and, in particular, how they effected change and transformed themselves into 'the new woman'. No reader can fail to be moved, for the contributors speak to us from the heart.

Their stories are told with a compelling honesty and directness. In the forge of suffering and challenging experiences, each woman has grown in wisdom, and we are invited to grow alongside them. By collecting the diverse stories in this book, Ritu Sharma presents a nurturing network of voices, voices that reach out to us as readers to empathise, and in doing so join them in an ever-growing band of sisterhood."

Dr Debjani Chatterjee MBE FRSL
Writer and Creative Arts Psychotherapist

∞

"This is a great book of some wonderful and amazing stories of powerful women.

The stories in the book make you think deeper and bring you an understanding that kindness is such an important aspect of human nature. We can never know what people are going through. It just makes sense to be kind whenever possible. I am so pleased that these women have spoken about their journeys, paving way for generations to come."

Christine Morlet, CSP
Speech Coach, Positive Influence Specialist

"It's a privilege to endorse Ritu Sharma's new book The New Woman.

What a great book full of inspirational short stories! We can learn so much from other's experiences and lives, as we come through the global pandemic; The New Woman gives us hope.

We all have been in the same storm but we are in different boats, inequalities have come to the surface like never before, yet with grit and determination we can still mend with our golden threads just like the Kintsugi bowls.

Reading about other women's stories has shown me that I'm not alone. We all are fighting battles that no one knows about."

Mandy Sanghera
Advisor at UNESCO MGIEP
Gender equality advocate and human rights activist

"The book is a reflection of this world's 'New Woman'. It is mandatory that men start to acknowledge and support women's journeys and struggles to create a healthy and harmonious world. These stories have depth of resilience, courage and love of authors for themselves and a lesson for others."

Sam Dossa
Emotional Intelligence Business and Personal Coach,
Founder of MenTell Health

"For society to function for the benefit of all, it needs to ensure that every individual irrespective of creed, colour or race has an equal opportunity to shine. This book shows that despite many obstacles and hindrances, it is possible to achieve - I applaud that through these collections of works, stories are being to inspire the next generation and remind them to treat all with respect and dignity and that good will prevail in the end."

Ninder Johal
Chair of The Wolverhampton Towns Fund
NED at West Midlands India Partnership, NED at WM5G
Governor at Wolverhampton University

∞

"Editing The New Woman has been an absolute honour. It has been such a moving and thought-provoking experience to read extraordinary stories from woman all over the world, from so many different backgrounds and cultures. All these women have been broken and then, in true Kintsugi style, have put themselves back together again, piece by piece, in order to become the strong, unbowed, resilient women they are today.

These highly personal and immersive accounts of hope, courage, determination, drive, and sheer grit will stay with you long after you have finished reading. These unflinching tales of fortitude are all stories that need to be heard and told.

The New Woman is a timely reminder of the power of the human spirit."

Olivia Eisinger
Editor

The New Woman

Stories of Kintsugi Experiences

Compiled by

Ritu Sharma

First published in Great Britain in 2021
by Book Brilliance Publishing
265A Fir Tree Road, Epsom, Surrey, KT17 3LF
+44 (0)20 8641 5090
www.bookbrilliancepublishing.com
admin@bookbrilliancepublishing.com

A CIP catalogue record for this book
is available at the British Library.

ISBN 978-1-913770-17-4
Typeset in Avenir
Printed by 4edge Ltd

I dedicate this to all the women who found their power within themselves and to those who are looking to claim that power.

Also, to my most beloved grandmother, Kaushalya Devi, whose life story became a guiding light for me during my transformation.

About Kaushalya UK

Kaushalya UK is a registered, not for profit, community organisation working to empower and uplift women. It is growing organically in leaps and bounds under the dynamic leadership of its founder and CEO Ms. Ritu Sharma, who has dedicated her life to bringing women of this world to rediscover their own power and true worth.

At Kaushalya UK, it is a core belief that all women are naturally empowered and at times need a gentle reminder and a little support to get back up and be who they are meant to be. Kaushalya UK is an inclusive organisation and embraces everyone. All women are important, no matter their race, language, faith, culture, nationality or anything else.

All projects run by the organisation fall under one of the categories of:

- Personal and professional development
- Health and well-being
- Financial education and entrepreneurship
- Social events

www.Kaushalyauk.com
Instagram: KaushalyaUK
https://www.facebook.com/calltowomanpower/

Kintsugi

Kintsugi, also known as Kintsukuroi, is the Japanese art of repairing broken pottery by mending the areas of breakage with lacquer dusted or mixed with powdered gold, silver, or platinum, a method similar to the maki-e technique.

The stories within this book illustrate how the women became broken and in their journey of repair, they have found golden threads that have made them whole again. As they transform, they are even more beautiful and have learned to know their value, just like the increased beauty and value of the Kintsugi bowls.

Trigger Warning

Readers may find some stories trigger an emotional and/or psychological response, with topics including rape, abuse, and domestic violence.

If you are affected by any of these, see the links below and get in touch:

Samaritans
www.samaritans.org

Refuge
www.refuge.org.uk

Rape Crisis England & Wales
https://rapecrisis.org.uk

NSPCC
www.nspcc.org.uk

Child Bereavement UK

www.childbereavementuk.org

Mind
www.mind.org.uk

Cancer Research UK
www.cancerresearchuk.org

Contents

Foreword

It takes a courageous woman to find, use and share her story. Too many women around the world are still silenced and when they speak out, it feels as if they are climbing Mount Everest. Marianne Williamson reminds women that it is not the fear of failure that frightens them, but the fear of being great, just like we are born to be.

When a woman reveals her soul to you through her story, it is clear to see the strength, capacity and resilience it took her to rise above her challenge. All women experience varying levels of adversity in their lives, and the stories within *The New Woman* exemplify not only this but her power within.

When women come together to share their stories, you can see the similarities that bind them. Whether you have experienced abuse, loss or mental health issues, or not, you will be moved by the tremendous honesty of each woman's words. Whilst many situations appear startling, the reader will marvel at how each woman found the strength to take action that would change her life forever. This is what makes *The New Woman* so inspirational.

The beauty that Ritu Sharma brings to this book is through the concept of Kintsugi – a Japanese art form. When a bowl is broken or damaged, they simply mend it with gold. Not only does this complete the bowl once more, but it is also found to be more valuable and beautiful.

As you sip your coffee and read each chapter, do not be surprised if a tear rolls down your cheek. For you will be moved to connect with these woman, thank them for their bravery and know that despite their plights, they have found that self-love is the key to change and moving forward.

Now that these women have dared to share their stories, they are also ready to rise, take their place and follow a purpose that makes a difference in the lives of others. Without the trials of their journey, they would not be able to stand in their power as The New Woman, ready to claim her crown and walk her path with decisiveness, dignity and determination to create a better world.

Lady Waynett Peters
Founder of The Extraordinary Achievers

Introduction

The New Woman: Stories of Kintsugi Experiences is a dream project.

Stories are essential building blocks of empathy and human connection. Sharing our stories become of utmost importance if and when these reflect lived experiences and are capable of both bringing healing and changing lives.

All stories collected in this book are those of transformation. These are stories of adversity and women warriors beating these challenges and coming out as winners. Many of these wonder women have now turned back to extend a helping hand to those still stuck in the black hole. This is the power of a woman – to have experienced the highest degree of pain, and yet still be capable of sharing unconditional love.

The New Woman materialised as a result of a strong calling to facilitate the sharing of these valuable stories. There is a need for a book like this to be read by many women, for various reasons. The main reason is that this book has the potential to become a survival guide for someone living a similar experience, giving them hope and power.

The sole understood purpose of the book is to create a wave of empowerment globally for women, helping them see that they are not their struggles; they are more, way more than that. It is possible to emerge from the storm as whole. Women must accept that their scars make them even more beautiful and valuable. There are undoubtedly other reasons for this book to be created, which I am not aware of unconsciously and are yet to be revealed.

I am truly thankful to Sam Dossa for his consistent support on this project.

I am blessed to have been joined by all the co-authors on this journey who have shared their very personal and extremely powerful stories in this book. Each one of you is a beacon of light for many. Your decision and courage to share your story is immeasurably valuable. You are going to be the reason for someone, somewhere, to believe in themselves and say,

'You are the reason I did not give up.'

Respect!

Ritu Sharma

New Woman 1

Illa Khagram

I Am Every Woman

"My love for you is a journey;
Starting at forever, and ending at never."
Anonymous

In 2009, when I was going through the most difficult period of my life, I met a beautiful soul called Michael. What occurred over the next few years was so significant, so deep and so profound, that I have to share this with you, dear reader. How I died the deaths that I did and more, to finally come home to my heart. Not to the I, the name, the titles, not to the me, the self-centred one that feels the world revolves around, but to "that", the one that truly comes alive! I discovered the Radiant Lotus.

I discovered myself, I let go of the inhabitant character of who I thought was me; brief and limited, to discovering the true habitant who lived in my body.

This story is a part of my life, my legacy of conversations with Michael, who challenged the assumptions that I was making; what happened – I woke up! The one who woke up is the one who is sharing her heart in this book with you all.

This book is not only about my love and respect but this is my gratitude to the one I refer to as "Michael, my father", for he saw me, not the shy, timid, unconfident one, but the one he called the "Radiant Lotus". I share this journey with you with my open heart so that you too can awaken within you what is yearning and crying to be heard.

To start this conversation, Michael asked me one question:

"Who is Illa?"

I couldn't answer, I didn't know. My heart shook like a chandelier on the ceiling that had just been rattled by a fast-paced train! I did not know why it shook, it just did! The shaking in my heart kept me awake for days and nights pondering on this question, for Michael did not ask me, "Who are you?" but "Who is Illa?"

If he had asked me, "Who are you?", rather than "Who is Illa?" perhaps there was something that could have surfaced, perhaps I would have known that there was more to me than who I think that I am, but I couldn't think what I could answer to "Who is Illa?"!

It was truly in that moment I didn't know who I was anymore!

I am every woman, and you are every woman and together we build a world; a world of love, peace and harmony. Yet, it was not always like this – not for me and perhaps not for anyone of you.

This is my story but I am NOT the story, and as I share a little piece of my story with you, dear reader, I hope that it can awaken you to understand your story and know that we are the shining diamonds that have had to go through fire to shine our light. I shine my light with you, and know that you will shine your light too.

Nothing happens without a reason for anyone of us. The reasons can sometimes be so unbeknown to us until later in life. These are the stories and the learning from them that have created my power of three:

- In an abusive marriage
- My five-year-old son taken away – I have not seen him for 23 years
- Left without hope

But it didn't just start that way; it started years ago when I was sexually abused as a child, but could not speak out. It hit me hard; I started to hide, and I lost my spark, for it was in those years I lost the identity of who I am!

I guess like many of us, I learnt to hide behind a veil, I learnt to only show the side of me that would in my heart be acceptable to the rest of the world; can you relate to this, dear reader? I hope that my words can touch your heart so that you can shed the exterior façade and shine your light to be you, the one that is so unique and pure, your true you!

So years passed after that incident of abuse, I guess somewhere I had hidden the feeling of inadequacy, of being not worthy, but I soon discovered that I had never forgiven the abuser or myself! Can you imagine how people hold pain from the past, and bring it into the present, that is destroying to the soul? I went through my teen years quite a happy youngster. I had beautiful parents who have loved me all my life and supported me in whatever path I chose. This was the greatest gift, for I had no idea how much I would need the love of my parents in the future. Look around you, for we are always gifted with those that will love us, even when we feel the world has crumpled around us. Know that we are given strength through them, so that you can awaken to your true self.

When I was 18 years old, my elder sister's two friends were going on a safari, and asked us to join them. We were excited; my sister and I were jumping up and down with joy when our parents agreed! I know today all things happen at the time when they are meant to happen. As we were about to go on holiday, I received a marriage proposal!

I didn't even know what marriage meant. I had a deep love for music, I was a dancer and I had a yearning all my life to play the sitar, an Indian string instrument. Well that was all it took! I was told that the boy's mother was a sitar player! I didn't even think about the fact that I was still a child; I made my mind up that was who I would marry!

Sadly, the day of my marriage was the worst day of my life, because I knew that I had made a mistake. I couldn't turn back now, at least that was what I thought! I felt so lonely throughout those 14 years of marriage. I had moved from the UK to tropical Mombasa, Kenya and my life was not how I could have ever imagined it – there was no love or respect for me, I was treated like an insignificant being. I was abused, both mentally and emotionally. Who is able to show the wounds of that unseen abuse?

I had to maintain a joyful and happy façade for the rest of the world. But I had already been doing this all my life anyway, so this came naturally. I was in a prison, I was imprisoned in my own body! The abuse continued, and finally rape followed. I died a very slow death that day, for how can I ever let anyone know that my own husband had too much to drink, got angry and forced himself on me...

My suffering was deep, so deep that I had contemplated suicide. In my eyes there was no life left, and I felt that I had nothing left to live for. But the thought of my parents kept me going. I never told my parents what was going on, for as they were faraway in England, what could they have done? So I pretended everything was great, and that I was happy. They knew, of course, in their hearts, that I wasn't happy and that something was wrong!

Marrying a man because his mother played the sitar, was a mistake; she would not even let me anywhere near the sitar. She gave lessons to others, but told me outright that she would not teach me, as I was not worthy of learning! Perhaps she only voiced what I already felt in my heart, for we project outwards what we resonate inwards, so the outside becomes a mirror. This went on for years; I started losing weight until one day I decided to take my own life. I didn't know how, and I also even knew this was the worst thing that I could ever contemplate, but I just didn't know what to do!

That evening, a torrent of abuse was thrown at me, and late at night, past midnight after my husband came to the bedroom drunk, I said, "I can't live like this anymore!"

He outstretched the lighter in his hand towards me and said, "Well if you're going to go, go!" I found myself in flames on the floor. He was kicking me and at the same time trying to throw water over me, to put the fire out. But he kicked me very hard and at some point, I passed out.

I woke up in the room next door and I was in agony, begging them to take me to the hospital, but they wouldn't do it and waited until morning. By that time, I was now an emergency case. They then rushed me to the hospital, where I was admitted to the ICU and operating theatre to save my life.

I was in hospital for 37 days recovering from burns to three-quarters of my body! My husband didn't mentally abuse me any less in hospital; in fact, the nurse looking after me told him to stop his behaviour, otherwise she would report him!

What kept me going was going within, creating the peace within, calming whatever was happening outside, not disturbing me on the inside. I found great strength in this and strength from the beautiful nurse who nursed me back to health; she was an angel in my life, she boosted my confidence. I confided in her about everything that was happening. She was another being sent to give me the empowerment to keep going; I am eternally indebted to her!

Soon after I was sent home and on the road to recovery, I conceived. I was so happy, at the same time apprehensive, but I accepted that this is a gift. My pregnancy was very difficult, and I was at a high-risk of losing my baby, but this little baby was my hope, my freedom to love and be loved, my joy. I did everything that was asked of me. I took care of myself, for this divine being inside of me was my hope!

My husband at that time totally transformed and although he still drank, he seemed to be kinder to me. I guess somehow this was his way of healing too – who knows? For I know we each have a story, and I learnt to forgive and accept!

On 21st October 1992, my son was born; this was the happiest day of my life, for it was a day that I became a mother. I had so much love in my heart and so many dreams, and I knew that I would make sure that my beautiful baby boy would see love, compassion, learn respect and more, to grow to be a gentleman, unlike his father, and would learn to respect women!

I breastfed my child for two years and cared for him, washed his clothes, always made fresh organic baby food – I did everything that I could, but two years later, the abuse started up again. I was put in situations where my integrity was pushed and then they started teaching my son to call me names, derogatory names. He believed he was doing the right thing, but he didn't understand until he saw the tears in my eyes, and said, "Maa, sorry, I sorry, Maa."

This continued but I made sure that my son would learn the right ways. But then the mental and emotional abuse started towards my son! In his own house, he was not allowed to be a child, because the daughter of the family – my husband's sister – also had a son, who now took importance over my son even though this was his birthplace.

When a mother constantly sees her child crying, she springs into action. The last straw for me was when the lights all went out in Mombasa, it was pitch black and my son was crying and wouldn't let me put him down anywhere. The food wasn't cooked, and my husband's sister was due to come and pick up food that she ordered me to make. But I couldn't do it as there was no electricity! There was a huge fight and I was told, "This is not your house, you cannot neglect things. You will obey the rules of this house. Do you understand?"

I was shaking in my body from fear and that was the day that I said, "That's it, no more!" and I begged the universe to help me get out of this life. A day or so later, my father rang out the blue and asked if I could come visit the UK as my grandmother was dying. To my amazement and a stroke of a human heart awakened, they said yes. Remember, I was totally reliant on them, I could not work as I was a British citizen.

When the day came that my son and I were travelling to the UK, I had already packed knowing that I was never coming back, but suddenly on that morning, my now ex-husband decided he was going to come too. My heart sank in despair and all I felt was that the prison guard is keeping the prisoner hostage!

When we landed in the UK, my home, my place, I felt peace, but when we arrived at my parents he started being abusive again and I knew this was never going to end! I told him, "This is it! I cannot come back with you! I can't live like this and cannot allow my child to grow up in an abusive home and be afraid that my own son will continue this way of being and thinking."

He threatened me, and I found a window of opportunity when he forced me to leave my parents' house even though I was there for my grandmother. He forced me to go and stay at his acquaintance's house. I had 10 minutes where he went out and so I packed my son's toys and clothes, then ran out of the house with my child. I left with nothing; no money, no clothes and no phone! I managed to walk to a place where I knew someone and asked her to take me to the nearest women's refuge. I begged her not to tell anyone where I was. "Please," I said. "They will try to hurt my family and me!"

When I arrived at the refuge, I called him to let him know that I was not taking his son away from him but as he was just five years old, he still needed his mother! I was not coming back and he needed to understand this! I tried everything, everything, to do this the right way but how can there ever be a right way when abuse is all that is there? He threatened to kill me, to kill my family, and every abuse that he could, and in the end the people at the refuge said to put the phone down as it was pure torture.

I stayed in the refuge out of fear as I was still being threatened, and then I received a court order that I had to attend a hearing as I had been accused of abduction – ABDUCTION! I couldn't get my head or my heart around this accusation. How could he do this to the mother of his child! If I was convicted, I would be sentenced to prison!

On the day of the hearing, the judge totally ruled abduction out and said that it was a very manipulative way of bringing this to court as there was no evidence or clear case of abduction. The judge said to my ex-husband, "She has called you over 10 times and was verbally abused and threatened by you. She was trying to sort this out. It is appalling that you have brought this case to the high court!"

However, the judge then said that due to the Hague Convention, this case of custody and divorce would need to be dealt by the justice system and courts in Kenya!

What happened to me on that day was I died inside a million deaths. I wept tears that I didn't even know I had anymore; all I could think about was how could they separate me from my child like this because of a law! Don't lives matter? My son was only five years old – he didn't deserve this!

The judge gave one month for us to reconcile. How do you reconcile after your husband is willing to put you in prison! There was no way back now, and I tried to see my son but he wouldn't let me anywhere near my own child!

It felt like my every core had been ripped out of me, when he was given his passport and fled back to Kenya with my son without any communication. That was 23 years ago and I have not seen my child since.

The trauma continued, the battle continued and I had to do the one and only thing that I could – I had to learn to forgive him, forgive them, forgive those who abused me through my life. My experiences and finding forgiveness has led me to the place I find myself in today.

I work with others to help them be happy and healthy. I had the honour of being a student of my Guru, Pt Shri Ram Sharma Acharya, and I met my most beloved Tao Grandmaster, Dr and Master Zhi Gang Sha, who is my teacher. He has taught me to be a Soul Healer. During this time, I experienced deep peace in my heart when I learnt to let it all go; there was no other way!

"In the end, only three things matter:
how much you loved
how gently you lived
how gracefully you let go."
Buddha

I learnt to forgive – unconditional Forgiveness brings inner Joy and inner Peace.

I learnt the power of service – to Serve is to make others happier and healthier.

I learnt the power of unconditional Love, Compassion and Light to be the NEW WOMAN.

Letting go is a deep and powerful process and know, dear reader, that your life matters but it matters not because of the experiences. It is the past – let it go and be free, for the experiences are what took you through the fire to become the shining light, the diamond that you are; please know that you matter!

I offer you my greatest love, from my heart and soul, love and gratitude, Illa.

New Woman 2

Tiffany Henkel

Birth of a Beauty: Transforming Into Your Whole Self

"Healing can get ugly, healing may come with a thousand tears. And that's okay.
Embrace that dark side of healing, so you tap into the light that's been buried deep inside you."
Michael Tavon
Poet

What do you love about yourself? If you don't immediately hear an excited voice in your head shouting all of the enormously amazing things about yourself, chances are your critical self is louder. You will know what this looks like if you've ever seen a woman minimise her achievements, apologise for asking for her needs to be met, and always supporting others tirelessly while denying the same support from herself. The story that follows is the result of seven arduous years of transformation, and is just one example of a journey from living for others, to living as a whole new woman.

I have always wanted to have a connection to someone who saw all of me and was only mine.

Ever since I was a little girl with wispy white blonde 'flyaways' snapped into bright barrettes, I longed for someone to play with that would always be there and always want to play the way I wanted. I grew up playing with my two older sisters and a few neighbourhood friends, so this inner feeling of not feeling whole, of missing someone close that I couldn't remember, was all the more isolating as it was confusing.

When I was around four years old, I knocked on my sisters' shared bedroom door to ask them to play. Instead of obliging me, they thought it good fun to push past me and run down the stairs, through the hallway and kitchen and down the basement stairs, running all the way into my father's workshop, whilst I followed them, then turning around and running all the way back up the stairs, turning off all of the lights and finally locking the basement door with me in the dark. I was barely able to reach up to pop the lock, wedging my tiny feet on the kitchen floor under the basement door to rescue myself, then ran crying to my exhausted mother about their mean trick. I would spend the greater part of my young life running from the dark of loneliness, chasing after others for their love and attention.

Over the span of my childhood, I only had a few close friends, all of whom moved on a few years after becoming friends. My first best friend moved after kindergarten, and my now lifelong best friend moved 500 miles away after seventh grade year. Both of these were significant early experiences of abandonment, as I had no control over their leaving. Crucially, in the fifth grade, my best friend Christina and I formed an instantly tight duo; we shared several common interests, laughter, and our academic accolades. For the next several years, we were constantly talking about books, writing each other short stories, ruminating on the next colour for our braces, singing songs in choir, playing our clarinets in band, and going to each other's house for sleepovers.

To me, I had finally found what I felt was missing, the companionship that I had so craved. We were invincible when we were together. With our protective best friend standing behind us, defending the other girl with their sharp wit and proud tone, there was nothing we couldn't overcome.

The harshness of our early years as women set in during our seventh grade year. This is the age when the crucible of society sets in to stratify young humans by socioeconomic status, appearance, ability, sexuality, to try and form socially accepted ideal women. Girls in our year were experiencing their periods for the first time, learning how to shave off the fine child hairs on their legs to escape gym class ridicule, and beginning to affect our appearances in other ways. We slathered on too much slippery lip gloss, coated our faces in glitter, and the rebellious ones outlined our eyes in jet black eyeliner, in a ritual of unbecoming girls and starting our years-long struggle with our bodies as women.

For me, this was the year I learned I was not desired, either by the young boys who called me "anorexic", a term they had only recently learned from our health studies class, or by the girls with higher socioeconomic status who rejected me on the playground, throwing sneers at me as I approached. This rejection would act as the basis of my perception of my own attractiveness to the opposite sex, and my lack of desire to form close female friendships with other women. By the end of that year, Christina and I would learn just how far into the world of adulthood some of our classmates were, with talk of drugs and twelve year olds having sex in suburbia. Through it all, Christina was there, until the fateful day her mother moved her and her sisters to Virginia the summer before eighth grade, leaving me defenceless to the bullies, and as I told her through tears 20 years later on our soul sisters' trip to Hawaii, abandoned.

I filled my teenage years in high school with enough after school activities to have a lot of acquaintances and several close friends, which helped me not feel so unliked. There was mild interest from the guys I encountered, but I was very headstrong about focusing on academics, and even more headstrong about my first kiss being with someone I really liked. With that, I passed into my college years without a first love or first kiss, until I was introduced to "Adam" during a fraternity party freshman year. Adam was the gallant young man who defended me from being pulled into a game of bobbing for beers and paid attention to me when his friend Steve, who had invited me, ignored me.

In the days following that initial meeting, I remember standing in the shower, when out of nowhere my mind was flooded with his name over and over in my head, overcome with light and an excitement about him. Significant people rarely come into your life without fanfare. I was so hooked on him that every Tuesday I timed my walk to class perfectly to coincide with his walk to the distant engineering campus. My heart would pulse in my chest, and my limbs would vibrate with excitement anytime a tall guy with dark hair walked into the freshman dining hall.

We started dating at the end of our first semester, a dozen red roses delivered at Christmas break announcing my first relationship to my parents. Adam was the first guy I had a crush on who liked me back, and the feeling of being desired was exhilarating! What followed were seven years of companionship, and a closeness to another human that I've never felt before or since. Truth be told, we formed a symbiotic relationship, soothing over each other's emotional void of lonely childhoods with strict church-going parents, with each other's affection and attention. With this being my first relationship, there was a lot I did not know about love and healthy relationships.

In the spring of my freshman year, after returning from our first formal dance for his fraternity, I noted that the campus buses, or Greenies, were still running which meant I could return back to my own dorm on the other side of campus, something I always tried to do when visiting him. When I mentioned it, he replied, "If you leave now, we're no longer dating."

Afraid of losing the closeness and attention that was finally in my grasp, I began quieting my voice over the next several years, following into what he expected and wanted to do, even when it went against my moral compass or desires. In a sense, I abandoned myself to continue to have the inner loneliness filled with his presence, even when I felt hurt by his criticisms. I remember him giving me feedback one day after a party at a friend's house, where another guy at the party mentioned that I seemed stupid, and which Adam said reflected badly on him. I was always like a lovesick puppy, desperate to see him again during our school breaks.

After graduation four years later, I followed him to Kansas City to escape the pain of being apart. In the beginning, we would go out to nice restaurants and out on the town with his new work friends. His desire to socialise quickly deteriorated over the next few years, as I saw him go from very outgoing to self-isolating behaviour, staying up late playing video games during work days, sleeping a lot, and overall ignoring me. I grew concerned that the drug habit I saw on occasion in college had fully taken hold, and when I confronted him about it, he simply said, "I'm not doing it all the time."

Even if I wanted him to not do it at all, I wouldn't have been able to persuade him to stop; I held such little persuasion over him by that time. Still, I desperately desired his companionship to do things I wanted to do, but I was very much denied, only going to loud rock concerts on occasion, and overall, far fewer outings. At the time, I lacked a car of my own, so it was very difficult for me to do things with my new friends at the non-profit organisation where I was employed. I knew we were quickly reaching an end when I turned to adopting the love of my life, Kevin, a Russian Blue cat, for the love and affection I felt draining from our relationship.

To this day, adopting Kevin remains the best decision I've ever made in my life, beyond the day I agreed to end our relationship when he suggested it; he was shocked as I called his bluff. He thought I would never leave! Truthfully, I anticipated it ending when he found a loft to move into, and I didn't even try to have a say in the decision.

The continuation of our relationship was based mainly on his feeling that he needed to financially support me, which ended when I obtained an entry-level corporate job through my own hard work, fostering a mentorship with a woman executive consultant, strategically gaining skills they desired, and my own networking efforts with a former employee of my non-profit, who happened to know the hiring managers. (Adam, of course, said it was all due to him.) The decision to split was further solidified when I went to a wine tasting with him after our break-up, and afterwards he stated, "I wanted to hurt you for talking to him." I didn't know what he was talking about but it turns out he was referring to me asking questions of the much older man who was our wine connoisseur for the evening. I left at the right time.

Starting my new career as a newly heartbroken single woman in the corporate world, I began to live a half-life. For anyone who has left a long emotionally abusive and co-dependent relationship, you know the pain of pulling whatever remains of you out of the wreckage of that relationship and having to survive as a person you do not know. During this time, my undiagnosed anxiety would cause me to shut down emotionally on a daily basis at work with only Autonomous Sensory Meridian Response (ASMR) to soothe me, coffee to motivate me, and flouncy outfits to help bring me joy. At one point, I remember feeling that in order to appear to be collected and put together, I visualised trapping the "weaker" version of myself somewhere deep in my mental space, choosing to "override the system" of anxiety, fear, and sadness by granting my ego full and steady control. I forced myself to be braver than I was, building an armour around my heart.

Meanwhile, I was constantly worried that everyone on my team knew I was doing a terrible job. I so believed in my own failure and comparison to others that I walked into my first annual review after only four months on the team with a full page of what I had done wrong.

One night not long after starting, a shift started to occur. I was awoken by a shrieking beeping sound, and as I clamoured around in the dark to plug in my dying work laptop, I heard a voice fire through my mind. "You can't save others, they have to want to save themselves." This message spoke truth to the emotional labour I tried to do to keep Adam happy, and was the first of many ethereal messages that came to me in the coming years. This supportive and wise voice would become more clear as I grew to know myself more, replacing my critical self-talk.

It was around this time that I sought out therapy for the first time, notably walking back to the office after one session seeing colours brighter than before. I was healing. Eventually, my hard work on a large California client earned me a leadership role on a larger nationwide client. My uncontrolled ego soared at the thought of proving my success by travelling around the United States to various project sites, having a corporate phone, and having a corporate card. I was also provided with an ample supply of stress, managing their day-to-day project load, which wreaked havoc on my mental health and sleep habits. Work and success became my sole focus, choosing to use my workload to numb my heartbreak. On that project I developed survival friendships, each of us working through our own traumas and raging about work stress.

Not long after joining that project, I moved out of my own small apartment into a new condo with one of the couples I had befriended. We learned to support each other through our mental health struggles, which proved pivotal one early December morning on what would have been mine and Adam's tenth anniversary. I awoke around seven that Sunday morning feeling happy and that there were so many possibilities for the new day. Only a few minutes later, Adam's best friend, Steve, called me on my cell phone to tell me Adam had died of a drug overdose. I quickly flipped from what I thought was an accidental dial to bawling large drops of tears and snot. As I was calling my mother, my friend Lewis had woken up to the noise of it all to come see why I was crying. He towered over me in my doorway and was hugging me so tight that when my legs dropped from underneath me, I still remained upright. In the months leading up to the call, Adam and I had started messaging again after years of silence. I had happily learned that not only was he seeking therapy for his anxiety and depression, but he had earned his dream job of working for a tech company in California and was to be planning a trip to Kansas City with his friend.

Out of nowhere, in the week leading up to the phone call, I had struggled through a severe instance of emotional pain, to which I placed heavy floor pillows on top of my torso to act like a weighted blanket to suppress my taxed nervous system. It was as if Adam's emotional pain had latched on to me across the miles. At that point, I had lost my first love for a second time, this time for good. With that, I went back into therapy.

Adam's death coincided with a pivotal moment when I was rekindling a relationship with the first man who gave me the same heart racing and nervous tingles as Adam. Damian and I started our romantic interlude in 2015, starting with us seeing two seals kissing against a deep pink California sunset. What I had been so eager to begin had abruptly met the emotional obstacle of a broken heart that unfortunately, we did not overcome.

There was something about us that made the world more alive than I had known it, an existence of magic and a soul level knowing had entered into my life. During our first date back in Missouri, I arrived at his house for dinner in my little red Chevy, and the moment I pulled into his driveway and saw him waiting in the yard with his dog Henry, I had an overwhelming sense of coming home. Shortly after this began our pattern of on/off separation, when I expressed my eagerness to see him again. Damian and I would connect multiple times over the next several years after each separation.

I began to believe in Twin Flames, two people born from a single split soul in separate bodies, meant to connect and transform each other's life. The fantastical nature of the sunset, the experience of the homecoming, and the synchronicities lured me into believing our connection was meant to be. We both would act so nervous around each other, causing a push-pull reaction as we tried to hide our affections.

One morning, as I was walking through the parking lot into work, I was mentally giving up on him again when he walked towards me out of nowhere, excitedly telling me about how he had spent the weekend learning how to play the guitar, jogging to open the door for me like a good Southern gentleman. The confusion of his feelings left me believing there was always something I could change for him to want to be with me, even though he would say there was no spark and he saw us just as friends. Having not learned my lesson of ignoring the uncomfortable truth about reality, trying to change myself to keep and believing instead in a fantasy, the universe saw fit that I finally listened to my intuition that his inconsistent affections were less than I deserved. The sole purpose of us meeting and igniting a connection like that was so that the universe could force me to accept lessons I was denying, flying me so high and crashing me back down to earth.

In the years that followed, I focused myself on the journey of healing, pushing my heart through a rigorous course, doing whatever I needed to do to push through the pain and darkness of loneliness to self-discovery. Lessons would seemingly speak themselves to me from the universe, and I would oblige. I built up my arsenal of self-love, learning about my attachment style, how to set boundaries, and how I handle unspoken expectations. This painful metamorphosis is something I pushed and dragged myself through over the next seven years, with the end goal being to find a loving relationship.

In reality, your end goal is to find "HER", your inner knowing. Transforming yourself into a new and whole woman is never easy; it is something you are forced into following adversity, and by need, you unlearn your old self into each new version of yourself. This journey will not be easy, but you have to do whatever you need to do to become the New Woman you are meant to be.

Dedication

This is for all of the versions of women I have been and will be on the journey to becoming a New Woman, and for the woman reading this that is just beginning her own journey. There will be light and dark, and you will make it through.

New Woman 3

Andrea Malam

Saving Dreams – Believe in Yourself

"I am an Achiever, a Believer, Empathy is my Super-Power".

"I was born in India – United Kingdom made me."

"I am going to be a charity founder," I said to my family and friends.

I want to make a huge difference to the lives of others by providing awareness and educating the community about the support we can provide to the needy.

I came up with an idea, started working on it and published it!

As work is no longer fulfilling me as it once was, I decided I needed to retire from my day job as a Law Enforcement Officer and start spreading the word on the charity and its aim.

This was the beginning of Saving Dreams – I was the Founder.

Its aims are:

1. to alleviate suffering and homelessness while maintaining human dignity.
2. to enable children and young people to escape poverty with education and support.

Saving Dreams is going from strength to strength with donations and volunteer support in the UK, India and Nepal. I speak from experience, and sometimes it can be lonely heading up a charity, but having a great support network also plays a big part in survival. And yes, we survive being achievers and believing in ourselves.

Being born to parents of British ancestry in India, like all Anglo-Indians that stayed behind after the British Raj, we were a community caught between two cultures.

I believed we had the best of both worlds. We spoke several Indian languages, adapted and tried to get along with everyone. We could savour the celebrations of each religion, which often involved lots of socialising, colour, and of course, lots of food.

My mother was a housewife trying to keep the family together, and my dad was a busy worker in the Indian public services. I was the youngest of six children. We as a family were close and tried to support each other in the ways we were able to. We had a history (ancestors) of diplomats working for the British Raj and the Maharaja, so there was this underlying belief that we were practically royalty and somehow this made us better than other Indians.

However you look at it, this did not last!

While I was in my teens, my brother Mark, a tall, fair and good-looking boy, was a victim of mistaken identity at a very young age. He was attacked from behind. I remember it as if it was not long ago. It was in the month of March just after his 18th birthday. Mark wouldn't ever show pain. He was strong, not just physically, but emotionally too. However, internal bleeding caused his death. He died on 13th March 1980. Mark's death was a turning point for my whole family. Despite catching the culprit and sentencing him for life, my dad was unable to make peace with what had happened. He stopped working and seemed to show little faith in the rest of his children. Life went on, as we all have to carry on, but it was never the same again.

I was the first person among my siblings to go to university. This did not mask my sadness, but it did give me a sense of purpose that showed me my path; I wanted to do something to help others. I knew I could do more. Yet how could I find my true purpose if I did not understand myself first? I wanted to learn more about the history of my ancestors. I thought that going back into the past would somehow help me make sense of the present and find fulfilment in the future.

Tragedy continued to unfold in our family as we lost members to very rare conditions at a very early age. Life was not easy. I was scared to dream. Every misfortune deepened my desire to want to give more to the world. I did not want to have anything to do with the glamour world. I was not willing to depend on my looks to get me places in life. I had turned down offers of modelling, even acting opportunities. My desire to help others further was my real dream and one I intended to follow. As they say, dreams don't just happen, you need to make them happen. Work on the ideas you have and implement on them. Easy to say but hard to do. It takes courage.

At 24 years old, at the lowest point of my life, I left India and set off on the adventure I had been praying for. It was a life I was dreaming of. This was my chance to get to know the rest of my family and make something of my life. I was intrigued by my ancestry so in 1990 I travelled all the way to the UK to find out more. With each discovery I made, I realised what my heritage meant to me. I had no idea I had maternal relatives that I had not known anything about when I came to London. DNA Ancestry helped me find relatives unknown to me. A great-grand aunt, an uncle, an aunt and first cousins. It took over 25 years for this process to reveal its results. Imagine being in the UK and not knowing there were close relatives a few miles down the road from you!

Before I met my husband Sanjay, a British Indian in London, I had started to give up on the idea of ever getting married. I wondered if I lacked the maternal instinct. But I married Sanjay and we had two lovely children.

One of the biggest joys over the years has been holding my children in my arms after giving birth. As time went on, his family started to appreciate my authenticity. Being raised in India, I knew more about the cultural rituals and practices of both our shared traditions. I thought I was happy doing all the things women do or are meant to do. I was married with two wonderful kids and had a steady job in the Law Enforcement arena of the Civil Service. But was that enough?

As a family, we have had our ups and downs. But my role as a woman, wife, mother and daughter in the family always seemed to carry many cultural burdens. Nobody asked how I was feeling. They just needed me to be strong – and that was it.

I lost my dad late in 1994 and within 18 months, in 1996, I lost my mother. I was devastated that I could not attend the funerals as we were in different parts of the world and I had young babies. The family had depended on me to hold it together for too long and it was making the world of my responsibilities feel like a very small place. Especially when you see loved ones being diagnosed with terminal illnesses such as cancer. This severally affects you and your family emotionally, psychologically and financially.

I was too close to people suffering and knowing they had not long to live. I have helped numerous people including family and friends, to come to terms with the unavoidable and inevitable. I was a good listener. This is where Empathy played a big part in what I did and I knew I could help and support others going through the same experience.

I was fed up. I needed to reach out. This was the start of the new woman inside me. It was time to reach outwards into the wider community. It has also helped me to remember my deeper desire to nurture people and help those who were in need. Raising a family was just one part of the journey; the other was me wanting to serve the world! It was time to reach out to the wider community.

We had a platform.

I had the opportunity to work in Law Enforcement. The problem was nobody in the BAME community trusted or had faith in the workforce staff associations. The organisation wanted to appear inclusive to the rest of the world. It seemed ironic to me that we were working on a project to build greater diversity in the workplace, and yet, in practice, my voice was not going to be heard. It took me years to overcome the bullying and gender gap in Inclusion, Diversity and Equality.

I experienced many diversity issues at work. There was a huge focus on grade and rank in the law enforcement industry, which bought out subtle, yet rigid hierarchies. Where was the voice of its members? How does the saying go? If you cannot beat them, join them?

I did join them, becoming part of the Executive committee. I even became the Chairperson for the Ethnic Minority Support Network, the Diversity Staff

Association. This was the only way my voice would be heard and support colleagues. I was busy helping, mentoring and supporting others. This was driven by me wanting to make a positive difference in this world. I started concentrating on what I could do instead of focusing on what I could not. I did this by joining other staff groups, becoming a Workplace Support Officer, a First Aider at Work and had awareness of Mental First Aid. I was the "go-to person" for any staff who had issues or wanted support in the workplace.

In 2017, I received the Queen's Medal for Long Service and Good Conduct within Law Enforcement. Shortly after, I was also featured as one of the 100 women highlighted in the civil service campaign: "100 years, 100 women, past, present and future". This put me in the spotlight. As if this was not enough, I also received the Diversity and Inclusion Role Model award in the National Crime Agency (NCA).

"It only takes one person to take a chance and change follows."

Fundraising changed the way I saw the world. It has changed the course of my life. In 2005, I started volunteering for a local children's charity and at the same time did my first fundraising run, running 26.2 miles in the London Marathon for charity. I am grateful to my children, Sharm and Sheena, who understood my desire to do something for others and patiently waited for me on Tower Bridge to cheer me on through the miles in London.

"We are raising funds for a charity."

When you are running for something you believe in, you are more motivated to train harder. Crossing the finish line after my first ever marathon was one of the most exciting and painful experiences of my life. When I crossed that finish line, I realised that one person can make a difference. That was the beginning of more than a decade of fundraising. Every time, the adventures grew in different ways. The next challenges included trekking the Great Wall of China, 100 miles coast-to-coast Hadrian's Wall Trek and then the 18 days Annapurna circuit of the Himalayan range in Nepal, to name a few.

My personal fundraising continued alongside my volunteering work with charities in the UK and NGOs in India. I recognised the immense value of the work the charity was doing, not just in the UK but also in India and Kenya. It was not long until I applied to join the executive committee having different portfolios.

My dream of making a difference for others was starting to become a reality. I had begun volunteering with specific non-government organisations, one of which was called Lok Seva Sangam. As their work involved helping people with leprosy and TB, many people would avoid getting involved because they feared infection. My sister was a head teacher at one of their schools in India, in the slum areas, which is how I came to learn about the NGO. Enhancement of Education and Family Development Projects were causes I wanted to support, with all my heart.

My sister then retired and ended up becoming an expert on TB, sharing her knowledge through debates to help increase awareness. The years that I am unable to visit, I continue to fundraise from home. This was the motivation behind my charity jumble sales in the UK. The money raised through these went straight to purchase educational assets for the children and young ones studying at the NGO centres.

The second NGO that I supported was the Dhanwantari Medical Trust with their Gift A Smile project. They support children who are terminally ill with cancer and do not have anywhere to stay after their free hospital treatments in Mumbai. Most people did not consider that aspect of care. The Trust offers shelter in their Dharamshala for the families with a small rent fee of 100 rupees a month – the equivalent to £1. This meant that the family could be located near to the hospital and have easy access while also living in their own space. A mission was also started where grain and other essential items were purchased for the families, including days out for the children.

Towards the end of year 2019, I took ill, collapsing on the floor at home and ending up in hospital. I had to undergo surgery that meant having just under six months off from work. This experience had affected both my physical and mental health.

Yet this pain also became my inspiration for the next calling, Saving Dreams.

2020/21 has been very different from other years. I have been supporting my local councils as a Community Champion in times of the Covid-19 pandemic, helping with the distribution of PPE to schools, care homes and care workers. I also found myself helping with the Covid-19 rapid testing and the delivery of the vaccination at different pharmacies and surgeries. I also run a food bank collection with family and friends to help the homeless and people under the poverty line.

Due to poverty and lack of affordability in countries like India, it has become challenging for students to access classes due to varying timings such as the Covid-19 pandemic and homeschooling. We are currently supplying tech assets such as laptops, iPads, smartphones, stationery and even care kits for them while they keep up with their studies.

We as a community at Saving Dreams are trying to extend our support towards safeguarding the physical and mental health of key workers, front line workers and students in these challenging times. I was awarded the Valiant Volunteer, Community Champion and Lifetime Achievement Award. It felt good to be appreciated.

What an Achievement and Satisfaction this is!

I think you should believe in yourself and follow your dreams. My aim was never to reach the height of any career. In fact, I became far less interested in that kind of progression and felt more valued through the help that I offered to people in need.

To make a difference, you do not need to aim high. I focused on the community, listened to my heart and followed my true calling. Take a chance – I did!

"Achieving your dream is the start to making a difference."

"Believe in yourself and follow your dreams."

New Woman 4

Hafiza Khatun

It's Okay Not To Be Okay

"There is help out there. Seek it.
It is okay not to be okay."

My name is Hafiza Khatun. As I write this little 5% of my life biography, it is January 2021, and we are in the midst of the biggest pandemic history has ever known.

I am 45 years old, married, five foot two and ¾ inches in height, and a perfect size 14. Just thought I would put that in so you can get a better image in your heads. Please do excuse my dry humour.

My friends describe me as a very caring, helpful, affectionate, sympathetic individual with lots of common sense. They also call me 'the witty clown'. I will go out of my way to help people and not expect anything back from them because I believe by helping people, you gain higher rank from your Lord. I used to find it extremely difficult to say 'no' to people until just recently, when I learnt that it was very bad for my health and the fact that people may start to take advantage of you.

With God's mercy, I have given birth to three beautiful children who are all grown up now: one daughter and two sons. I have done my bit for society now, three is more than enough for me. It is very hard work and never-ending, but saying that, it is also very rewarding and very worthwhile – especially now that they're adults.

I am not quite sure where to start my story as I have a lot to say, but on this occasion, I am going to concentrate on the mental health part of the journey.

It all started after I gave birth to my firstborn, my daughter Nazifa, who was born exactly a year after I got married. I was living with my in-laws at the time. With my mother-in-law's help, I just had to concentrate on looking after the baby, while she took over the majority of the housework. I was enjoying being a new mum.

By nature, I am a very anxious person, always looking for perfection. If I am going to commit myself to something, it has to be done to perfection. Well, as near as possible. I had a very strict timetable with my baby which I had to follow to fit in with the responsibility of living within an extended family too.

I was getting along quite well, until four months after the birth of my daughter when I found out that I was pregnant again. Oh, my goodness! What a shock that was, because it was totally unexpected and unplanned. Now my body was acting with all the normal pregnancy side effects: morning sickness, severe fatigue, dizziness and no appetite. You still have to look after your baby no matter what you are going through, and I also had to show my in-laws that I was managing very well.

At that point, a certain person stopped talking to me for some weeks, because they said that I shouldn't have got pregnant. The person is question was an elderly male in his sixties. But I forgive him; I put it down to ignorance, nothing more. How I wanted to tell them that all the precautions were taken but it still happened! However, that conversation was never going to happen with this person – it was simply not possible – and quite frankly, it was really none of their business. This certainly had an effect on my mental well-being.

So, nine months had passed, and I gave birth to a very tall, beautiful baby boy on 31st October 1997; he was a Halloween baby. The very first thing the midwife had said was, "Oh, my! What a very tall baby". He is 23 years old now and over six feet tall. He is now completing his pre-registration year in Optometry with Boots the chemist.

When I came home with the baby, I was so overwhelmed because I had a 13 month old waiting for me and this new bundle of joy in my hands. To be honest, my mother-in-law didn't expect too much from me, I just did what I could around the house when she would sit and play with the kids.

The hardest part were the nights. I would put one to sleep and the other one would wake, so feeding, changing, putting them back to sleep, would go round the night. My husband is a teacher, so he would need to be out the house for 7 am and he was a heavy sleeper, so he was totally oblivious of the night-time activities.

I struggled but I managed. In a few weeks, I started to feel very lethargic, miserable and had a lack of motivation. I started feeling desperate for something but did not know what. I felt like crying all the time. I wanted my mum; however, that could never happen because my mum was elderly and not well within herself. She has never been well since I can remember. She herself had her own battles.

I don't really know what a mum is. I've never had a mother-daughter relationship at all because of her illness. From the age of six, I remember looking after her and taking responsibility of my three-year-old brother. After the birth of my brother, my mother fell severely ill with what I now know to be severe postnatal depression; she was hospitalised for six months. She never really recovered throughout the years after. I remember taking care of my father as well as my younger brother, making them breakfast, then getting my brother ready for school and making the after-school tea. Every Friday after school, I would hand wash mine and my brother's uniform because we didn't own a washing machine. My mum couldn't sleep at night, so she would sleep during the morning and into the early hours of the afternoon.

My mother had a very tough life. Before I came along, she had already lost four boys. They all died in infancy. I am the eighth child, and my brother is the ninth and was their last child. My mum was in her fifties when she had me and my brother came three years after me. I always wished I had younger parents, because in school, all my English friends' parents were so young and energetic. They used to take them to school and pick them up again. We had to make our own way to school and back. In a way, we were their support, because on top of their age, they didn't know English, so we had to understand every situation first and then translate it to them.

I am in no way complaining about the situation I was in, because it made me very independent, which helped me in my later adult years.

Anyway, back to when I became a mother the second time. I just was not feeling right. Aches and pains were a constant thing, frequent headaches and dizziness were an everyday thing. I visited the doctor several times telling them all my symptoms. After a few visits, he did blood tests and found nothing. Every time I visited the doctor, he would say that I was too young to have aches and pains. He also said that he didn't actually know what the matter is. Eventually, I stopped going to the doctor and carried on with life, bringing up my children and trying to be a good daughter-in-law too. It was very challenging at times with trying to be dutiful and keeping everyone happy, but I just accepted what fate had in store for me (my ailments). It had become second nature to feel dizzy all the time and living with the pain.

Cutting a very, very long story short, the time came for us to move out. Nazifa was three and Saeed was two. We managed to get a council house. I enrolled Nazifa into nursery and put Saeed's name down too. My three-year-old daughter cried for four months straight. She used to be stuck to the nursery door pouring her eyes out, but I knew it was best for the both of us. At the time of writing, she is 24 years of age, divorced, a qualified Level 3 Nursery Practitioner, and now working as a qualified Optical Assistant with Specsavers.

It was absolutely wonderful to have our own place. I enrolled in a computing course in the local Women's Centre. I knew the childcare I would receive for Saeed while I did my course would be very beneficial for him; it would help him to settle into nursery when the time came. I enjoyed my course, made friends, started going for walks and absolutely loved shopping. Life was good, but I was not feeling good. All the usual symptoms returned, and I went back to see the doctor. This time, he prescribed me Amitriptyline and said it would help with the headaches. I took it for about a year but it didn't help much, so I came off it. Now I know it was the very first set of antidepressants that I was prescribed.

Boy! Little did I know there was a lot more of these coming my way.

When my kids got ill, the anxiety was even worse. I would have severe anxiety of 'what ifs':

- What if they get worse?
- What if they die?
- What if I can't make them better?
- What if they have something serious?

To make things worse, both my children used to projectile vomit every time they caught a cold. Also, they used to take hours to feed. By the time you had finished one meal, it was time to prepare the next meal; it absolutely exhausted me and when they projectile vomited it out, I used to cry with them. Then I'd get up and start again.

I used to crave for my mum. I just wanted someone to put their arms around me and tell me I was doing okay. That I was going to be okay. Being a mum was extremely hard work. I so much appreciated my mum, but my mum was not well within herself to support me. Even to this day, I actually don't know what a mother's love actually is. I would so much like to talk about my father, but this is not the right time. Someday, I will put that to paper too and believe me when I say, I really need to.

Six years passed after my second child when I got pregnant with my third child. This time, the usual morning sickness lasted for three months. Otherwise, the pregnancy was not that eventful. Generally, I gave birth quite naturally. That is what my mother-in-law used to tell me. When she used to come to visit me and the baby, she used to say, "You don't look like you have had a baby, you look so fresh,"; she said this three times.

This baby was a boy we called Nabeel, a healthy 7lb baby. He cried all day and night for the two days I was in hospital. I got no rest at all. The nurses didn't take him. They said he was my third baby, so they wouldn't do any babysitting. I came home and I was so confused. I had three kids to look after, cook and clean, all at the same time. I told myself I can do it - so many other women do it all the time – there's nothing special about me.

I slowly got to work, made sure they were fed and cleaned, did their homework, reading, and made sure everyone got everything that they needed. I would put the school kids to bed then feed the baby and get him ready for bed. Then me and my husband would eat and get ready for bed at about 11pm. As soon as my husband hit the pillow, he would start snoring. But I'd take a lot of time to fall asleep, so as soon as I would start to drop off, the baby would start to cry. I would calm him and put him back to sleep, but then he would start again. It became a vicious cycle: all night, every night. I would wake the kids up at 7.30am to get them ready for school, while I was having no sleep at all.

Every week the midwife would come, and she would always ask about how I was feeling. I used to say, "I'm fine, thank you", and she used to say, "You look exhausted." I would always reply, "No, I'm fine."

This went on for a month. Finally, when the midwife came to weigh the baby, I saw her and started to scream, "This baby doesn't sleep! And I can't sleep! I feel so scared of everything! I don't want this baby. I am going mad! Nothing makes sense!"

She looked at me and took the baby off me. She sat me down and gave me some water and said, "Hafiza, you are not going mad. This is quite normal. I think you are suffering from postnatal depression."

I said, "What's that?"

She said, "I'm going to give you some leaflets and get you referred. The doctor will come and visit you early next week, then you will be referred to a Community Psychiatric Nurse (CPN)."

As promised, the doctor came the following week. While sat in my living room, he said, "New parents do feel overwhelmed at these times. But never tell anyone that you are feeling not right. They will think that you are not coping and that you are going mad." I just looked at him and thought, 'I don't bloody care what people think of me. I'm not feeling like I can cope. I need help.' After telling me that everything will be okay, he said the CPN would be in touch, then left.

The following week, a CPN came to my house and talked to me for an hour. Then he prescribed me Venlafaxine, which the doctor would have to give his consent and signature for. One per day, to be taken at night (I cannot recall the actual dose as it was 17 years ago). I took it for a week. My heart used to beat so fast, then it would start shaking, then the palpitations would start. I was told to carry on, and that the side effects would wear off. I took them for a month and still had the same effects. I was getting paranoid. I would not let my husband go to work and would tell him that I was scared, and he should stay at home.

When he used to ask, "What are you scared about?", I used to say that I have lost my ability to sleep. I used to cry all day and all night. I couldn't eat and lost a lot of weight. Every time the CPN used to visit, which was every two weeks, he would tell me that I needed to eat. I used to reply, "No, I need to sleep."

I simply could not fall asleep anymore. I started getting severe panic attacks. At the time, I didn't know what panic attacks were. I thought I was dying because I couldn't breathe. I used to have pain in my chest, and was suffering from dizziness and nausea.

On the third month, I was really bad, but I still managed to look after my children. My CPN referred me to Dorothy Pattison Hospital in Walsall to see a psychiatrist. He put me on Citalopram 20mg daily, and he told me to come off Venlafaxine because of all the side effects I was having. At the time, I was totally gone and didn't care much for myself. I was not taking care of myself. Personal hygiene went out the window. I lived on bananas and milk. But I knew I had to keep going for the children so I would swallow a cup of milk and half-chewed banana every three hours.

During this time, my husband got very worried. He told his parents that he was going to send me to my brother's place for a while. He wanted me to get a bit of a breather because my sister-in-law offered to look after the baby at night for a while. When my family heard about my illness, one of my brothers, who is way older than me – about 18 years older – went around telling people that I had too much free time on my hands. His ignorant allegations were that: my husband had given me too much freedom; my in-laws didn't give me enough work to do; I had brought this on myself. A kind of an empty mind devil's workshop thing. Another brother of mine said, "Come and see how much housework your sister-in-law does. Come and work with her; your illness will go."

How I could have had too much free time on my hands, with three kids, a husband, a house and myself to take care of, is far beyond my understanding. I remember my husband saying to himself, "If she has so much free time, then she should be happy and well," which of course, I was not.

My brothers did not understand at the time. Their situations have since changed. Their mindsets have since changed. I do not hold anything against them. This way of thinking, back then, was very normal because people had no or very little knowledge of mental health back then. Even now, to this day, mental health is a taboo subject. People still struggle to understand it, especially in our Asian community.

Look, I kind of believed what they said, and I was prepared to go. By the way, my brothers live in Newcastle upon Tyne, a four-hour drive from Walsall, where I call home. When my mother-in-law heard that I was going with the kids, she suggested that I shouldn't go because the older children would miss a lot of schooling. She offered for us to move in with her for a few weeks and she would do babysitting at night so that I would get a block of uninterrupted hours to get my sleeping pattern in order. Nabeel was not sleeping at night. He would only sleep for 15 minutes at a time throughout the night.

We moved into my in-laws, all five of us. Space was not an issue because they have a huge five-bedroom house between the two of them; it's actually a massive house. We settled in quickly. My father-in-law would take the older two children to school and bring them back. My mother-in-law did the cooking and between my husband and my mother-in-law, they shared the night shift.

My shift was from 10am to 11pm with the kids. I would do everything that needed to be done for the children to thrive. From 11pm, my husband would take over from me to look after the baby. I would make the extra bottles and leave them in the fridge from 11pm to 2am. He would do his shift, then he would hand Nabeel over to my mother-in-law as he needed to go to work at 7am. She used to go to bed at 10pm so she would have already had a chunk of sleep ready for her night shift. From 2am to 10am, she would be sleeping when the baby slept. She was a very heavy sleeper who had the ability to drop off anywhere at any time, so she wasn't really bothered about not having uninterrupted sleep. She would also sleep during the day too.

This was a Godsend for me. I will forever be indebted to them. Even though I couldn't sleep, I wanted to train my brain to get into a routine. It took months to get some sort of reasonable sleep back into my body.

I took Citalopram for two months while also having appointments at the outpatients psychiatric hospital. My psychiatrist changed the antidepressants to Fluoxetine 20mg daily because the Citalopram wasn't working. I was still unwell, with regular panic attacks, a lot of muscular pain, no appetite, constant headaches, constant dizziness and very little sleep. I stayed with my in-laws for nine months. Nabeel had just started to sleep for three to four hours in one go.

After about three months of staying at my in-laws, I felt confident enough to bring all the kids after school back to our house, and do everything for them there. Then, we would only go to my in-laws for the night. I wanted to give my in-laws their space back and so that she would not have to cook for us.

I eventually found out why Nabeel would not sleep through the night. It was because he had a nasal condition which wouldn't let him breathe properly. Numerous times, I took him to the doctors because of his constant crying. After a long time, they said that he has a very narrow nasal cavity which they told me will improve as he gets older.

Ramadan was approaching so my mother-in-law said that we should move back into our house because things get a bit difficult while fasting, which was kind and understandable. So, we moved back in. The thought of being in the same room as my baby frightened the living daylights out of me. I just could not have him in the same room as me. On the first night back, I tried but I couldn't sleep. I kept checking in on him. Every turn he made, I kept looking over the cot checking upon him. I was awake all night.

The following day, I said to my husband that he would have to sleep with him in the same room while I slept in the spare room, because I started to panic again. He agreed. I would give Nabeel his last feed, get him ready and put him to bed at 11pm. This is the time when my husband went to bed. I started to go to bed at this time too, so I could get some sleep and take over from 7am when he would get up for work. Nabeel had one feed in the night, and the other noises he would make didn't bother my husband because he was a very deep sleeper like his mum. I think half of my problem is that I was a very light sleeper. Any noise or movement wakes me up.

I was still having appointments from the hospital because I still wasn't getting better. On top of my Fluoxetine in the morning, I was prescribed Quetiapine 50mg at night. I still am today and will be for the rest of my life. While still having regular appointments at the hospital, I visited a new GP who was a locum, a beautiful Chinese doctor. She was called Dr Tia. After looking at my records, she told me not to have any more children. She said in her own words, "We have managed to stabilise you, but if you have another child then the chances are that we will not be able to bring you back. You will mentally not be with us anymore."

This routine lasted for three years until Nabeel moved into the same room as Saeed. I finally moved back into my bedroom. Nabeel is now 17 years old and studies well in sixth form. To this day, I am not well. But I have learned how to manage the illness, along with the catalogue of other ailments that I am suffering from. The post-natal depression was later diagnosed as clinical depression. I still get regular visits from the monster inside me, but he has become weaker – though it can still make me ill for weeks at a time.

With help from family, friends, doctors, community nurses, therapy and medication, you can still have a decent life. There is help out there. Seek it. It is okay not to be okay.

I have promised myself that when my daughter or daughters-in-law have children, I will make sure they eat and sleep for weeks so they can heal from the pregnancy and the birth. I will be their babysitter, God willing. This truly is only 5% of the story.

Now, at this time of my life, young, old, middle-aged people come to me for advice on how to cope with anxiety and depression. They say that they want to understand the illness. I basically tell them what to eat, and how important it is to keep yourself hydrated. I focus on the importance of getting enough sleep. Essentially, I draw on everything I did and still do to this day to keep myself healthy.

I believe we are all afflicted for the benefit others, but at the time of our suffering, we just don't understand the wisdom behind our suffering.

New Woman 5

Jenni Harris

You Can Handle It!

"I am thriving."

This is a story of hope, strength and showing up. As you read through this, you will learn about how my happy, vibrant life was soaring; how it then blew up in mine, my husband's and my sons' faces; and how I am slowly putting the pieces back together.

I sat by the window returning from an amazing all-expenses paid trip to Iceland. The plane was sat on the runway and I was anxious; there was something I had to do when I returned home, yet I was scared. If the truth be known, I should have dealt with it about six weeks before, but I had been busy. The nagging voice had got louder and louder, particularly over the last week, so I had to make it a priority.

My life was great; in fact, I was soaring. Seven months previously, I had partnered with a network marketing company in the health and wellness sector and I was having phenomenal success. My business was growing and I was helping others do the same. I had experienced early success and my hard work had been rewarded as a Founding Member and Executive in the UK. I had spoken on stage at our Grand Opening in London, had been rewarded with a Five* all-expenses paid trip to Las Vegas and had a suite at the Venetian Resort where I stood up on stage and spoke to 1,500 people. I was on fire; literally everything I touched was turning to gold.

I remember feeling a little irritated when I decided to go the doctor. He had no idea why the pain was in that place, yet he was trying to dismiss me. There I was, sat feeling irritated whilst he started tapping on his keyboard. I was having a conversation in my head. "Shall I say something? No, leave it," and then

I heard my voice. My voice was polite but firm, call it divine intervention or intuition or simply someone was watching over me that day, whatever it was that made me say something. I will always be grateful that I had the courage to use my voice and speak out.

Back home, the ground was covered in snow and I was sitting on my sofa working on my laptop as it was much warmer in the lounge than my office. I was working away minding my own business when I noticed a missed call from a No Caller ID number. I didn't care – I was sick of PPI claims people calling my number. But then the caller tried again. I don't know about you but I don't answer the calls from No Caller ID numbers so I ignored it. Then it called again. WOW, this person is insistent, I thought, so I answered the call.

Boy, I wished I had let it ring. Moments later, I came off the phone and could literally hear the blood pumping in my ears. I couldn't breathe, my heart was racing and I wanted to stand up but for some reason the message had not been received by my limbs so I was stuck, and then I heard my husband's voice. The voice that was like a warm duvet and always made me feel safe. "Jen, what's up?" I didn't answer – I mean, what on earth could I say? I didn't want to say anything because then I would hear it and it would be real. At this moment, the normally encouraging supporting voice repeated, "Jen, what's up?" But this time, it sounded different and I didn't feel safe. Someone who I didn't know had just detonated an almighty bomb in our lounge and it had exploded in our faces. Our lives had literally been blown into a million tiny pieces and for the first time in my life, I didn't know how to fix it.

I walked upstairs as I needed to shower before leaving the house, and I could hear my mum's voice which was odd as she had passed away five years before. But she was with me. I stood in the shower and let the water wash over me and tears rolled with the water because I knew. I knew exactly what they were going to say and I was terrified. I kept saying to myself, "Why wouldn't they just tell me on the phone?" After showering, I put on a little black dress and went downstairs. "I don't want to go," I repeatedly said to my husband. He put his arms around me and said, "Let's go."

Sitting in the chair, I looked around the room. When the nurse came into the room, her face was kind and she had that look about her; professional, yet caring. My mind was all over the place; the doctor's mouth was moving but all I had heard was, "Mrs Harris, you have cancer." What kind of sick joke was this, why was he saying this to me? This could not possibly be true! I was fit, healthy, a healthy weight, I didn't smoke. Yes, I drank but only in moderation. It must be a mistake. His mouth was still moving and I just about made out the words, "It has spread to your lymph nodes."

I then asked the unthinkable question that no one wants to ask or hear the answer to. My eyes darted from the doctor's face and as I turned, I saw a silent tear roll down the beautiful face that I had loved for 20 years. Then an even scarier question popped into my head and almost as if our minds were connected in that moment, we both said, "How are we going to tell the boys?" It was bad enough that we knew this but how were we supposed to tell our beautiful boys who were only 17 and 19?

In my previous career as a police officer, which I will tell you about another time, I have delivered much bad news to families but this was the hardest message I ever had to deliver in my whole life. I cried and stumbled but I just couldn't finish the sentence and my poor gorgeous, strong husband had to deliver the message twice. The look on my children's faces will stay with me for the rest of my life.

It was a cold January morning and I found myself sitting in yet another chair; this time, all the gory details were being given to me. I was still reeling – I had no lump and I had gone for a routine mammogram a few months before so how could this pain be cancer? I had a gazillion tests and scans and the results came back: I had stage 3 breast cancer and I needed to start treatment fast. But what about my son's birthday? We were going on holiday to Lanzarote in four days' time to celebrate his 18th birthday. "Can we start this after the 19th?" I asked. The soft caring voice soon changed to an emphatic, "No, you cannot travel! If I could start your treatment tomorrow, I would." The words kept coming but I was stuck on repeat. "You will lose your hair, you will lose your hair, you will lose your hair." This was a big deal for me – there was so much information and I simply could not take it all in.

It was only when we got home that it registered that I was going to be on an 18-month journey of various different treatments and after my six months of chemotherapy, I would have to have a mastectomy. A mastectomy!

"Oh god, Jen how do you feel about that?" If I heard this once, I heard it several times from my friends who I know were not being unkind, but were simply terrified.

To be honest, if I had listened to them, I think I would have ended up having long-lasting mental health issues. However, I had faith and the logical left side of my brain had reconciled with the fact that if I had skin cancer I would want the mole removed, so having breast cancer made sense that my breast was trying to kill me so I needed it gone. I did have moments when I felt that losing my breast would affect how I saw myself; of course I did, but this was not a time to feel sorry for myself. I had a disease that could potentially take my life but that wasn't my only thought. I had to be here for my husband and my boys. I wanted to be there on their wedding days. I wanted to see the lucky women who would win their hearts. I wanted to be there when they got the keys to their first homes, when they passed their driving tests and had their children. I wanted to be there for it all. That was my JOB.

When my friends would ask about whether I needed a mastectomy, I could see that they felt awkward and I could see fear in their eyes of some of them. They would literally touch their breasts and say, "I don't know if I could cope with losing a breast," to which I would laugh and reply, "I don't think I can cope with dying." It's really all about perspective. You see, I don't know if it was my mind helping me to cope with the thought of losing a breast, but dying was not on my agenda in any way shape or form. So if I had to lose my breast to stay alive, then "tough titty!"

So where is this story going? I decided that the only people I would tell were my immediate family and close circle of friends as I was hosting a big ticketed New Year Kick-Off event with over 100 people attending and I could not cancel.

On that cold Sunday morning, I got up four hours early as I couldn't move quickly at all, my speech was slow, my hands shook and it felt like there was a kaleidoscope of butterflies flying around inside the whole of my body. The burning pain around the centre of my chest was a constant reminder of what I had done six days before; yet it was also a symbol of hope. My body was in a war zone and I was watching it in slow motion. I had carefully chosen my outfit; a beautiful fitted, designer black shift dress with jade-green killer stilettos. I carefully applied my makeup and as I looked in the mirror, I knew it was me but it didn't look like me. It was then I realised the old me had gone forever – my life had been blown apart. As I wiped the silent tears that threatened to ruin my makeup, I picked up the final part of my outfit. I carefully pulled it onto my head – it felt weird and strange but somehow comforting at the same time. I would have to make sure I didn't hug anyone; having just had chemotherapy, my immune system was at rock bottom and any kind of infection could have a detrimental impact on my health. The other reason was just in case someone inadvertently got a bracelet or watch caught in my wig so making sure it was straight, I smiled weakly.

I was ready and it was show time.

You see, despite the tremors and the darkness I felt inside and the fact that my world was falling apart today, I was giving others hope. I was choosing to show up and deliver a first-class event. I put my beautiful jade-green shoes in to my large tote bag, picked up my car keys, and quietly left the house. I could have cancelled the event and stayed curled up in bed but I knew that really was not an option for me; my children were watching me. I knew they were watching how I was coping, I knew that my behaviour was literally giving them hope, and I had to show up.

Sometimes I would catch them looking at me when I came downstairs in my gym clothes on my good days, or when I was shuffling to the bathroom after treatment on bad days, and the sadness was written all over their beautiful faces. A sadness that would tug at my heart and immediately send a message to my brain, reminding me I had brought these boys into the world and I had to get through this for them. They were just starting to navigate life as young men – how could I not be there when they bought their first home, got married or even had their first baby? The sadness in their eyes told me they were scared, as their only experience of someone prior to me having been diagnosed with cancer had not been good. Their uncle Steven, whom they loved dearly, had passed away in 2012. So their experience was that cancer was a killer and I wasn't going to make it, so I had to prove them wrong.

They both dealt with me differently; one son found solace in speaking to me every single day to check I was okay. The other created distance and stayed away after a few treatments when the compound effect began to show. I noticed there was a pattern to him being absent but I understood. My boys were in pain and there was nothing I could do apart from survive. My words were just that – words – and that did not make them feel better. I remember them both saying to me, "You're Mum – of course you are going to tell us it's going to be okay, that's your job! You would not tell us the truth."

Deep down inside, I knew they were right; it was my job to protect them from the harsh realities so yes, I would tell them everything would be okay. But more than that, I truly believed I would survive and could handle anything that was thrown at me.

We lived our lives in three-week cycles for six months; it just became our way of life and my husband did everything for me that I couldn't do for myself. He was 'steady eddy': he cooked, cleaned, kept people away from me, gave me my medication like clockwork. He really was my rock, and he 100% stood by those vows we had made on 28th August 1997 in sickness and in health. He was my ears at many medical appointments as I didn't remember everything that the doctors and nurses would say. He would listen attentively and share the information when I asked. None of it was plain sailing. I had a couple of hospital admissions, one of which I woke up from and was told I had been asleep for two days! I clearly needed the rest; my poor body was doing its best to repair.

Radiotherapy had gone really well. I had even taken a picture with my medical team on my last day – I was ecstatic! Another step closer to recovery. A few days later, I was sitting on the train travelling to London for a meeting, and my chest was burning, despite the fact I had a great big pad covered with gel. I was wearing my lightweight prosthesis as I didn't want the pressure on my chest wall but I could feel the heat – surely this was okay, right?? The next day, I was in the hospital as what had started out as heat and pain was now literally burnt to a crisp and had fallen off, leaving my skin raw and exposed. The pain was excruciating but I knew I could handle it; I mean, what choice did I have?

I finally completed my treatment on 2nd May 2019. The day I rang that bell on the oncology ward will be a day I will never forget. Whilst my physical intervention treatment had finished, the mental journey was continuing and to be honest I don't know when it will end. You see, surviving cancer is one thing, but the fear that hijacks your mind is quite another. It's insidious; you will be happily going along one day and something of no real significance which can be totally unrelated, will trigger a voice that says, "What if it's back?" I have a little mantra that I say to change my thought pattern.

I am so grateful that I am here, alive and able to share this snapshot of my story with you. I am thriving too. In 2020, I was a finalist for two business awards; I didn't win the awards outright but for me it was a huge win for tenacity, a win for strength, and a win for courage.

You see, I could have given up all hope when I was diagnosed. I could have crumbled when I didn't feel strong, and I could have not shown up when I was meant to, but I did all of those things, and more. Cancer has not defined me and as I write I have started two new businesses in 2021, businesses created to help women find hope, find their courage, and show up. I am also a grandmother in waiting, as I await the arrival of my first granddaughter! I am so excited for my future and I hope reading this chapter has inspired you to know that if anything happens, "You can handle it!"

New Woman 6

Azmina Jiwa

Freedom To Be Comfortable In Your Own Skin

"The key to changing the world, to changing your life and empowering those around you is authentically – the willingness to be yourself – the willingness to be vulnerable – the willingness to feel – the willingness to live. I am simply reminding you of who you truly are, supporting you into self-love and acceptance by eradicating the judgement that you have imposed on yourself and society has imposed on you."

Panache Desai

Who would have ever imagined that this small, shy, meek girl who came to England from Uganda at the age of 17 is now a fearless, visible and vibrant woman?

This girl is ME!

Born in Uganda, the eldest of seven children, my grandparents migrated from India for a better life. I don't have many memories of my childhood. The ones that stick in my head are those of my dad not being a very affectionate person. He would often get angry with us, if he thought we were misbehaving or were noisy. I remember him chasing one of my sisters with a stick, as she was often the one who refused to conform. I also remember being slapped on my face a few times. My mother seemed to fear him, as she was always asking us to be quiet and stay out of his way.

I was extremely shy, to the extent that I would not even sit at the same table if we had guests; I would not go to parties and I would not look up, especially around boys. Even as a teenager here in England, I would not cross the road at the crossing unless someone else needed to cross, as I was conscious I would draw attention and also did not feel worthy for the cars to stop just for me to cross the road. At college, I found it very hard to make friends. I only had one friend and she was from Uganda as well.

I qualified as a podiatrist by getting a loan and through my part-time work. My parents, who were financially supporting me to start with, had to leave Uganda overnight, leaving all their assets behind, with only $50 to rebuild their lives in America. Whilst studying, I stayed at the YWCA hostel, sharing my room with five other girls. I had three evening jobs during the week, doing babysitting and clerical work. On the weekends and holidays, I worked as a cleaner and helped out in the kitchen at the hostel. I remember the matron at the hostel saying to me once, "You are so tiny, but full of vitality!" She saw something in me that I did not see!

After I was married, things were great in the beginning. I was confident as a wife and professional, but things soon changed after I had my first child. I took on the role of a conforming wife. I became overly sensitive to passing comments instead of voicing my opinion or being assertive. What I later realised was that those close to me were simply expressing their opinion, which I was interpreting as an expectation on me, and I pressured myself to meet their 'demands'. I began to live in fear of being rejected if I did not do things expected of me and constantly felt anxious about not being home on time.

I have to mention here that it was not all doom and gloom. We went on holidays and met and entertained friends. But emotionally, I was not feeling connected. Now looking back, I feel that I may have become mechanical, a bit like a robot. I also realised I had learnt to be a 'people pleaser' like my mum, who lived in fear too. A fear of being judged or not being liked by others, possibly partly because of her own upbringing. With Mum being how she was and with my previous fear of my father, I adopted this mental attitude of fear towards others around me, particularly those who were vocal and domineering, so I felt compelled to conform to others' wishes. This was history repeating itself from my father to my husband. I was reliving my childhood fears, which were resurfacing in my adult life.

However, somewhere amongst all this was also a daring, resourceful, and ambitious woman. I believe every one of us has qualities to help us thrive in life; I just could not see them at the time. I want you to know that you have them too; you possibly may not have discovered them as yet.

I love the quote by Rumi: *"You are the light that shines the world."*

My journey of becoming that shining light started in my forties. Prior to this, I used to wake up in the morning with my heart pounding in my chest, just at the thought of getting through the day. I was increasingly tearful and anxious about driving or leaving the house at times. I was drained of energy, and did not want to do much, apart from the bare minimum. This lasted for four months. I was wondering if life was even worth living if I was going to keep feeling this way. When was this going to end?

I wonder if you are going through something similar in your life?

I was not able to see my own worth despite frequent assurances from my family. My husband often pointed out to me, "You have everything you can ever want. A beautiful house, garden and a profession. How can you feel unworthy after all that you have accomplished? Many people would love to be in your shoes!"

My children, who were now in their teens, would also make comments on my achievements and how proud they were of me. But despite these encouraging words, I could not see my own self-worth.

We often strive to achieve things that we believe will make us happy, such as a house or car, but I came to realise that although these made me comfortable, they did not give me the inner happiness and peace that I longed to experience in my life.

Later in my married life, I was the Head of Religious Education classes, which were held every Saturday. After that I became a Board member with my faith community, which is considered to be a prestigious position. On reflection, I certainly had the confidence to do what it took to make sure I qualified, despite no financial or family support and later even took on senior positions within the community. I was like a 'Jack in the Box'. I sometimes had that courage to be visible to do the things I wanted to do, and at other times I wanted to hide and be safe.

Throughout all this, I still remained unhappy and anxious, feeling unworthy.

I went to see a doctor who pointed out that I was pre-menopausal and asked if I wanted anti-depressant medication. Somewhere within me, I knew that this was not the answer as I felt I needed to look within to find some answers. The doctor also offered me medication to slow down my heart rate due to anxiety, which I took when needed.

One day, I found myself down on my knees, sobbing. I was crying and praying for some guidance, some help. My chest felt heavy and tears were streaming down my face. I was praying for this heavy feeling in my chest to pass, for this anxiety and tears to pass. I was praying for this darkness to pass. I wanted it all this to go away. I did not want to face another day of this horrendous pain, being tearful, feeling worthless and so unhappy.

So while on my knees praying for some sort of relief, a ray of hope in the form of a book caught my attention. This was a book that I had read in the past, and in that moment, reminded me that menopause is a time of self-reflection. A time for self-care and to look within, especially when not living your life for yourself, but for others.

Once I had this realisation that I needed to look within, and started to look for answers, I found them everywhere I looked. Isn't it amazing – power in seeking for answers? Gabrielle Bernstein says, "The universe has your back."

Suddenly, the universe had my back. This was proven to me time and time again. On one occasion, I came across a promotional leaflet for a seminar called 'The Zest for Life' and I thought, "That's exactly what I need! Yes, please! I want to live life and not just exist."

I was absolutely mesmerised when listening to how my life could be transformed by using some very simple but powerful tools that Dawn Breslin was teaching. So I registered for her one-day workshop. I was quite apprehensive, not really knowing what to expect and fearful of being vulnerable.

Dawn was very gentle, and made us all feel very comfortable and at ease. I remember sitting in the front seat; being small built, I often have a preference for sitting in the front to see the person talking. However, at the same time, I was feeling very vulnerable, being seen by and in full view of the speaker herself.

For over half of the morning session, I was extremely emotional, crying the whole time. I was reconnecting with who I was by looking at a photo of myself as a child. In this moment, I realised I had completely lost the sense of who I was. This beautiful child with so much potential, who knew what she wanted in life. Where was she now? She was hidden, like the core of the onion with all the layers of conditioning added as she was growing up. This was my time now to peel away the layers to find the gem that I was. I learnt some powerful tools during the workshop and by the end of the day, I knew that I also wanted to share these tools with others by becoming a trainer. I did wonder why these tools were not commonly available and in fact not taught in school.

I was not living my life; I was living the life of others, my husband and children. I constantly feared rejection and judgment. I was terrified if I did not manage to do something I was asked to do. I kept saying 'Yes' to people when I really wanted to say 'No'. I thought no one will like me if I said 'No.'

I did not know what I wanted; I had no idea how to listen to my inner voice. I was often unclear of my feelings and was not comfortable making the simplest decisions such as preferences for places to eat. Before my intuition had a chance to be heard, the voice of fear kicked in. I would start worrying about what others will think and say. My logical mind would wonder if they would like it or not and if not, then it would be my fault. On and on would go my chatterbox or 'monkey mind', as some people call it.

I am in such a different space now and am grateful for where I am, with the self-help workshops and continuously reading and reflection. What I know now is that by practicing and using these tools once I was ready for change, I was able to create my new reality that was free from all control. I was able to take charge of my own life and happiness. There are some things which we cannot change in our lives, and I now understand that it is about accepting and embracing the reality, and looking for the positive in the situation. And there is always a positive. It just needs the right lenses to look at it.

I have learnt to accept both myself and those around me.

If you are in the space of feeling powerless, stuck, have low self-esteem, tired of always being there for others and not for your own needs, with feelings of being taken advantage of and many more, let me tell you that there is light at the end of the tunnel. If I can do it, so can you!

I started putting into practice what I was learning and it finally gave me the freedom to be ME. These were the simple steps of how I began:

I started a daily practice of writing a gratitude journal and 10-minute meditation. This slowly started to shift my attention from my bad feelings to all the great things that were present in my life.

I would like to share three tools that I found most powerful, in changing my life from being a prisoner of my fears, my unhappiness and unworthiness, to being happy, energetic and feeling connected.

1. What am I feeling and thinking?

I started becoming aware of my thoughts. I changed the negative thoughts to positive statements. I used to have a little book of writing these affirmations. For example, one of them was "I am now learning to listen to my inner voice," and then I wrote three statements of how this would change how I felt and my behaviour. On some occasions, I was not in a good mental state to do those practices, so I would do some vigorous exercise, shouting out loud "Yes, yes, yes!" This is about changing state, as taught by Tony Robbins, or I would even do some laughter yoga.

I needed to remind myself, "I am unique and special, with my own individual gifts."

My low self-esteem and unworthiness were coming from my own beliefs and thoughts. If I changed the way I was thinking, the way I was feeling would change.

2. How to feel the fear and do it anyway.

This was from Dr Susan Jeffers' book of the same title. I learnt that everyone feels fear. I used to think that if I was afraid of doing or saying something, it meant that I couldn't do it. And just knowing that we all feel fear

– even the great inventors felt fear and still did what they wanted – gave me the confidence to let the fear be there and speaking and voicing what I wanted any way. The more I practiced, the easier it got. Now I know that the only way to get over fear and step out of our comfort zone, is to go and do it.

This has allowed me to speak to audiences of 200 people when beforehand I could not even speak to a group of three people! When I went to pick my children up from school, I used to sit in the car until they started to come out. I was worried that if I stood where the group of parents were waiting and chatting, they would think I am silly just standing there quietly, or if I said something, they would think that it was silly.

I believe that all these feelings of mine that used to come up to the surface were just pushed down, as they were too painful. I would busy myself with making the dinner, children's homework, cleaning and then, tired, off to bed to start all over again the next day. This was the treadmill of life for me, as I am sure it is for many of you.

At the time, I was able to push my thoughts away, but of course they did not go away, they just got pushed inwards. I now have come to believe that during the hormonal changes in my life, I could not push them away like before; I guess I was not as busy as before. The children had flown the nest. So this was now my time to go within and take care of me.

I also learnt that most of my fears were False Expectations Appearing Real. All the 'what if's' – when I say this, they will get offended, or they will not like me. Ninety per cent of the time, this is not true.

I learnt the truth about fear from Dr Susan Jeffers' book, *Feel the Fear and Do it Anyway*, and later on became one of the trainers for her book. The other big lesson for me was that I am responsible for my happiness; when I blamed others for not listening or not letting me do what I want to do, I was giving away my power.

3. I am responsible for my own happiness.

I cannot change anyone else. I am the only one that can change my responses to people and circumstances.

I used to blame those around me for not allowing me to do what I wanted to do. I used to blame others for asking me for favours, and I used to blame myself for making mistakes.

When I started to believe that the ball was in my court, what would I do with it? I became more assertive, said what I felt without blame, and forgave myself for what I did not get perfectly right.

I'd like to say to you as I say in my training sessions, "You are perfectly imperfect." How often have you felt that you are not good enough until you get it perfect? That's impossible; nobody is perfect!

I suggest asking yourself: "What would I do if I was responsible for what I want in life, and what am I willing to do to achieve this?"

With practice, persistence and commitment to myself for change, slowly but surely, affirmation by affirmation, my life has changed.

I feel I am living life, I feel excited, I am fun to be with and I am expressing my full potential.

I am doing more things that I love doing. I am being who I want to be. I feel energised and am truly able to give to others without resentment or blame.

I know that I am not the only one who has been through these struggles. If my story resonates with you, then I would urge you seek within to find your true self and live your life fully. Do not let others stop you!

Imagine looking into the mirror when you are 80. What would you say to your younger self?

How would you feel if you did not choose to have this freedom to be YOU?

My journey has led me to become a trainer for Dawn Breslin's workshop, Zest for Life, as well as Dr Susan Jeffers' book *Feel the Fear and do it Anyway* and Azim Khamisas workshop's on forgiveness. I am also a life coach, a neuro-linguistic practitioner, an international speaker, and author of the book *Freedom to Be Me*. I am now embarking on enabling and empowering others, with my Five Keys for Freedom to Be YOU.

Dedication

I am most grateful for my experiences in life and for my husband Salim's support during my transformational journey.

New Woman 7

Donna Joseph

Lost and Found – A Story of Faith, Love and Forgiveness

"Once you realise that you have unconsciously created your own path, with its twists and turns, you realise you can now consciously take the steering wheel and drive yourself down the path you choose to go."

I didn't realise how lost I was until I started finding myself. Now I'm searching all the time because I realise there are many gifts of faith, love and forgiveness to find along your life's journey.

My hope is that my story will encourage you to find and accept who you are, so that you too can feel the freedom that forgiving yourself and others brings. And maybe like me, if not already, you'll share your story one day.

Truth is, if I didn't have faith in myself and if I didn't love and accept myself, I don't think I'd have been able to write this chapter. The fact you're reading this means I beat the pesky voice in my head that still occasionally says, "Donna, you can't do this," or, "You're out of your depth." Thankfully, through learning to quieten that voice in my head, I've now achieved something I have always dreamed of doing.

So thank you for being here and reading my first published story, *Lost and Found*. I believe we've all felt lost at some point in our lives, some more than others, and my hope is this story will encourage and inspire you to let go of what's gone so you too can find and believe in the beautiful human that you are.

The hardest part is looking back and confronting yourself with what happened in the past. I'm learning how to free myself from the emotional pain because I finally figured out it no longer exists in my current life. It's in my past, yet still a part of me struggles to accept. This in itself is an act of forgiveness.

I was adopted at three months old. My birth mother knew she'd likely be giving me up for adoption, or that it would be difficult if she kept me. It was in the seventies that she fell pregnant with me, an unmarried white woman with a mixed race child inside her belly. She wasn't with my biological father for long. I've now found out my biological father was married at the time, but that is another story...

Knowing what I know now about those first few months of my life, I wonder if I was feeling lost then, maybe even as far back as being in the womb. I don't and never will know this. However, I do know that the first night at my new adopted home, I slept the whole night through, even though my adopted parents were told that I didn't sleep well at night. I can't help but wonder whether at three months old, I felt that I was finally where I was supposed to be.

From the moment I arrived at my new family home, my adopted parents loved me unconditionally. And if I'm honest, I believe this foundation of unconditional love throughout my life, thankfully continuing to this day, has saved it. When I arrived at my new home, there were just four of us: my new parents and their own son. After two years, my parents started fostering children, which made for a very exciting childhood indeed. We had a big house with a playroom where we were allowed to cause chaos, as well as a huge garden with a climbing frame and lots of chickens roaming around. I have so many fond memories; in fact, I remember thinking our Christmases had to be the best in the world!

I had no personal issues in those first few years. My first experience of feeling lost started when I realised I was different to everyone else. I'm pretty sure I'd not have noticed so early on if others hadn't. But my brown skin shone like a beacon because everyone else, including my adoptive family's skin, was white. I received a lot of compliments about my skin being a lovely olive tone or coffee-coloured. But it was the fact that everyone seemed to look at me differently that I didn't like. I didn't understand it, I didn't like it, and I just wanted to be accepted like everyone else.

It was at this time that I started daydreaming a lot about my birth mother. I didn't blame her in anyway; in fact, I remember thinking of her fondly and putting her up on a pedestal. I imagined her with long blonde hair and I used to wish and daydream that my hair stayed like it was when it was wet and full of ringlets, but it never did. It always went back to being a wiry mop of an afro that I couldn't make any sense of and neither could my parents. How could they if they weren't shown in the first place?

The only other person I saw with similar colour skin to mine was the TV presenter (now Baroness) Floella Benjamin. She was a children's entertainer on TV and watching her is likely why I also daydreamed about being an entertainer or TV presenter one day.

I didn't realise the power of these daydreams until much later in life...

When I was 12, my wish to see what my birth mother looked like became desperate, so much so that I begged and cried for my mum to ask social services to help me find a picture of her. My mum didn't like seeing me this way and I realise now that she thought she was doing the right thing at the time by helping me. What she or I didn't know, was that my birth mother was dead and seeing the picture would be the start of another level of trauma which stayed with me for a very long time afterwards.

The picture I'd dreamed of seeing was not the picture I saw on that day. What I saw was a washed-out newspaper clipping of my birth mum who had been found dead at the bottom of a canal. I don't think my mum and dad would have wanted me to see or know such graphic information but as it was a newspaper clipping I'd been shown, it would have been hard to keep the truth away.

Finding out about my birth mum's death was the start of more trauma. Any hopes I'd had of meeting her one day were gone, and with this the love I'd held for her and indeed myself had gone. I also held a lot of anger towards my adopted parents for adopting me. I felt it was their fault and if they'd not adopted me in the first place, maybe I could have saved my birth mum. I now know that this was not the case; however, at the time I felt totally on my own and incredibly unloved. And I believe this was the start of me losing any love I may have had inside for myself.

Sadly, trauma doesn't usually just stop in its tracks; it usually results in more trauma, and for me that's what happened. I replaced daydreaming, with drinking alcohol and smoking cigarettes and doing things that a girl my age shouldn't have been doing.

Because of the imagined lack of love I felt in and around me, I craved love and attention elsewhere, which resulted in experiences of abuse and domestic violence in later life. I left home at 17 and went to live in London with a guy I thought would love and protect me. But he didn't – far from it. My feelings of emptiness and rejection continued in that relationship for five years. I felt trapped in this volatile, abusive relationship, until at 21 I decided to find out more about my birth mum. It was in 1992 that I set up a meeting in King's Cross with the social worker that had informed me of her death years before. Up to that point, I'd been scared to leave my abusive relationship. It's hard to leave when you don't believe you deserve any better. I thank God I went to that meeting because as you'll read on, it changed my life forever.

Whilst it was heartbreaking to hear about my birth mother's death, I now believe she saved me from going down the same road as her. I found out that she had also been in an abusive relationship and that this was likely why she died. Only she and maybe one other would know exactly why she was found at the bottom of that canal; however, I believe she committed suicide. Hearing about her life before she died was like looking at myself in the mirror. History was repeating itself, even though I'd never even known her.

As I share the rest of my story, I'd like you to think back to the daydreams I've mentioned. As well as finding out about my birth mum and her death, I also found out I had a brother who was two years younger than me. Knowing I had a younger brother that had also been adopted and was the same colour as me, filled me up inside with a good feeling I'd not felt for a very long time. Finding out I had a brother was exactly what I'd wished for when I was younger. For the first time in a very long time I felt I had something to live for, a purpose. Up to that point, it had felt as though I'd lost everything. After that meeting, it was like a door opening with treasure inside and the treasure was my brother. And there was no way I was going to let my brother see me in the abusive relationship I was in. To put it bluntly, that day's discoveries gave me the strength to leave the relationship. And I believe I had this new-found strength that glowed around me that day, because he didn't threaten me or even scare me; he couldn't because I had something in my life now worth fighting for.

Going back to that meeting with the social worker in King's Cross, I also found out the name of my biological father. The surname was familiar: it was the same surname as my then-boyfriend's best friend. Years later, that surname would change my life forever and I now see it as a blessing that it was a further 15 years before this massive shift and change in my life occurred.

If I'd have discovered that day what I found out 15 years later, my life may not have been as positive as it has been. It was positive because on that day, I walked out and left! I remember as clear as if it was today – walking away, not looking back, and also vowing with such passion that I would NEVER be in a relationship like that EVER again! And boy, I meant it; I'd got my strength back. Knowing I had a brother helped me to find a piece of me again. And because I'd felt so lost, it was a massive piece...

I don't know when I started saying, "It was meant to be," but it's a phrase I use and mean a lot. I believe it was meant for me to find out about my younger brother. It could have easily been a shut door when in fact the door was wide open as the social worker had an address of a lady who knew where my brother had been adopted. I wrote and within a few days I had the address of where my brother lived. As he'd turned 18, I was allowed to make contact and so I wrote to him, and although he took a while, I did get a reply. I will NEVER forget how receiving his letter made me feel. In fact, as I write this I can feel the emotion as it comes back to me. It's quite a journey writing this chapter!

It was such a beautiful experience finding and then meeting my brother. Even now, we have laughs about certain memories we hold from that day we first met at Birmingham Coach Station. We have a good relationship and I can't help but think our mother has something to do with that.

So I don't know whether you've figured it out yet about my daydreams? If you haven't, I'm going to tell you. They all came true! All of them! I wished for a picture of my birth mum – I got one. I wished to have lovely hair – I've got that now. I wished to be an entertainer and I am one, a children's one at that, just like Floella! I wished to be a presenter, and I'm now a radio presenter and podcast host. And an obvious big dream was I found my brother, but actually what I wished for was plural; I saw lots of brothers and sisters all the same colour as me. In my daydreams, I imagined *The Cosby Show*...

Fifteen years after meeting my brother, a mutual friend of ours started dating a guy that turned out to be my younger brother from my biological father's side. There's a HUGE story here that I will write down one day. For example, the circumstances to me arriving at the pub to meet my friend, how I went straight into the toilets to find her and how within minutes she was showing me a picture of her new boyfriend on her phone. It was as though I subconsciously knew I was on the path to finding my other brother! And it turns out I was, because not only did I discover my friend was dating my brother from my biological father's side, but I also discovered I had a further eight siblings!!

I also found out that night that my late biological father had left 16 brothers and sisters, my new aunties and uncles. It doesn't take a rocket scientist to work out that I now have a big family, all the same colour as me. And remember my previous partner's best friend? Well it turned out he was my cousin all along! And this is why it was good I didn't discover this when I first found out. If I had, then this may have meant I would not have left the abusive relationship when I did. Instead, I met my brother and 15 years later, he led me to my biological father's family. Just another reason why I believe everything is meant to be.

It was in 2006 when I found my biological father's family and I'm still finding new family members to this day. It wouldn't surprise me if I'm not meeting new relatives when I'm in my eighties. What is exceptionally wonderful is the love that my three sisters and I all have for each other. I could never have dreamed this was possible. Or did I ?

You can hear me talk more about finding my family on my YouTube channel.

One more dream I want to share that came true is meeting my husband, Eric. We've been together for 28 years, and he never has, and never would, physically hurt me. If anything, in the past it was more likely to be the other way round. Not a lot of men could have handled me back then but he managed to and we're good now and we are blessed to have our lovely son.

If nothing else, I hope my story will inspire you to daydream. This chapter is a good example. I've had so much adrenalin and felt so many emotions whilst writing it. In the past, I've had many doubts and fears that have stopped me but this time I saw another door and opened it. And now I've experienced it, I just know in my heart that my second chapter or book is a lot closer than it was before. Another door to open through using my imagination. I honestly believe this works; try it. What have you got to lose?

However, as you've read, it's not just about daydreams. Recalling all the different aspects of my life has meant revisiting the emotional pain that's been getting heavier and holding me back. And with the many traumatic twists and turns in my life, this hasn't always been easy. I realise letting go is an ongoing journey. Writing this chapter has shown me emotions inside to deal with, so I can now work on them – how fabulous is this! Writing is healing!

When you start this process, you realise life is for living, not fearing I now see my life experiences as gifts and this somehow changes the energy around the experience; it helps me to see situations from a different perspective. You go from thinking, "How can I get revenge for this?" to "How can I learn from this?"

Once you realise that you have unconsciously created your own path, with its twists and turns, you realise you can now consciously take the steering wheel and drive yourself down the path you choose to go.

This is how I've gone from feeling lost as if I didn't belong anywhere, to a place of faith, love and forgiveness.

I truly hope my story inspires you to do the same.

New Woman 8

Mirabel Ngong

Stereotypes: The Fight for a Dream

"Take the small steady steps to that goal with determination. Above all, never forget to be grateful and to appreciate yourself for every step you take. Keep going – the world needs you."

There is much humanity one can learn from children: a mindset of limitless possibilities, unconditional love, genuine curiosity and openness. That is how great and untainted we are born before social norms and stereotypes consume us, defining and shaping our lives in different ways based on our environment. In patriarchal societies, being born a girl is a major game changer as gender plays a pivotal role in your development as a human being: especially how you are raised and treated.

In this chapter, I chronicle my journey through girlhood to womanhood, a path fraught with excitement, but also challenges. As you will see, in overcoming these barriers, I have gained practical and vital lessons for life. In fact, my story attests to the saying that success is best enjoyed when preceded by the stench of failure.

I was born and raised in Kumbo, a town in the North West region of Cameroon, with a social system where women are considered 'the backbone of the country' with men being primary power holders, leading in roles of political leadership, moral authority and property control. Kumbo is the capital of the Nso Kingdom and known for its rich cultural heritage that brings people from around the world annually to participate in the prestigious Nso Cultural Festival in honour of the founder of the Kingdom called Ngonso. Growing up here, I enjoyed the stories of our cultural heritage, the Ngonso festivals, and I also became aware of the cultural and patriarchal expectation for women and girls.

In as much as we love the beauty of our cultural heritage and traditional values, some of its labels and expectations immensely affect the lives of women, hence the need to preserve beneficial values and to drop or reform aspects that harm or limit its people. Patriarchal settings often expect women to develop, dress, and respond to life in certain ways thus ensuring that they stick to cultural norms for acceptance, regardless of their views and choices.

These expectations often vary as every culture around the world has its own standards and requirements.

My family believed in the power of education for both boys and girls, with equal opportunity for all siblings to learn and explore their potential. It is a great thing for society when fathers can stand for their daughters, be good examples, and believe in them to grow and create positive change; when brothers can bond with, grow and learn with their sisters treating them as siblings, no more, no less. Girls become unstoppable when their fathers stand with them. Just like the presence of an outstanding and loving mother figure can set the stage for a daughter's relationships and behaviour patterns, the active presence of a father can be a game changer; and it takes more than just the title.

The silver lining for me was having a supportive and engaged father who believed, and still believes, in the benefits and power of educating a girl. My father constantly encouraged his daughters to own their voices and explore their potential. "Go to school and learn. If you want to be something, go for it and never stop learning. You can make it." This support became a strong backbone as I pursued my studies, built my self-confidence, and the drive to always keep going and never give up even when I failed at something.

Supportive and engaged fathers or male role models for girls serve as a reference for what a 'good man' is like. I respect and salute the amazing and wonderful women who have sailed through in life successfully without father figures or supportive fathers, because it takes a fight and the grit to stand against the challenges.

"It takes a village to raise a child," they say; and I believe it also takes a village to silence a child's dreams and potential when their voices are hushed and when no one stands with them, especially at the significant ages of life. I grew up seeing some of my friends given into marriage at tender ages without their consent, being raped and having to be silent not to soil the family's reputation or to reduce their chances of getting a husband. Some of the girls gave up on their dreams as they had also been convinced to believe those dreams were too much for a woman. So they would let go, settle and live quiet lives that focus on the family, having limited engagement in society and taking on traditional careers acceptable for women.

However, that was not for me. With hard work, unwavering faith and determination, I received my national diploma and degree, regardless of the challenges. It was always a process of one step at a time, one success at a time and overcoming one setback or failure at a time.

As a student and later a community worker, I travelled a lot within Cameroon. I was always catching buses for family or work-related travel to rural and urban areas within the country. The experience of travelling by national bus agencies to urban cities was always quite different compared to catching buses or motorbikes to rural areas. Rural travels came with some considerations regarding seating arrangements, like the passenger's body size and gender, with front seats often considered for men. A dispute would arise every time a woman tried to take the front seat of the car. I always made sure I was early to pay for a comfortable seat and hold on to it for the entire journey.

Working with non-profit organisations has been a great opportunity for me to contribute in the development of communities, learn, develop my skills and an opportunity to do one thing I enjoy a lot: travelling. Some of the travels were great, some challenging and some in-between. I loved my work and it was always great meeting and working with various communities, municipal councils, government delegations and media organisations. There were rare occasions when I was challenged as a woman and reminded that some jobs and responsibilities were not just for women and that empowering women was creating insubordinate wives. Many of such ideas have subdued female talent and kept many communities behind.

One of the communities from which I gathered many wonderful memories was Mbessa, a village located in the North-West Region of Cameroon. My task was to accompany the municipal council to set up and train a water management committee to take care of the newly constructed community water system. To me, it was a great experience. I lived in a new community for many days, connected with the people and was part of their team working to provide portable them water.

On the second day of my stay, just after we had completed catchment site visits and the training session for the day, I began to put my flip charts and field material together so I could retire to my little room at the guest home. The water engineer and two other men were helping to tidy the hall for the next day. I was exhausted and starving after a busy day and couldn't wait to go freshen up and have dinner. Just before I could finish packing my stuff, one of the elderly women we had met the previous day walked up to my desk. I greeted her and she responded, "Hello, my daughter," with a motherly smile that made me feel at home. "Are you married?"

"No, mother," I responded with a curious smile.

Then she continued. "My child, you are doing some good work here but you should always remember your rightful place and role as a woman. You should be home taking care of your husband and giving him children, not travelling and mingling with men out here. It's not right. Do something about it, you hear me, child?"

"But, mother", I started.

"No word," she concluded. She looked at me again with a smile, turned gradually and walked out of the hall. I stood there trying to wrap my head around the last three minutes of this brief exchange. Then I picked up my bags and walked out feeling grateful for my own mother. I was stirred up to encourage the other women at the training to educate their daughters and give them the chance to not only marry but also add more positive impact to this world. Nonetheless, I was still starving but not discouraged.

These experiences, instead of dissuading me rather kindled my spirit. I was inspired to work harder, to stand up for myself, for other women and girls, and seek ways of bringing solutions and contributing to positive change in my own way. Being in synergy and working together with other people, especially women, who share a similar vision, has not only strengthened me through life but prepared me for my current work. I am passionate about encouraging young people, improving girls' education, and promoting women's participation in leadership positions for development and better livelihoods. The most beautiful thing about this is the fulfilment of seeing results, facing challenges head on, and connecting with the global community to seek solutions. It is a process of growth and continuous learning.

Imagination is everything and some of the greatest innovations in the world were once a thought that was nurtured, given a shape, an image, a name; in essence, turning them into an object or accomplishment. As kids, many of us have practiced deep visualisation without knowing until the world robs us of this wonderful treasure when they tell us to come out of our heads and face reality. It is all right to believe that one is created for a something bigger, it is all right to be ambitious and aim for heights, even if the people around you cannot see the bigger picture as you do. You were created for this world, with a gift to add value to the world, and that is why you can still wake up every morning.

Rising Above Failure

Many times, I failed at things, and failure really sucks, especially for those opportunities I poured effort, hope and my heart into, believing the best would come. Failure got me feeling bad or crying my eyes out and wallowing in self-pity on the shoulders of my family members and close friends.

However, I turned them into opportunities by reflecting on the failure; accepted that it had happened, learning from it, picked myself up and doing it again in a better way.

I remember one such moment at my first job. I called my mother to recount what had happened; she listened with so much love and attention as I recounted the situation. When I was done, she said with a calm voice, "Mira, I am sorry this happened and it is totally okay to cry about it, but the most important thing is to wipe your tears, get up, and do better...yes, you can do better, dear."

Those words turned everything around. Not only did I feel stronger, but my confidence was also boosted. Consequently, that evening I created my first vision board which served as an inspiration to more action and better performance at work. I was able then to transition from a volunteer to being employed as a full-time worker, and was later promoted.

My physical circumstances always had a different picture to what I could see every time I looked deeply within me. According to what I could hear and see in the physical world, I was just another girl growing up to fit into society's expectation. I came from an economically marginalised region of the country. The economy was getting worse and after our family business suffered burglary twice, things were getting tougher at home; resources were limited and challenges were screaming at us all of the time. However, every time I looked within me, I could clearly see something bigger than me. I could see myself speaking for myself and for many voiceless people. I could see myself bringing meaningful change in communities and contributing to make the world a better place. I could see myself meeting other great world leaders who were paving the way for the younger generation.

Over the years, my vision has enabled me to travel around the world and led me to meet and speak with some great leaders who have inspired me over the years, like Barrack and Michelle Obama, Atifete Jahjaga, Hillary Clinton, Linda Thomas-Greenfield, and more.

In 2015, I was selected as one among 12 Cameroonians to attend the Mandela Washington Fellowship in the United States. It was a big deal and I enjoyed every moment of my fellowship at the Presidential Precinct in Charlottesville, Virginia. Little did I know, one of my biggest dreams was to unfold from this experience: meeting my role model of all time, Michelle Obama.

Three weeks into the training, I was invited to speak at the Girl Up Summit in Washington DC. We arrived in Washington DC on the day of the summit and headed to the event venue where I joined the members of my panel. Our panel was briefed to get ready as we would be meeting the First Lady, Michelle Obama backstage before the event. I was speechless.

Just a few minutes after a couple of security checks, the moment came and here I was, walking towards Michelle Obama, who waited with open arms and a great smile. This was followed by a wonderful moment of sharing, encouragement and photos with the First Lady. That morning, I spoke on improving girls' education in the 'Let Girls Learn' panel following opening remarks by Michelle Obama.

It was a beautiful day. I had always hoped and prayed to meet and speak with Michelle since I was a student at the National Polytechnic in Bamenda, not knowing how it was going to happen. Then here the opportunity came, and so suddenly! The following months and years, I had more opportunities to raise my voice on issues that matter in crucial circles and to meet more leaders I had always held in high esteem. These experiences spurred me to carry out more work back home and to encourage more girls and young women to work hard and to hold strongly to their dreams and what they feel called to do.

The Power to Choose

The wonderful thing about life is that you don't get to decide how you come into this world, but you can always choose what you make of this world and how you go through it. You get to choose what you give to life and how you respond to life. Culture and environment can shape our thoughts and beliefs but we have the power to seek knowledge, to stand out and be different, if we choose to. We can be pacesetters and leaders who bring new norms and positive change in society, leading causes that celebrate our cultural heritage and at the same time, guide society to rid itself of harmful practices and beliefs.

Seasons of life will happen; the good and the bad seasons, which are all necessary for growth and renovation. The question is: how are you going to navigate the chaos when it happens?

How are you going to stay anchored amid the possibilities of panic, anxiety, and depression or losing control? Surrender to peace at every dead end when the tunnel gets dark. From childhood, I was raised with knowledge about God and over the years as I learn, ask questions and understand better, I see God through many situations in my life, leading to a deeper relationship that gives me guidance, peace and strength in challenging times. One thing I have come to know for sure is that God will keep you in peace when your mind has stayed on Him intentionally, acknowledging His presence and believing that all is well.

Half of the world's population is female. Imagine the possibility of empowering all women and men to explore our potential with equal opportunities. Challenges and failures are important in our lives; they are essential for our growth and maturity. There are no limitations except the ones we place on ourselves. Take the small steady steps to that goal with determination. Above all, never forget to be grateful and to appreciate yourself for every step you take. Keep going – the world needs you.

New Woman 9

Maureen A Lewis

A Black Woman Growing Up in Walsall

"Every obstacle, every challenge,
is there to shape the person you are meant to be,
so continue to believe in you and push forward."

I was born to Jamaican parents who came to England in the late fifties, as part of the Windrush generation. My story is about my journey growing up in Walsall, family life, the loves, the laughs and the racism experienced; my journey of learning, the struggles in fulfilling my dreams and aspirations, culminating with where and who I am today.

My early memories are of sitting upstairs by the front bedroom window, looking out on a busy main road as the world went by. I must have been about two or three years old. As children, my sibling and I were only allowed to play within the confines of a small terrace property which we called home. I would watch the cars and trucks and the large double-decker buses pass by, stopping at the bus stop just outside my home. People dashed to and fro to either catch the bus or just cross the road to get to the local shop on the other side.

I am the middle child of three siblings. We grew up very close, we looked out for each other and would often create our own imaginary games when our parents left us alone to go out to work.

My parents came to the UK and settled in Walsall as part of the Windrush generation, who came over from the Caribbean islands to help rebuild England after the Second World War. They were very industrious people like many of that generation, who were willing to do all sorts of manual labour to make a living for themselves and their families, both here in the UK and back home in Jamaica. Part of 'making of a better life' was the belief that England was the 'Mother Country'. Many from the Caribbean believed that as 'children' of Queen Elizabeth's Commonwealth, they would be welcomed with open arms. Nothing really prepared them for the racism they would endure and their fight for survival.

I lived and grew up in the north of the borough of Walsall, a place that was predominately white. I grew up not knowing many from my own African Caribbean and other ethnic communities. Most of these cultural communities lived in the south, an area that I never ventured into until I attended senior school; there I encountered a diverse ethnic mix of communities. It was great because it was a melting pot of learning of new cultures for me and a sense of belonging.

Both my parents worked very hard. I cannot recall any time that they were out of work and were reliant on the state. My father was the main breadwinner, and on occasions when my mother could not go to work, she looked after young children of friends and family, helping support these families so they in turn could go out to work and not worry about childcare. Their strong work ethic was something that I, including all my siblings, emulate even until today. This notion that racist people speak about, "that immigrants are lazy and are taking their jobs," is nonsense in most cases. In the fifties, sixties and even up to the present day, most people come over to the UK for work and in many cases, do jobs that people who live in the UK will not do.

I grew up with my younger sister and my older brother to parents who loved us greatly. However, our lives were often disrupted by various incidents of domestic violence. These episodes were a horrible experience for me as a young child.

One vivid incident was when my bedroom was nearly set ablaze from the use of a paraffin heater. The heater itself was lit and I remember flames blazing high as the single bed caught fire. There was a sense of panic and all I can remember next is the heater being thrown out of the small back room window, landing on the concrete outside and the flames from liquid paraffin blazing across the ground.

That one incident made me realise that experiences like that are imprinted in the memories of children, and it is something they may live with for an exceedingly long time. I have also learnt through my own experience and that of others, that when there is an intention of violence in the home, children are usually told to "go to bed" or go into another room, and there is a notion that they would not know what is going to happen next, not hear the beatings, the screams, and everything else that goes with domestic violence. But how wrong parents or adults can be!

Writing this book has made me realise that my experience of that one night, although there were many others, made me have one reoccurring dream for many years, far beyond my childhood. It was quite scary... The dream was always the same – being trapped in a burning house, trying to escape but not able to, flames rising high in every room with no way out. Added to this, I also had a sinking feeling of falling. This was also a regular occurrence, especially at nights just before I fell asleep.

I had to try to survive the situation for my own sanity. Things got that bad for me, I would shake frantically and the local doctor was called out to help me. I was prescribed anti-depressants, and as a child that was major. I had to decide whether to take them or not and I thought no... It is funny how things I had seen as a young child on TV about the effects of taking such medication from research and news reports, made me realise I did not want to become like other people who became addicted, and with the long-term side effects; I did not want to be part of those statistics.

Dealing with domestic violence continued into my late thirties/early forties, and still having to go and deal with the disagreements was quite wearying. However, I grew to understand that people of that generation took their vows literally "for better for worse, in sickness and in health, till death do us part," and the notion of separating was not something they would consider.

I remember driving home after one incident and saying to God, "I can't take this anymore; how long is this going to continue?" The whole experience made me an introvert who lacked any self-confidence. From that day on, I would not say that the violent incidents stopped, but they were not as often, and I was given added strength, until it all went away without me even realising it.

I have never really talked to anyone about my experience, received any counselling, or anything else. The only one I was able to talk to, who understood and helped me through this, was God. My siblings had their own experiences, and I cannot explain why, but we never really shared or discussed how we felt, and how it has affected us. We just knew it was part of our family environment. Despite all this, I decided that I was not going to be a statistic and I was not prepared to let this affect me in a negative way.

There is a happy ending to this part of my story – my parents continued to grow old together. As I said previously, people of that generation are from the old school, of those who took their vows of marriage seriously. During the latter years, the love was very evident. My mother cared for my father as his health deteriorated, and my father could not believe, that despite what he had put her through, my mother showed such care and love for him. I recollect one day as he laid on his bed, he turned towards her and said, "Thank you, I love you." This was the first time in their 60+ years of marriage that I ever heard him say those words to her.

This experience and my journey growing up, has helped shape me to be the woman I am today. I am grateful that despite the bouts of trauma, love conquered and we could overcome the hurt of past years. The experiences, like many others, have made me live by this quote:

"Every obstacle, every challenge,
is there to shape the person you are meant to be,
so continue to believe in you and push forward."

My life certainly has not been easy. I lacked confidence for most of my life, but the continued journey has seen me overcome it.

After finishing senior school, I made a conscious decision that I wanted to work in Walsall. Most of my peers decided to leave to go on to university or work in other parts of the country, like London, as they felt that

Walsall had nothing to offer them; but for me, I wanted to give back, and so all my growth and development in relation to work, has been in my hometown.

I enrolled in college to do a BTEC in Business Management. I also managed to take on a part-time job working at the local McDonald's, just to fill the gap while I studied. After I qualified, I applied for numerous positions in the business field, but had no joy and was constantly rejected because of my lack of experience, as I was told I continued to work at McDonald's and did see an opportunity for progression because of their internal training programme that encouraged personal development. I expressed to my then-manager that I would like to be considered for a management position in the near future as part of my progression.

From working on the shop floor, I was soon promoted to a trainer, a position that required me to train all the new staff that came into the organisation. This is something I thoroughly enjoyed. I did this for some time and ended up working another five years. I had to leave in the end because my request and desire fell on deaf ears. I knew I was a hard worker, striving for that day that I would be considered for a senior role. The penny dropped when a young man whom I had trained was soon promoted to supervisor and then floor manager, while I remained where I was... I was so annoyed, I went straight to my manager and reminded him of what I had said and asked how come someone who had just come into the organisation and whom I trained was now considered above me. I just remember him looking at me and shrugging off my question, like it was nothing. It was then I knew I had to leave. It did not click that maybe it was because of the colour of my skin...

I continued to apply for several jobs, but again, I was met with the same barrage of excuses. I then had to resort to agency work and temporary positions to keep me going. I was never given the opportunity to fulfil my career goal.

It was within one of these jobs I met a nice mature Black lady, who for some reason took a shine to me, took me under her wing and provided motherly advice. When this temporary contract came to an end, we kept in touch periodically and I recall one day, she called me to tell me of an admin position that was available at a local charity run by local Black women. The lady became the manager of this charity and needed an Administrative Assistant; she felt I would be the ideal candidate, so I applied and got the job!

The charity was set up by a group of local young Black women back in 1986. At the time, there were inequalities and lack of opportunities for people from the Black community, so they thought they had to do something to help their own. With determination, continued persistence and lobbying at Walsall Council, the organisation was soon rewarded, when they secured government funding to enable the set up and delivery of projects, including one to support single mothers to find employment and training opportunities, and a supplementary school to address the underachievement of Black boys.

The ethos of the organisation was something that intrigued me because I never really mixed with my own community, as the area I had grown up in was predominantly white and the stereotypical image of Black people was a negative one.

I started working in the voluntary sector after having my third child back in 1991. After three years, the organisation was struggling with funding, and having just a small pot of money, the manager left as the funding had dried up and the organisation could only afford to keep me with reduced hours. So outside of my remit, I stayed on and worked to develop the organisation with the then management committee, taking on the task of raising funds, something I had never done before. I had to learn on the job. I was successful in securing a three-year grant, which enabled the organisation to deliver more projects that addressed local needs, disparities, and inequality of Black communities living in deprivation.

My main obstacle was believing in myself. As stated, I was a shy child, who really did not have any confidence. However, I have grown through the ups and downs of running a charity, developing in character and abilities. Starting with basic admin duties to now being the CEO has enabled me to remain humble.

After nine years, I left that charity to work for another local charity, which I did for two years. During this time, I was headhunted by a statutory body to take on the role of Community Development in a number of localities within Walsall. I thought, "Yes! I have now found my ideal job!" Working within local government, I thought meant that I was set for life, but again, how wrong was I!

I was treated differently to my white colleagues, although I was very good at my job. I experienced plagiarism – work that I had done being copied and claimed as someone else's. Lies were told to my line manager. I had to fight for my rights and kept a paper trail just in case I was called again to question. At one stage, I felt the whole establishment was against me, an establishment which was not prepared to fight the cause of a Black woman or defend me. The system was not built or prepared to tackle the undertones of racism, as they could not see it. So once again, I had to leave.

Luckily, the Black women's charity was in need of a CEO, so I returned to the organisation that helped me on my career path. The difference of working for this organisation is that it was about making a difference to people's lives, and that is what I love, outside of the bureaucratic systems and structures that stifles real growth.

Knowing that this local women's charity is still here after 30 years makes me feel proud, especially seeing the work and lives that we have helped to change. Working within the voluntary and community sector, I can say that I have now found my passion for helping people who are less fortunate.

It took a Black organisation to propel me to fulfilling my dreams and ambitions. I can now help others who have faced the same discriminations, and through our work, we can make a difference. Racism was something that I was oblivious to. It was through working for a Black charity and my experience of working within local government, I then saw the hoops we have had to jump though, the disparities, discrimination, institutional racism at play, that has now made me realise this is no way a level playing field.

The young women who started the charity witnessed first-hand the racism and discrimination that existed in Britain, so took matters into their own hands with a collective voice to ensure that we were able to fill gaps and give Black people a step on that ladder of success. I appreciate the support this organisation gave me, the belief in me and the community to make a difference. Having a purpose is all it takes. They gave me a voice and the passion to continue to help impact change, empower people and promote a Walsall that is inclusive of its diverse communities.

New Woman 10

Nina N

Never Apologise For Who You Are

"It really is incredible to see what a woman's spirit can endure when she is called upon."

I have found my voice and I choose to finally tell my story and speak my truth, in the hope that it will encourage others to do the same.

My parents divorced when I was five years old and my only reference for a relationship was theirs: shouting, fighting and misery. As a child, I just absorbed what was around me without any thought and accepted my surroundings as the norm, until I was 30 and sat in therapy; I didn't realise the damage and dysfunction it had caused. At school, the boys always picked the white girls over me, making me feel second best. The first boy I liked at 13 years old told me he had feelings for me but couldn't make me his girlfriend because I had brown skin and his friends would mock him.

* Before you feel sorry for me – don't. Now I turn heads just walking to the corner shop...

At 17, I met a boy. He was the type of boy your parents would warn you to run away from, but I didn't. He was older, charming and dangerous – I was young, naïve and infatuated. He was my first boyfriend, so I quickly got sucked in and swept up in the whirlwind romance and drama that this 'bad boy' was offering. I didn't care that he sold drugs and was a career criminal; all I knew is that he wanted me.

The first six months of our relationship were bliss. I was on cloud nine, we spent every waking minute together, falling in 'love' and making plans for the future. Then, my hastiness caught up with me – I fell pregnant and within a week he was sent to jail.

I decided to have an abortion but was still so in love that I wanted to stick by my man, despite the fact that jail changed him. It brought out an ugly side of him I hadn't seen before. He became paranoid, nasty and aggressive. I would visit him weekly and for the first 90 minutes of the visit, he would relentlessly accuse me of cheating and lying to him. I would sit there lost and confused, desperately searching for a flash of the boy I had once fallen in love with, whilst he would berate me for having had an abortion, taking out all of his frustrations and anger on me. Like clockwork, just as the visit would be ending, he would grab me and say, "Baby, I'm so sorry. You know I love you. It's just so hard in here being away from you."

Stalin once said when referring to people and populations: "If you treat a bird badly, plucking it of all its feathers, but throw it some food now and again, that bird will follow you around and accept the pain you are inflicting on them if it knows that once in a while, it will receive small crumbs of what it wants."

In that year he was locked up, I didn't miss a single phone call of his. I was glued to my phone nervously waiting for it to ring, in fear of what I would hear on the other end if picked up too late or, God forbid, missed his call.

When he came out of prison, his control began infecting my life insidiously. He became violent, abusive and manipulative, leading me to doubt my own sanity. Everything was my fault and my doing. In each argument, I would see about five different personalities surface, never knowing which one I would get. To this day, I remember the gnawing twist in my gut and the hot wave of dread that would brew inside me knowing what was coming. Sometimes it would catch me off guard and I would curse myself for not paying more attention. Other times, I would remain silent but this would just fuel his anger. Everything was my fault and therefore my responsibility to 'make things better.' If I ever hinted to have a break or that I wanted to leave the relationship, it would be chaos. He would threaten me, threaten to hurt my family and terrorise me, ripping out any remnants of the happy, young, carefree girl I used to be.

"Married couples don't just give up, Nina, so why do you?"

By now I had dropped out of college, left a job because he would repeatedly turn up and embarrass me in front of my colleagues, and I was desperately trying to find a way out whilst living with my mum. I decided to enrol on a course to get me into a university far away. So far away that he wouldn't be able to get to me. I promised myself I would make this happen.

Eight weeks after starting my college course, I fell pregnant again.

"Those contraceptive pills are making you crazy. That's why we always fight. I'm throwing them away, give them to me, you're never taking these again, it's ruining our relationship."

By this point, he was abusing me daily, threatening me, controlling my every move and had become an absolute monster. I was completely suffocated. He would follow me home then later at night stalk me to ensure I was still there, waking me up and forcing me to come to the window to prove it to him. If I didn't reply to messages fast enough or answer the phone within two rings, he would drive straight back to my house, sit outside in his car and repeatedly sound the horn to scare me. I would be shaking in my room begging him to stop and not cause a scene or worse still, tell my family.

My mum and sister were oblivious to what I was involved in; they thought I had left him and by now I was too humiliated to tell the truth. I had become a compulsive liar and was leading a double life; managing him and his volatile nature, whilst also trying to maintain some kind of relationship with my family, pretending life was going well. I was a mere shadow of a person; 19 years old, weighing 7 stone, eating one packet of crisps a day and relying on cigarettes as my only comfort. I was barely keeping myself alive, whilst desperately keeping my hellish nightmare a secret. He knew how much my family meant to me and he would use them to taunt me continuously.

"You want to leave me, yeah? Okay, how about I slash your mum's tyres and get your mum's house robbed to show you who you're dealing with. You think I'm a joke don't you, Nina? Okay. Let's see how much of a joker I can be."

His words were chilling. He would see the terror in my eyes and it would be as if he was aroused by it.

I remember once we were on the motorway. He had one hand on the steering wheel and with the other, he had grabbed my head and was dragging me around by my hair and smacking my head into the dashboard. I remember how much I judged myself that day for not just opening the car door and jumping out.

At times, the thought of my family knowing my reality scared me more than the violence I was enduring. I could barely face it myself.

Whom had I become? What would everyone think? How would I explain why I went back to him?

When I found out I was pregnant for the second time, his abuse had become unbearable and having his baby was a death sentence – there could never be an escape, we would be tied forever. There was no choice for me, so I made the appointment and got it over and done with as soon as I could.

The shame I felt on that day, I can't put into words. Shame is the lowest of all human emotion. It is the emotion that drives people to suicide.

As far as I was concerned, I was the lowest of the low.

I was nothing.

Insignificant, invisible and worthless.

What had I allowed to happen to me? How had I allowed myself to be in this situation… again? Whom had I become?

When someone continuously humiliates, belittles and degrades you, you enter this mindless limbo of existence. No purpose, no identity; you just become numb, because it is so much easier to feel nothing than it is to feel something.

It's easier to feel numb than feel the hands wrapped around your throat.

It's easier to just lie there than it is to accept you are being raped.

It's easier to look away than to look your predator in the eyes.

And it's a hell of a lot easier to say nothing than it is to speak up.

It took me eight years to get away from him. The police were involved and I was forced to come clean to my family but every few months, he would worm his way back into my mind and my life, so I would end up back there, engulfed with even more guilt and shame than the time before. I didn't understand for years why I couldn't gather the courage to leave him for good and why I never seemed to have the strength to stay away.

It is difficult to understand why women go back to these men but as anyone who has ever experienced abuse at the hands of a partner knows, the deeply complex web of self-hatred and shame that you become entangled in takes a lot of courage and bravery to see, let alone untie. As time goes on, your own voice in your head is replaced with theirs; no matter how outrageous, cruel or untrue their words are, you begin to believe them and you start seeing yourself through their eyes, with their judgements and their hatred.

They say that on the other side of fear, there is freedom. One of my most freeing realisations as an adult was accepting that it wasn't actually him that stole my self-respect and crippled my self-esteem; it was the fact that I never had any to begin with.

Responsibility is an incredible thing. The ability to respond or be responsive to something. The power in taking responsibility is huge, and understanding the true beauty of this concept has changed my life forever. It doesn't mean passing blame; it doesn't mean it was my fault and it doesn't mean that I am the reason why all these bad things happened. Responsibility is a decision. It means I choose to take responsibility for not loving myself, for not having boundaries, for not showing myself the respect I deserve, and for making the unacceptable acceptable.

After responsibility comes forgiveness.

And after forgiveness comes freedom.

I realise now that he took out every single one of his own insecurities on me; he hated women and was so sick with disgust and hatred for himself, it oozed from every cell in his body. His misery, unhappiness and the disdain he had for his very existence, turned him into a sick and deluded man.

For years, I was bubbling with blame, rage and anger. Brimming with resentments, I blamed him for every struggle I faced. Now I will tell you what harbouring those emotions did to me.

Six months after ending my relationship for good, on 27th March 2015, I had a stroke.

I was rushed to hospital and underwent a three-hour-long invasive brain operation to remove the life-threatening blood clot that had formed in my brain. During those two weeks in ICU, I underwent probably every single test and scan under the sun to find out why such a freak thing had happened to me. After a week in hospital, they found a hole in my heart.

Looking back at the years leading up to my stroke, I now see the damage I was doing to myself and my body. I had been living in a pressure cooker and inevitably the lid had blown off. A stroke is an event that takes place when your body and organs are put under high pressure and extreme stress. Most stroke patients suffer from high blood pressure and are over the age of 60... I was 25.

Years of internalising my trauma and suppressing deep unhappiness meant my body had finally had enough. It needed to rest.

It took me a while to realise the magnitude of what had happened to me. I couldn't believe I wasn't paralysed, let alone that I had survived and honestly, neither could the doctors or my family.

The next few months, I experienced a variety of struggles; though I had working limbs, they were extremely weak and I was fatigued to the point of collapse. I'd wake up, brush my teeth and become so tired, I would just fall back asleep. For the first time in my life, I was forced to honour myself and listen to my body. I took each day as it came, put no pressure on myself to do anything and I gave myself permission to rest.

The surgery left me with a level of brain damage so I had lost some of my memory and had forgotten how to read – but the beauty of the human brain is incredible. For months I diligently forced my brain to practice and remember and I did it. I knew I had a long road to recovery, but I was free.

We say in yoga that gratitude is an attitude and I now truly understand that. Because that is what carried me through. I was alive. My limbs were weak but they weren't bruised; I was unwell but I wasn't a prisoner; I was no longer trapped and I was my own person, maybe a sick person, but I was ME: as lost as they come, no idea who I was, what was happening or where my life was going, but finally on the way to figuring it all out.

The next part of my story is probably my darkest time. It left me in the deepest hole that took me years to climb out of. By 25, I had endured violence, abuse and survived a stroke that could have killed me, but believe me when I tell you, nothing is as ugly as cancer.

Within a year of recovering from my stroke, on 16th March 2016, I was diagnosed with thyroid cancer. I couldn't believe it.

Hadn't I gone through enough difficulties? Hadn't I already learnt all the lessons to make me appreciative and grateful for the most basic of things? Apparently not, and I felt utterly defeated.

In over six months, I underwent two surgeries to remove the lump in my throat and my thyroid too. The surgeries were a disaster and the surgeons messed up repeatedly. They burnt me during the operation, my wounds kept getting infected, I was in and out of hospital constantly, and my scar took months to heal. I had taken my stroke in my stride, feeling like a medical marvel and it had been a novelty that I had survived. But this was different. I felt dirty. Cancer is such a dirty word and one that no one wants to be associated with… but I was.

I could feel that old and familiar feeling of shame and worthlessness creeping back into me. I was the girl that had a stroke and then got cancer.

Who would ever want to be with me? What boy would ever want to get close to me? The sick girl; the unhealthy one; the one with all the problems. I couldn't stand that that was me. I was so angry and ashamed and just furious at the world for having dealt me such a horrible card. Again.

I didn't want to be strong anymore, I didn't care to be. I was tired.

It turns out that when you mute your truth, swallow your feelings, and ignore your pain, that combination will sooner or later poison your body. And that is exactly what had happened to me.

Over the next year, I faced many difficulties. Physically, mentally and spiritually, I had been broken. I couldn't understand why all these rare and awful things kept happening to me. I was so desperate to be doing the things other women my age were doing and live my life how I had dreamed when I finally escaped from him.

People say when you go through hard times, you re-evaluate your life, purpose and perspective.

I just wanted to get drunk.

I went on a hard core, two-week, alcohol-fuelled bender with my best friend and let loose. I drank my pain away and felt physically free.

Soon after, I quit my job to go and do the things that were important to me. My mum came to this country as a refugee so the refugee crisis was something close to my heart that I wanted to get involved in. I volunteered with a charity and then travelled to Calais, Greece and eventually the West Bank in Palestine to work with refugees and teach English.

For the first time in my entire life, I felt like I was living my true purpose. My heart was full and my life finally had meaning. I felt proud of myself.

I spent the majority of my twenties deeply distressed and unaware of my pain. I lacked boundaries, didn't nurture myself in any way and made a habit of burying my true feelings. Out of sheer desperation to get my life back, I convinced myself that I was okay. I was not okay.

I have looked the shame, guilt and fear that consumed me for so many years in the face, to finally free myself from it. Through therapy, yoga and a 12-step program for trauma, I have let go of the anger, the resentments and the rage towards life and the hardships I have been dealt. I have been more brutally honest with myself than I ever thought I could be and it really has changed my life.

Today, I am an English teacher working in North London. I live a life according to my own values and wake up every day with a heart full of gratitude – for my freedom, my independence and most importantly, my health. Honestly, the simple fact that my limbs work and I have the ability to jump out of bed if I want to, puts a smile on my face.

Sometimes I look back to remember how far I've come. Today at 31 years old, I have learnt not to be embarrassed or ashamed of anything that I experienced, felt or endured because I know now, that freedom is what you do with what has been given to you.

It really is incredible to see what a woman's spirit can endure when she is called upon.

Someone once told me, you should never apologise for who you are. Because that is who you will always be. And that is unapologetically me.

New Woman 11

Sangeeta Patel

Colour Is All You See

*"The battles we are challenged with,
eventually make you stand up for your rights."*

Life can be so unpredictable, especially when you least expect it as a young adult, just starting out on your education and career. Who would have thought when growing up, that the world around you would be so cruel and frightening? Unexpected situations arise and you are faced with racism and prejudice on an everyday basis, although I have only brought a few to light here.

In my eyes, life was the same for all. Whether brown, blue, or green-eyed.

We all talk and walk the same. But do we?

Weakness dawns! Stuck in a bubble!

When will it burst and set me free?

Will I be safe?

I was the shy, reserved, timid girl at school. I daren't speak up in class, afraid everyone would laugh at me. There were characters who were much stronger and more powerful than me, I thought. I knew I didn't fit in. With my friends, I was a different person, happier and more relaxed. I was able to express myself and my wittiness came through. I just couldn't find my voice in the classroom. My head was full of things to say; answers to the questions asked, and even though my answers were correct, that voice just didn't emerge.

At home, I had to be quiet in the presence of my father; I was sometimes even sent to bed to give him space to freshen up, relax and have his evening meal, as he had worked all the hours God sent. He chased job after job from the moment he touched the ground in the UK, in the late fifties. Mom was a housewife. Weren't they all? Keeping everything afloat with housework, raising the family and attending to her husband. Don't get me wrong, my dad was a good hard-working man. Just very strict with a temper.

My parents went from renting small overcrowded shabby flats or houses of very poor-quality and sharing with extended families, to finally settling down, after all their hard work raising the deposit for our home. As an Indian-British born child in the early seventies, I didn't know any of the struggles my parents faced in their life until they shared their stories, when I was much older, of living through discrimination around them.

How hard it was to maintain a job in such tough conditions, or even to buy a home. Education for children wasn't their priority. They knew that we would learn from attending school. I learnt a lot from watching my mom, keeping the house, cooking, a woman's role and to appreciate what little we had. Saving money, repairing clothes even sometimes until they were totally worn out.

We lived in the Walsall area; I remember it was heavy with crime and drugs. The streets weren't safe to walk in alone. Cars and homes were regularly broken into. The Asian communities were an easy target based on their ethnicity. Without any help or support, we slowly settled in this area.

We personally had two burglaries; the first when we were all asleep in bed – thankfully we weren't attacked! The second was when we went on holiday to India (my parents' homeland). They trashed our home and took the little we had saved or managed to possess.

If you stood on the front doorstep on a hot summer's day with the heat waves passing by, you could smell the aromas lingering in the air. Vehicles parked on street corners with windows slightly open adding to the air we breathed in. This was the way of life.

I had no idea what career path to follow. I merely went to school and came back home again, not really thinking of my future. I had no guidance. Careers advisors suggested a Youth Training Scheme would be suitable for me. Not even exploring my true ambitions or talent. These regular meetings became pointless. Even the careers advisor couldn't see my potential and probably felt YTS for an Asian girl would be the correct career path to take. I wasn't happy or comfortable to take their word for it. Something inside was telling me not to settle with the advice given. I flicked from course to course to find myself. Business Administration, Secretarial, Office Management, Typewriting and even a Database Analyst. But it was all around the same area which didn't feed my hunger at all. There was something missing. What was that something else??

My position as a receptionist for the Community Health Council (CHC) shone a light in the right direction. A colleague pointed out that I was wonderful at interacting with children as we completed our rounds on the children's wards and children's centres, writing reports of compliance to meet government guidelines, policies and procedures. A suggestion led to undertaking my diploma as a nursery nurse at the Walsall College of Technology. My character was slowly materialising.

The diploma was demanding and I found myself quite competitive with my fellow students. With good organisational skills and preciseness, I began to own my skills and ability. My family placement as a nanny was with a lovely, friendly, warm-hearted family in the Goscote area, which became daunting to attend. My journey to and fro wasn't so simple. As I walked through the streets, cars tooted their horns, pulling faces and showing hand gestures, shouting from their open windows, "You Paki, go back to where you came from."

'Oh no, what was happening?' I asked myself. What universe had I stepped into? I'd dread the thought every morning as I woke up. I knew what I would have to face on my journey in the morning and afternoon when I left, two bus rides each way.

My palms became sweaty, I was shaking with fear, my heart racing to the hilt. I was scared. I had nowhere to hide or run, or even pick a different route. What if they turned the car around and came back? All sorts of thoughts running through my head. As I panicked, I picked up speed to get to my destination. There was a feeling of comfort once I entered the home. My troubles drifted away. The children were beautiful. My skills developed, the creativity, the communication, even the interaction, came through so naturally and my affections began to grow. Leaving all this behind, I would have to step back into the real world.

At times they would throw cans at me, laughing, making rude sounds. I wished I was invisible. I'd stand back as far as possible, in the bushes of the hedgerow hoping to be camouflaged, not to be seen. If I heard loud engines backfiring in the distance, I knew the 'boy racers' were back.

Passers-by would shake their heads, staring with disgust on their faces. I watched, afraid that they would say something or attack me. I had no one to call as we didn't have mobile phones in those days. Still, in the distance you could see in their eyes the hatred. Tears rolled down my cheeks, I couldn't stop. 'Someone take me away from here and tell me I am safe', I thought. A quick glimpse here and there not to miss the public transport. Again, a sense of relief once I stepped onto the bus.

College didn't understand or even explore my predicament, so I continued for the term with my learning.

My arranged marriage proved to be another challenge. Leaving my family home and the community where we became the same, a togetherness, was all disrupted again. My husband and I settled in a prominently white neighbourhood in Staffordshire, where everyone was a stranger, even my husband to a certain degree. You'd think that as time passes, people would be more tolerant with people of different races. My family grew, with two beautiful boys. It was time to occupy their little minds, so we explored and found playgrounds and playgroups to attend.

With my two very young boys, indoor activities were perfect – community halls and centres. They had a somewhere to develop and interact with others. They explored their surroundings, in their new world, with brightly coloured toys and fun activities. We engaged in laughter as we played. Their little faces lit up as they babbled away. This was heaven for them, a warm comfortable atmosphere; little did they know!

Activity groups were like Chinese whispers. 'Glares and Stares,' I called them. We continued to enjoy our time. We had a lot of space around us. Other groups joined each other, at a distance. Moms stood back in their little areas; I could hear soft sounds of laughter, chuckles and whispers in the background. As I looked up, they'd stop and turn away, not engaging in any eye contact. Nervously, I continued to interact in play with my children. They giggled and knew no different. We weren't aliens after all and we were here to stay.

These brown-eyed people! Week after week, I was determined to attend these sessions and slowly but surely, we became part of the group, with some! I wasn't going to allow them to drive me away or my children to miss out on the activities. I had already left my life in Walsall, so I had to try and make the most of my new life here as it was a new beginning for both my children and myself. Alone, I faced the battle.

Even the town of Stafford had no coloured people around that I could remember. I once bumped into an Asian woman at the counter of Asda; how strange we felt when our eyes met! The expression on her face, a smile with pure natural happiness, and her eyes gleamed, to see one of her own. It was a 'wow' moment.

Time came for me to return to work. A slight career change, still working with children as that was my life – I couldn't move away from that. But now looking more in depth at the development of a child, a holistic approach including safeguarding. I studied to enhance my career alongside watching my babies grow. I moved back to Walsall, my family home. My boys started at a new school and new friendships were to be made, for all of us. My new position took me to work in Tipton. I was extremely excited and apprehensive at the same time. My team of colleagues were wonderful, very welcoming and I felt really accepted. I had a lovely, enthusiastic role model who showed me my role in a flash. I learnt very quickly from her achievements. I admired her qualities of positivity and confidence, which in turn helped me gain my strength. 'Why did we get on so well? I asked myself. Perhaps because we were from a similar minority group.

Soon, odd comments flew around here and there as I completed my daily work. Not everyone was the same. "What does she know?" one said. "How can she say that there is a misuse of drugs in that household?" as they spoke amongst themselves. I proved myself with knowledge and handled it professionally. But I really felt like saying, 'I come from a ghetto, so I have that life experience'. But I didn't, of course. Quite quickly, people can be very judgemental not knowing one's background. This didn't faze me at all because I knew I was right and we had a job to do which required exploring. The safety of the children was my priority.

Socialising proved to be uncomfortable and lonely at times. Even with the same age groups and sharing similar interests, acceptance was ignored. Working together was one thing and a nightlife to be seen together was another. Little clicks formed and drifted away; I was excluded. I started to develop a thick skin. I was determined to enjoy myself just as much as they were, since I was there in the moment. I started to accept myself and consider their behaviours. I was not able to control how people felt and to make myself go through pain and hurt for the sake of others all the time. I had to stop and think. 'I can't let them walk all over me,' I thought, 'whether it was in the workplace or out of work.'

I found remarks crept in. Surprisingly I took a step back. Brushed it off and concentrated on my work. I realised that, depending on their own upbringing, their era or where they came from, made a big difference to the way they thought and behaved. They were uncomfortable around people like me. Slowly but surely, there were more and more of us!

I remember been challenged with everything I did. A person couldn't accept anything, even when the work completed was correct. I felt I was fighting a battle that I just wasn't going to win. This behaviour made my life unbearable. I became a nervous wreck. That dreaded feeling, when you wake up in the morning trying to drag yourself out of bed to get ready for another day. I became totally miserable and so withdrawn again. 'What is happening?' I asked myself. I couldn't think straight.

One particular person was on my case constantly. She came from an upper-class area, was of course a knowledgeable person, whom I had actually admired, but nevertheless very much a snob and it was a very awkward atmosphere. She definitely looked down on coloured people, as I wasn't the only one who faced this offensive behaviour. After a few months of this, I asked to be moved to another site. I was wasting my time and energy in this environment and it wasn't healthy for me. I wasn't going to let her carry on and get the better of me. I reported her but I don't think anything came of it.

My new team at the new site were wonderful. I felt at home. The energy and team-working was effortless. The respect for an individual, no matter what race, colour, age, religious beliefs or ethnicity. I started to enjoy my work once more.

Many times we hear phrases like:

"You're just a number."

"You can be easily replaced."

"You are not academic!"

People don't realise how hurtful and demeaning this is to a person. You face the hardship of been accepted all the time. It is a knock to your confidence. You pick yourself up and then wham, you're down again!

"So tough," is what I say now.

"I am here to stay!"

"We are here to stay!"

"We will not let your words bully us."

I have learnt over the last 30 years that there is no escaping these behaviours. I have tolerated and accepted these forms of discrimination, but no longer. I can't wash my skin and make it better for their eyes to see.

We are all human beings after all and God has given us a fantastic opportunity to be on His earth. So, make the most of it! Enjoy and embrace your life and the people around you. Be His outstanding student so He will bring you back because believe me, if you upset Him, He will treat you as you treat others.

We are still facing discrimination and prejudice all around our world. Much less than we have done, but that doesn't make it okay! There's no need to be horrible and cruel. We hear stories about violent attacks and abuse, which is terrible and so disheartening. Even though we move through times, prejudice and racism will always exist with narrow-minded people.

The battles we are challenged with eventually make you stand up for your rights. With all these events happening in my life, I feel it has made me a much stronger person. I hope that in the future, racism is no longer a reality, but a thing of the past. Nations have improved as we've moved forward, yet there are still some who will stay stuck in the past. Although things are changing, we still need better education for our future children to change their mindsets. We wish for better relations between all races. We are all facing this and hopefully we will become one.

New Woman 12

Ruth Cyster-Stuettgen

Ready Or Not – Here I Come

"One day you will tell your story of how you overcame what you went through, and it will be someone else's survival guide."
Brené Brown

For the umpteenth time, I felt as if I have been dragged through the mud, but this time, I had thought to myself, never again.

Even after all this time that has passed, I am still struggling with an overwhelming sense of unbelievable uncertainty. I have yet to fully resolve the reasons why I have been through what no person wants to go through or to endure. I had reasoned that I was on a good wicket but somehow felt that God has other plans for me.

Here I am fighting against obstacles scattered along the path I find myself on. Here I am doing events again, coaching again and speaking with you and the women who have supported me throughout all the ups and downs, waiting patiently for me to step boldly back into my courage and my truth, to reclaim and to own the stage of who I am and what I do.

Am I a glutton for punishment, or dare I believe that I am merely following my life's calling, my purpose for being here?

I can no longer deny that God is instructing me to continue to walk down this path, but heck, I had not in all my dreams signed up for this. I just cannot help myself though. I know that my divine redemption is for me to embrace becoming a New Woman. I courageously step up and shine again and to achieve that, I must first have faith to dip my toes into the waters. Will I make mistakes? You betcha! Will I rise again? Yes, I will!

Have you ever experienced being pulled through the mire of life's challenges, convinced that you will never be able to climb back out of the slums of feeling defeated, betrayed and not heard? Have you ever felt as if the light flickering at the end of a long dark tunnel was impossible to reach? And as you rise, have you ever admitted to yourself how much you love what you are destined to do?

When we let go and release our fears and doubts, it becomes clear what path we are meant to walk. What we have overcome in our past, are going through presently and will go through in our futures, is meant to be.

Your book of life has already been written to be the woman leader you are meant to be, inclusive of all scars of life's experiences etched into your thoughts and being.

There comes a time when we can no longer permit fear or rejection to hold us back. We must own our vulnerabilities in knowing that we do what we do to the best of our abilities.

There is no other who can do what we are meant to do in the way we do. We are on this earth to perform our plan as we seek out those we are destined to serve.

I share my story to encourage you to keep rising despite challenges. Know that you are not alone in being the chosen one, to stand tall in your belief of self. In opening our hearts, we learn to heed messages of when to keep pushing forwards and when to retreat, so that we can replenish our energies and gain clarity of next steps.

After walking away from being a victim within my abusive marriage, my life changed dramatically.

Something had to change to enable me to reinvent the narrative of my life. I have always worked hard at finding ways to uplift myself. I know that no matter my suffering, there is never a wavering in wanting to fulfil my purpose, and this time was no different. I wasted no time in honouring my freedom by equipping myself with knowledge, with professional and personal development. I worked relentlessly to better myself and my situation.

In my concerted efforts to create a life of positivity, I had somehow overlooked one important factor. In my eagerness to take care of everybody else, my beloved children – bless their hearts – and my parents, I had forgotten to include myself into the self-care equation.

I then felt compelled to put pen to paper, with a desire to help others see the real possibility to live happily, free from the shackles and pain endured during a destructive relationship. To know that we are capable of creating the life we deserve, without depending on others. It is our own inner peace of mind that will ultimately carry us through a life lived in contentment and joy.

To that end, I penned my life journey and shared my wisdom by birthing my first book, *From Misery to Mastery: Journey to Freedom and Empowerment*. The euphoric sense of accomplishment I had felt in hitting the 'send' button with my manuscript, was overshadowed by having to be rushed to hospital during the early hours of that same morning. I was discharged later that day, only to be readmitted by ambulance the following day, as the pain in my rib area had worsened dramatically. I was consequently hospitalised for a week with the diagnosis of a blood clot on my lung. I could have easily died, I was told. 'Perfect!' I thought. In the nine endless months to recovery, I was blessed and grateful for the help received from family and friends caring for me and the children. I felt profoundly reluctant to ask for help but had little choice. My body was too weak and I had been instructed by doctors to rest and heal. Days of turmoil followed where I fought against what my body was telling me not to do and what my mind was telling me I could do.

Was it God's way of nudging me to take note of the signs He threw my way, to just rest and recover? The long-term effects on the body, mind and spirit of our souls whilst enduring an abusive relationship, are devastating and cannot and should not be trivialised or ignored. It is imperative that we take the time to process the state of our well-being and to heal properly, something which I am guilty of not having done, or at least as well as I had been telling myself I had. I had plunged straight into wanting to carve out a new way of life for myself and my family. Everything I tried seemed unobtainable despite my tremendous efforts. I realise now that it was due to me not taking the time to work on myself from the inside out.

So, my due and timely advice to you, is to take the time to heal, physically, mentally, emotionally and spiritually.

Sometimes we fool ourselves into believing that we must experience certain things for ourselves, but for real, take heed of this advice from one who has been there and done that. Lean into me and my shared experiences. There is no need for you to reinvent the wheel, as the saying goes.

I implore you to take it step by step. I repeatedly told myself the false narrative that I was doing just that, when in hindsight I had not been doing it enough. I was not putting my health or well-being first. I had not considered myself to be a valuable priority. I would rest briefly and then release that pause button to then continue pushing myself on along that path of self-destruction. All I ask is that you pay attention, as you are a precious soul, so worthy of self-care and caring.

When you do not put your health first, the consequences of that lack of care for self, are devastating. That lack of care had simply distracted me away from the path towards wellness, taking me down a dark and challenging road for a while. In some ways that had been literally off the road as well, as I was not permitted to drive due to the high doses of medications that I had been prescribed and their after-effects. Being such a stubborn, sometimes hard-headed know-it-all kind of woman, who thought she was super woman and could therefore do it all, I had failed to pay close attention to common sense and before long I had been off and running with a view to doing and creating again. Knowing I had so much to do and telling myself that time had been the right time, had not served me well at all, as far as my health was concerned.

Even though I am speaking about me, do you recognise yourself in this? Do you think you can do it all, all the time, without any detrimental effects on your emotional, mental and physical health? Have you experienced hitting rock bottom and risen again, without giving yourself the space you needed, to retreat and heal? My life may well have turned out differently if I had put in the effort of healing properly. However, I am also profoundly aware that the road ahead of us is not always straight and void of twists and turns. The things I had consciously put into place for my healing journey were not enough.

Not even two years since the publication of my first book, I felt a seed was planted for me to create another book. As I sat in a workshop, my immediate response was to reject my mentor's offer of a publishing package. I returned home but the offer kept nibbling away at my overactive imagination. Days later, I was ready to step back into my next venture. I was certain that the signals I had been receiving were from above, and that I needed to carry on working with my creativity and skills to empower those that needed me. This time around, I felt it needed to be more than just a book about my story but one that would include the stories of other women. That is how the concept for *The Book of Inspiration: For Women by Women* came to life.

An intense and prolonged period with a flurry of mental and physical activity followed as I fully threw myself into this project, with it swiftly consuming me 24/7. Apart from my book mentor and publisher, I was alone in attempting to succeed with this inspirational book project. I have always worked in solitude before and felt confident in being able to co-ordinate hundreds of women to publish their inspirational pieces with me. I spoke to each of them, with an invitation to come on board. When I was not on the phone or social media, I was busy creating content and doing videos. My laptop was my constant companion. The logistical nightmare of it all soon reared its ugly head and this beautiful idea snowballed out of control as the women begun to sign up. Stubborn old me still thought that I could do all on my own. For a time, I remained blissfully unaware of the enormous pressure I was under with this project, plus working full-time and raising my two younger children who were still at home. It was pure adrenalin that kept me going. I barely survived with only four hours of sleep, with the additional stress of my finances taking a hit as my ex-husband refused to contribute to child support.

In attempting to ease the pressure, or so I hoped, my children and I moved in with my parents so that they could support me along this journey, for which I will be eternally grateful. But in reality, my responsibilities tripled as I dutifully and lovingly cared for them, both in their eighties and with my father's health steadily deteriorating. To avoid the burden of paying school fees, I was homeschooling my son too. Always fascinated by this concept now, suddenly the reality of it felt like a heavy burden, even having come from a teaching background.

Despite the downward spiralling of my health, I kept on pushing through, thinking I had it all under control. There was no time for self-care as my plate was already filled with work and responsibilities. Despite regular loving warnings from a dear friend to be mindful of my health, I laughed them off to the point of being sleep deprived to where I would fall asleep whilst driving my car! It felt exhilarating to be juggling calls between different continents of possible co-authors, who were all amazing and the deep connection that was developing between us. I refused to let go of this huge vision I knew would come to fruition.

If only I had taken the time to stop and listen, to reflect, to practice what I had preached about in my first book. When I look back at photographs of me over that time, I can see that I was not doing okay. It is amazing how much the body absorbs into fooling the mind that you are coping well. The project was amazing and could have been even more so, had I done so many things differently. I should have had a team behind me to assist me with that massive project. I did seek help halfway through, but the help and time was still not sufficient. How I had ever managed without the help of my three amazing virtual assistants and a dear friend, also co-authors, I will never know. I had certainly needed to take a tad more time to plan. I was crumbling with having to wear so many hats simultaneously. As a mum, daughter, carer, friend, author, publisher, writer, coach, teacher, employee, driver, volunteer student mentor, church volunteer, cook, and as a businesswoman plus more, it was full-on.

With the date of the book launch looming, my event planner, co-author and friend encouraged me to focus on the book and to leave the planning of the event to her. I trusted her knowing my time was taken up with so many other aspects of making this a success. What a mega task to accommodate the varied personalities, characteristics and demands of hundreds of women, all of whom were inspiring, uplifting and ready to impart words of hope to those who were in need of it. Some women voiced strong opinions. I had the added stress of their book cover rejections and was accused of showing a lack of professionalism in dealing with the whole project. To then receiving threats of being sued and taken to court, it was a horrendous nightmare to deal with.

Overall, that whole experience has taught me how to be resilient, empowered, confident with an inner strength, and so much more. It has taught me that we as human beings, as women, can choose to be as nice or as horrible as we decide to be. The experience had ups and downs (more ups than downs), but those downs had proven to be of a calibre that knocked the wind out of me each time, from which it has taken me a long time to recover. I accept that as the leader of the project, the buck stops with me. We are none of us perfect and sometimes in trying to bring light to others, we set ourselves up to be targets from negativity and lack of understanding and compassion.

From external appearances, many assumed that everything was rolling along incredibly well, and we were all prepared for a wonderful evening with the launch of the book. Beyond that, I had planned other things like a television show to highlight these beautifully talented women, annual retreats, and so forth. I had visions of creating this massive global empowerment circle of women.

The book launch evening was incredible, and the women amazing, with co-author interviews the following day. I am grateful to all the women and girls and those who flew in from other countries to celebrate our massive achievement, from as far as the UK and New Zealand.

It was an honour to have my father attend the launch of *The Book of Inspiration*, to see his daughter shine in her passion for what she had created. He had clung on to see me achieve one of my dreams, the fruition of all those hours I had worked my fingers to the bone.

Little did we know that his time on earth was fast coming to an end. "You did good. You were great last night," he told me the next day. Words that will forever be imprinted into my mind, and every time I remember that twinkle in his eyes and that proud grin of his plastered all over his face. Thank goodness we have some great family photographs from that night. Six short weeks later, my father passed on. I miss him and yearn for his presence and approval to this day. I was honoured and thankful for the last few months spent with him.

The passing of my beloved father had been the final straw for me in terms of my mental, emotional and physical health. Disheartening occurrences had happened both during and after the project and as visible as I had been during the creation of the book, I now felt an uncontrollable need to be private and unseen. I shut down completely. I desperately wanted to protect the privacy of myself and my family.

Social media will always be good for many reasons and without it, my vision may not have been so successful. But with me needing to recuperate in private, away from the public eye, with it came repercussions. Despite the successes, some less sensible decisions were made behind the scenes. I had been overloaded to the maximum, physically and mentally drained.

As I was mourning the death of my father so soon after such a high, I was unable to deal with anything more to do with the book project. My enforced but necessary absence on social media became unbearable to many and the commitment of ensuring copies of the book were sent out to the co-authors was delayed several times. In the state I was in, I could not respond to their enquiries. I simply could not find a way of getting myself out of this suppressive fog of depression that was engulfing me. Strong opinions were voiced within the private Facebook group, and as much as I take full responsibility for my actions, reading those shocking comments felt like a stab in the back for me.

As I slowly picked up the pieces, I know my intention was and will always be to try to make a difference. I will continue to learn how to arm myself with confidence and purpose. I know I am protected by the Grace of God and The Holy Spirit. I am a strong woman and with the learnt experiences of what I have endured, I am now a New Woman.

By no means have I conquered all the lessons I need to learn, because my journey is not yet over. That is my reality. I do not wish for you or me to be living the same experiences over and over until such time that we are forced into learning the lessons from those repeated traumatic and painful experiences. We are all but human beings and sometimes we need those difficult life lessons to teach us to be and do better. I implore you to be brave and dip your toes in and step into your purpose. By doing so, you will experience and become a new woman.

Dedication

I dedicate these insights to my girls, Laura and Emily, and my son, Tim, with the hope that as you carve out your place in this world, you will step into it confidently and with assurance that you don't have to know it all and that there are no mistakes, only growth opportunities.

New Woman 13

Samantha Pearce

The Path to Unconditional Love

*"Growing up, I had not a care in the world;
I believed and created a world
around musicals and fairy tales."*

Since 2006, I've never really been the same. My life changed in the most devastating of ways. The manner in which I thought and how I viewed the world completely changed. Bearing in mind I won't even be touching on my teenage years, and yet nothing prepared me for what I was about to go through. I do not know how you will think about parts of my life, and to be honest it's my truth; it's not written to be liked, it's written to help someone, anyone who may see a glimmer of hope when they are going through some of their darkest times. It's not about exposing anyone else's truth, not without permission first anyway! Whether you see it as good or bad, I walked it, with my head held high, all of it, even the bits I didn't and still don't like, because whatever I experienced in that moment, was to prepare me and equip me for moments to come; that and the fact that I'm loved by those who matter.

I was 22; it was 2006, the best summer I remember ever in the UK. Music was and will always be my healer. 2006 playlists reminds me of what was. I still listen to it even now on my not so good days. I was five months pregnant; round and hot and sweaty, and round and hot again. I also met my ex-husband, and my baby wasn't his.

Like any young mother, I was worried about all the usual fears a first-time mother experiences. I knew my life would change forever but couldn't wait to hold my baby and love him/her unconditionally. I would finally be loved like how I love, I would have my own reason to live. Nothing would have prepared me for what was to happen next; I was oblivious to the fact that my life was about to change with the most unnatural, devastating turn of events.

No loving mother should bury her child. Almost 14 and 13 years later, I still can talk you through everything that happened on that day, the day before and the day after, even down to some of the conversations I had. I think because I'm a talker I was able to articulate how I felt to those that loved me and just listened: my bestie for life Becki, and my beautiful sister-in-law Sarah, were my rocks in those times right through, in their own ways. Being able to express my feelings in safe environments helped me heal.

I waited 45 minutes for an ambulance and walked the corridors alone that night, fearing and preparing to hear the worse, yet praying and hoping to hear my baby was okay. Remembering the story of when my mom was rushed to hospital because she had complications, my big sister was still here. She was early and she is perfect, literally, so my baby will be perfect too. Can you imagine? Born asleep, I like to say, she was here for her purpose; she remained an angel and will always remain my angel. I learnt so much about myself and people, and how those around you have a direct bearing on how you deal with life and how you view the outcome of your future. Learning to let go, especially of the things you can't control, and that nothing in this life is guaranteed but death, so live life every day to the fullest. Live each day as if it is your last, and make sure you give life your very best EVERY TIME.

In April 2007, I found out I was pregnant again. Considering the heart-wrenching experience I had with Mya Leigh, I was still so excited and still full of hope. Surely God wouldn't let my heart break again. In December 2007, I had Josiah, my second child, my only son; he was early, breathing, gaining weight, and we even had conversations about transferring from an incubator to a cot the day before. The day before the world broke me, God broke me again. In my head, my son was going to be like my dad: handsome, loving football and the kindest man I'd ever known. I couldn't sing Beyoncé's *Daddy* for years after, without tears filling my heart first, then them translating into physical tears. How hard it was to let go of the idea of my son. He had the biggest eyes and after Mya Leigh was born asleep I never got to see her eyes, but I know they would have been big, like mine. Josiah (TJ) grabbed my finger; he had wind and had the most beautiful of smiles. I had conversations with him and made up the answers whilst resting my head, falling asleep against the incubator.

When we got the phone call on our way to the hospital, on 13th January, he was 13 days old. For the second time in the space of 15 months, the world crumbled around me, and swallowed me whole. Not again, not my baby. For a hot minute, I thought I'd be better off opening the door and sliding out of this world, whilst we were speeding down the road, than to walk through those hospital doors and go through this pain again, putting my family through this again.

I'm not going to lie, I was so angry at God this time but even more; it really happened again. Oh, I had some fierce conversations in the hospital car park, talking to the open sky, not holding back either. I was so angry and I wanted God to know. I said, "God, I need a minute and you can't get mad. When they killed your son, you turned your back on the world, well, so the Bible says." I learnt not to let my anger drive what I say or to make me do things I may regret at any moment in time later.

From here on, I was tested on my learnings and quickly realised if I can sit in a cemetery in the middle of my babies (the council gave me a space opposite each other so I literally sit in the middle when I used to live up there), I can stand and face any situation.

I was a walking, talking, living, smiling zombie; I literally stopped feeling. I didn't want to feel; with all that hurt I was still piling in more on top of everything else, so I shut down for years. When I say shut down, I'd still go to parties, I'd still visit family, I'd still enjoy bedroom time. I was existing but I don't feel like I really started living until 2017. I always know what it's supposed to look like when you are happy in a relationship.

I was raised by King Solomon and Queen Naamah: Yvette and Canel Pearce. I have to talk about them later because the foundation I was raised on is what I use to this day to walk through life with an understanding of how unconditional love works, and how we have the power to shape our own future. I could focus on all the negative aspects of my life but I am a firm believer of what you give energy and attention to, is exactly what will be, and that life and death is in the power of the tongue.

Before I discovered the true me, I was being guided and given the tools to equip me for my purpose. I have been able to use these tools and guidance throughout my life, subconsciously, in some setting or another, to help heal those ready to let go of hurt and pain. If I hadn't gone through some of these things in life, I wouldn't be able to help and offer peer support to the countless messages, WhatsApps and direct messages from people just crying out for unconditional love,

God's love and someone to simply listen, without judgement.

I started to live the lie, over the years, allowing and accepting less than I knew I was worth, because rejection cut me that deep. Even down to lying to myself and excusing friends and family's actions and shitty behaviours – but that's for another book!

I became the ultimate 'yes' girl. I wanted to please everyone. I didn't want anyone to feel hurt or be left alone to face anything by themselves. I had no idea or understanding of the world of energy and energy transfers, certainly not to the depth I know now, and am still learning through reading and seminars. I grew up in a Pentecostal church. Anything apart from the holy spirit is 'juju'.

I digress! Sorry!

Still to this day, my eldest piece of sunshine amazing doctors with their findings and annoying anyone older than her when they realise she's literally not your average at the time six-year-old, now 12 – she isn't your average 12-year-old! She was growing inside me and living detached away from my oxygen supply. I was in hospital for weeks before I had her. I say God and she were having their one-to-one time before she came to change the world with her beautiful ideologies, spirit and love for humanity. This is around the time when it started, the time I became attached to nothing, yet connected to everything.

Bearing in mind I was going through mental and emotional turmoil at home, while in hospital my ex-husband and I would often argue and he or I would storm off. I am literally a Jekyll and Hyde kind of woman once a month so BEWARE, almost werewolf-like, but that's my business and I stay away from the world during those times and home-in on my creativity.

For three weeks, I didn't look at my child, I didn't sit near her, I didn't even change her or form any kind of attachment with her; she was only going to die and I had to pick up all my broken pieces and put my life back together again. I say this because it's important to know the depths of my zombie state and where some of it stemmed from. I still continued to pile on the hurt. Through life choices and allowing people to use and abuse my love, I was hurting myself trying to heal the ones I loved, while broken and living in a zombie state myself. You can't help others until you learn to help yourself; you can't be hurting and help anyone.

However, Seriah came all the way through and still amazes me today with her mind and her love! During that time, my on/off marriage was taking my focus from healing and raising my baby, my wanting to be the perfect wife and keeping the promise I made to God, so I did what I thought at the time was right. I communicated my feelings and concerns, lived open and honest, respected, honoured and obeyed the direction my husband was taking our family, even cooked and cleaned (in this zombie state, mind you!). I didn't even know what I wanted for myself, let alone to fulfil needs of another adult human being.

When dealing with anything external from self, having expectations is setting yourself up for disappointment; dealing with people and the baggage they have carried with them most of their adult life, some from childhood, without addressing their feelings. I once had counselling due to clinical depression and loss of appetite. They all wanted to put me on medication and all sorts, but instead I insisted on counselling and by the end of our first session I was counselling the counsellor! That's when I realised I had to turn my life into purpose, I had to turn all my pain into power, but first I had to heal.

My second ray of sunshine is Nevaeh. To this day, I laugh when I think about everything and how she came into the world, because of how my waters broke. I was in hospital at 29 weeks pregnant and she was delivered two weeks later. Let's just say sex was wild with my ex-husband. If he's reading this, that was then!

I chose to focus on my rays of sunshine and the lessons I learnt around their existence. If I'm honest, without them I would still be in that zombie state and allowing life to happen to me.

Fast forward a few years, I left my ex-husband, experienced more heartache, and more pain, mostly self- inflicted. I had to fix my relationships with men. I moved back close to my mom and best friend and began to live again. I started to dream again and Soul Therapy began, literally and metaphorically. I started to unpick all of the elements of my life I was unhappy with and slowly, one by one, got down and dirty with myself and each insecurity. I didn't hate men, not at all; I did not want to trust another man, to depend on him again. I will be honest; there's nothing more healing than platonic, unconditional love from a friend of the opposite sex. That's what the love of three strange men did for me: Ashley, Ronald and, in the beginning,

Matthew. I invited Uncle Ron into my home. I don't even know if he knows to this day how he helped save me. He's not blood family but he's Uncle Ron for life.

On 7th January 2018, my last ray of sunshine, Keziah, appeared. My 'likkle' miracle birthed from a union I call divine and even though it's not been the best of rides, her existence and mine is up there. When asked what is the pivotal moment that changed my life, it was to see God in everything.

I didn't feel like I had control of my body the day Keziah was born. I knew what could happen; it had happened twice; my baby could have lived or died based on my personal odds. During the emergency C-section that evening, I felt like I was zoning in and out. I put it down to the anxiety, the epidural and the fact that the father of my child was not there as he lives in another country. When removing Keziah, they removed a blood clot the same size as her that was sitting behind my womb. My blood pressure was so high that day.

I wanted to take my children to see their baby sister after weeks of anticipation, but I was told I couldn't leave. If I even walked to the ward, they feared I would have a heart attack or stroke and I was advised to organise childcare until they could bring my blood pressure down, which took a week. I cried. I got home after weeks in hospital, my sister the perfect role model; she's my go-to example for my daughters.

2020 has forced us all to do one of 3Fs, in my opinion, words of wisdom from my mom. The day that changed my life, the day we, my children and I almost, died in a car crash. I felt all three of the Fs at once: fight, flight and freeze.

Growing up, I had not a care in the world; I believed and created a world around musicals and fairy tales. I still love them both to this day and encourage anyone if they haven't watched a musical in a while to do so; it does wonders for your mental health! Trust me!

Everything had a perfectly pitched soundtrack… each person a principal role and the ones I didn't know would be automatically in the chorus.

As I got older, I realised everything really does have a soundtrack. But I also learnt as I got older, it's not every song I enjoy listening to.

I was given the gift and the curse of unconditional love, a physical interpretation and the exact definition of the word. Never hearing an argument growing up in my family home allowed me and my younger siblings, brother Stuart and sister Sianna, the freedom and the courage to explore and see God in everyone and everything. My life has taken many turns that helped me forget some of the experiences I've lived and endured but after I felt what was a blink of an eye, I saw my whole life flash before my eyes; every heartbreak, every disappointment, every tear, every moment in time that broke my heart, came flooding back to memory, like I was watching a blockbuster film. Not only the bad moments, the good ones too; the moments that helped shape the woman I am and the woman I am growing into today. The moments that can't be fully described but only felt. The moments that I'll remember forever.

New Woman 14

Poonam Karwal

My Angels

"I will not allow myself or those around me to become broken by the uneducated minds of others."

I think the best way I can describe my life is as one crazy roller coaster: the good, the bad, the highs and the lows. But, hand on heart, it has made me who I am today. This is my life, and I am finally in control; loving life and ready to deal with whatever is thrown at me.

I was raised in a humble loving home with a devoted mother and amazing dad. We were a big, mad, party-crazy family and all nine of us would squeeze into Dad's pride and joy, the Granada. Six siblings would squeeze into the back and my little brother was once again volunteered to sit at Mom's feet in the front seat; honestly, these day trips were some of my best days: humble little day trips with the family, ham sandwiches at the ready and almost certainly some old Punjabi tunes. Oh, the nostalgia. Dad loved his cars and would race every car in the third lane on the motorway; flashing his lights for them to move over; I was fascinated by his every move.

We would sit together around the dining table every evening for whatever dish Mom had prepared and then on into the lounge to channel surf between BBC1, BBC2 or ITV; we watched one programme together and somehow, we were content. One dish, one programme, simple, and that's how we liked it. It was myself and the little brother that were always allowed out, on the bikes, in our little gangs; but back as soon as the lampposts came on. We used to get paid a pound each for washing Dad's cars; this was so treasured! We would go to the local shop, excited and undecided as to how to carefully spend our earnings. Blessed! I remember the pride I would feel washing the car perfectly to impress my dad. I was raised like a princess; Dad (my guardian angel) gave us everything we wanted. He worked hard at the plant; but would always come home to a home-cooked meal prepared by Mom; she worked from five in the morning until at least eleven every night. I think that's what embedded in me; the desire to graft and work hard for my money.

We lost Dad at 51: what an unjust age to leave your legacy. Devastation is an understatement; I'd never felt grief or emptiness before in my life. He was my warrior, my protector, and never let me come to any harm. Days passed leaving a massive hole in our perfect family; we were lost without him.

Our culture dictated the need to be married by a certain age; if not, was there something wrong? Too ugly, too fat, pregnant, a rebel, something that the aunties would sit and snigger about. So now it was easier to follow the path that had been dictated for me, and marriage was on the cards. Luckily, he was a handsome man; strong, good-looking with a perfect jawline, just perfect. Dad had always been big on morals: respect your elders, do good and good will happen, be a good daughter-in-law and of course, the main one – never lower your standards for anyone. So I dived in head-first taking all these morals with me. Now I would learn that some people have no morals; so how does that work? I had no experience, as my previous life was built around dreams and just a lovely world; how do I deal with these people? I think demoralising me was their key goal. You know the fairy tales with the wicked stepmother and the ugly stepsisters? I felt like I had just been hurled into one of those.

On day one, we had the Presidential Suite; I felt like a queen. VIP treatment all the way. Yep, I was looking forward to life with him; he was loving and attentive yet strong and kind all in one. Again, that overwhelming feeling of being blessed came over me. We came home at 10:30 in the morning rather than 10am which had been dictated to us by his vile sister who was not willing to speak to me as I had defied her rules by 30 minutes. I had not really learnt to deal with confrontation as I had a pretty easy life up until now so what should I say? I didn't know, so I said nothing. My husband didn't speak, and as time went on, I began to realise that this was the norm; they would bark, and he would watch. Don't get me wrong, he loved me – there was no doubt about it, but is love enough?

Things began to get worse and at every turn they barked; still, none the wiser, I could not stand up to them, I couldn't deal with the negativity. I fell pregnant and by this time the only way he could deal with them was to wait until they left and take it out on me; so I walked out the door. I left him. I was devastated, as he was the love of my life; but I couldn't live in fear of anything happening to our baby. Days went by and he pleaded for me to come home; promises after promises that he would not raise his hand. Of course, I went home, so many times…

One evening we sat at the table eating with our three boys; he was drunk, and I felt an unbearable pain in my shoulder. He had smashed his pint glass into it. He was in a rage and then left the house; my baby was three weeks old. I scooped the baby up and sat him in the car; my other two boys had been quickly rushed into the car without their socks or shoes. I drove to the hospital, one arm hanging painfully, scared for my life, and was then treated with a fractured shoulder. I spent three weeks without him; my heart used to break thinking of him alone at home. I would spend days convincing myself to leave and then run back to him over and over; I was in a cycle that I had no idea how to break. Three sons later, I was still doing the same thing. I would spend the whole night fearing for my life and the whole day getting the courage to leave. I was desperate to be strong enough to do the right thing.

I felt a crazy mindset of overwhelming love for my man and the greatest fear of not waking up from his frenzied attacks on a bad night. Night after night, I would lay in my bed and in my head, I would scream as loud as I could for my dad to come and make him stop. I was now bitter as my dad was my protector; in the midst of all the anguish, I could not understand why my dad was not stopping this man from lashing out. The worse things got, the more I grieved my dad.

One night whilst sleeping, I dreamt that I was going into a prison to visit someone. When I walked through security, I went to the cell and saw my dad, kneeling on the floor; he was hanging his head down in despair, broken. I could not understand why; he was always so strong. I knelt next to him, his hands handcuffed behind his back. He looked into my eyes and it was at this heart-crushing moment that I realised that my dad had gone and that he was helpless. His hands were tied and he could do nothing; I was alone. I woke up and sobbed inconsolably for the first time in my life. This unbearable realisation hit me with the most excruciating pain I have ever suffered in my whole life.

I woke up one morning, head swollen from the night before. I could not lift my head and so scrambled for my phone. I called 999 and asked for an ambulance. I knew it was over and was ready to leave; it had taken me 13 years. Deep down inside, I knew he was trying to be a wonderful man, but he could not stand up to them; they ate and ate at him until everything was lost. The morals I had learnt from Dad had no chance in a family who had a dog-eat-dog mentality. They were ruthless; the times I pleaded with them to be my support, my strength... I have lost him to them, and this is my only regret.

Time went on and I regained my strength; I moved to a new area. It was a week before the new September term so I called a few local schools who could not help. I then called this little school to whom I am eternally grateful. The humble, caring headmaster directly took my call and I explained my situation to him. He told me to come in the following morning; him and his deputy headmistress, who was also his wife, welcomed me and my children into their school with loving arms. They had arranged uniforms and stationery for my sons; they were my rock. I now realise at certain parts of my life, my guardian angels always appeared and I think these two were definitely my angels.

My passion and my background were helping the vulnerable and I was offered a job at the school to help others. This would be the first part of me rebuilding our life which we had left with just the clothes on our backs. I know my path was laid out and then met with my next building block: an opportunity to help the vulnerable and homeless. I had now built up the strength to enjoy a healthy challenge, so welcomed this opportunity.

My first help was to a boy who had been in the care system since the age of eight; he was so troubled and was so much trouble but there was so much love in him to offer the world. I worked closely with him for months and supported him to be the best he could be. He grew from strength to strength and would proudly say that he was now happier than he had ever been. This gave me the irresistible urge to help others and never stop. I have now helped hundreds of young people in the care system and have made a difference to their lives. My sons have also learnt a lot through my experiences at work and have the passion to help others where they can. They have been involved in soup kitchens and charity events many times, trying to make a difference. My mom continues to look after us all; continually helping and teaching us her learnt lessons. She is what I aspire to become; she is my guardian angel.

I strongly believe there have been many guardian angels helping us on our life path and they sometimes appear where and when we least expect them. My dear brother-in-law Rajesh, who was the only person in that family who helped me and stood up for me. My dearest sister-in-law Deepika, who was taken so early from my little brother and their three beautiful children.

I have never found comfort in discussing my private life and have always struggled to confide in anyone about my feelings. My amazing sister Raj and my mom have really encouraged me to finally start facing what really happened and to begin by writing this piece.

So now I stand tall; three fine sons that I have raised (my guardian angels), respectful and humble. They have embedded in their souls that it is not okay to treat anyone as any less than they would expect to be treated. And I will continue my journey with my head held high. I will continue to help myself and others; and I will not allow myself or those around me to become broken by the uneducated minds of others.

We have dreams now, little tick lists, to be together, the four of us; this we have accomplished. To own our house with a cute little dog and a feisty bird; this we have also achieved. We will build our own house in the countryside soon where we will continue our journey. We are content and grateful, and my children are loved. So, I would like to think of myself as a humble success story and will endeavour to help where I can.

God bless.

New Woman 15

Sonal Dave

Finding the Strength in Disability

"When you focus on someone's disability,
you'll overlook their abilities,
beauty and uniqueness.
Once you learn to accept and
love them for who they are,
you subconsciously learn
to love yourself unconditionally."
Yvonne Pierre

Once upon a time in a land far, far away, a young child was born to loving parents who absolutely adored and protected her. Adoration of your child is quite the norm, but the protection of your child as a parent can be, of course, quite a large spectrum and for this young child, it was at the higher end. You are probably asking why I mention this so early in my chapter but it's important to set the scene and understand much of what comes later as I tell you more about my journey.

As a baby, it was apparent to my family that I was in constant pain when they played with me. I was taken to various medical appointments where it became clear that congenital hip dysplasia was the cause of my pain. Now I have to explain at this point that this diagnosis was established outside of the UK and was back in the late sixties, when medical knowledge and intervention was not as it is today.

I was put in plaster in what was commonly called the 'frog leg' position with the hope that this would realign my left hip to stop the pain but also to avoid future concerns. Regular visits were made to the hospital to see the doctors so they could check my progress, but it was a time of intense anguish for my parents and lots of tears and screams for me as a young baby.

No parent would wish for their child to be in discomfort, and definitely not for months. My parents had to endure this and from what I have been told, it was a tough and uncertain time.

I came to the UK with my parents when I was a young child and the appointments and check-ups continued in a UK hospital. What was now clear was the long-standing impact of the initial diagnosis would be with me for life. My parents were advised that there would be a likelihood that this would affect my growth and that I may have a leg shortening. This was back in the early seventies, and at that time conversations or discussions around disability did not take place. In fact, it was such a taboo subject, that it was felt your child would be treated differently so it was easier not to say anything. On reflection, I do wonder why the doctors did not mention it to my parents and can only assume they did not know themselves. At least, I hope that's what it was.

As I grew older into my teenage years, I never quite understood why I was not allowed to do the things other children were doing and why I was always told no. I wanted to do things that might be a little bit physical or possibly a little dangerous and as I saw other teenagers doing it, I found it hard to understand. It just felt unfair to me as I just did not know why. On one such occasion, my friends were going ice skating, and as much as I really wanted to go with them, I was told, "Definitely not!"

What I did not know at the time was the reason behind that no, was my parents were protecting me from any harm that may happen to me, as they knew that it could put me back in hospital. All I wanted to do was be a teenager just like my friends but this was not going to happen.

When I reflect on my school years, I recall playing football in the playground and being quite a tomboy. I was allowed to do gymnastics in PE which did not make sense to me, as I was not allowed to go ice skating. I wonder if my parents had not said anything to the school, but then why would they if no one had labelled my condition? What I do know is that when I wanted to do a dance and drama course, I had to get medical consent and this was not given.

It was only when I came back from a trip to India and started working in the early nineties, when a colleague and I were having lunch together, and she asked about my background and wanted to get to know me more. It was then that I first mentioned my situation as a baby as well as growing up. My colleague mentioned the disability charter and that it was in place to support people like me.

I had no idea that this existed or what it was. I started to have a look to understand what it meant. The more I read, the more I understood that this was what I was dealing with. I needed help and support for my work and daily needs. I knew that I would not be running downstairs in an emergency. I needed the right desk set-up with a chair, and I needed people to understand my personal situation, especially my manager. However, I was also worried that if I told anyone, they may treat me differently or maybe I might even lose my job. I must have read the disability charter and the guidance so many times to ensure I knew what to do, how to do it and what I could expect to happen. I wanted to have the knowledge before I said or did anything.

Initially, I found this hard to make people understand as people did not have an awareness of disability themselves, but they also had no idea about what needed to be done. To be honest, if they had never been exposed to someone who had a disability, or had any training, how would they know what to do or what was required? I knew I needed to use my voice and new-found knowledge to help them understand.

In the UK alone, 1 in 5 people has a disability, with 80% of those having an invisible disability.

I wonder why there is a feeling that if you or your child has a disability, you should keep it quiet, you should not tell anyone, as they will treat you differently. I have even heard some people mention that if you or your child has a disability, then God is punishing you. This will be followed up by a variety of pujas and prayers as if to say by doing these acts your disability will vanish. Surely, if you are born with a disability or have one later in life, a puja or prayer is not going to change that. Why do people still listen to the old wives' tales that ultimately harm an individual who has a disability? Surely acceptance and support are the right ways to help them.

This reminds me of the following quote:

"Disability is natural. We must stop believing that disabilities keep a person from doing something. Because that's not true . . .
Having a disability doesn't stop me from doing anything."

Benjamin Snow
Disabled activist, film maker and public speaker

So what is a disability?

A disability is any condition of the body or mind (impairment) that makes it more difficult for the person with the condition to do certain activities (activity limitation) and interact with the world around them (participation restrictions).

Did you know that there are also hidden disabilities?

A hidden disability is a disability that may not be immediately obvious. Hidden disabilities don't always have physical signs and include learning difficulties, mental health as well as mobility, speech, visual or hearing impairments.

So why is disability such a taboo subject that people will not talk about it? Now when I say they will not talk about it, this also means to their family, friends and even their doctor. I sometimes sit back and think, maybe it is a lack of understanding, a fear of the unknown or even a fear of society and what they will do or say. It is a little unclear, but I am hoping that by sharing this chapter, it will help people understand why it is so important to communicate and talk to others to get the right help to support you. If you do not find the power within you to share, then you will find yourself living and facing the disability in silence and the only person that will hurt more is you.

So, moving on with my story. I have now accepted that I have a disability. In my life, I have also had three road traffic accidents. I should also say that they were not my fault. One as a teenager, the second that resulted in injury, surgery and long-term effects, and the third that resulted in yet more injuries and long-term effects, each one making it more difficult to do the things that I enjoyed. Following the third road traffic accident, I found myself struggling in life and getting tired quickly with lots of aches and pains that I have not had before. Initially, I put it down to just being too busy and not sleeping well. As time went on, I realised that there must be more to this. I went to see my doctor and following a year full of appointments and tests, I was diagnosed with a hidden disability, fibromyalgia.

Fibromyalgia, also called fibromyalgia syndrome (FMS), is a long-term condition that causes pain all over the body. Wow, now that was a huge shock to me? How was I going to manage all the symptoms of fibromyalgia **and** my physical disability? I had so many questions I wanted to ask the doctors and I just did not know where to start.

I was also very concerned about what others would think and say. I mean, how is it possible to go from a physical disability to a hidden one? That can't happen, right? Surely you can't have one then the other, or even both at the same time? An additional worry for me was that I was starting to feel that life as I knew it had ended for me now! I was also worried that people would think that I was lying and making things up. Even close friends would make comments such as, "What's wrong with you now?", "Are you ill again?", "You are always in pain," "You're not fun anymore. It's your fault, you don't eat properly," and so on. I know that if I had asked them outright, they would have said, "We were only joking," but many had no idea what the hidden disability was, as fibromyalgia has not been heard of by many people – but also they were not thinking of how this could impact me, their friend! But on the other hand, why should they? I myself had not heard of fibromyalgia and they were not having to deal with it on a daily basis.

The difficulty with hidden disabilities is that they can't be seen but they can take over your life in many debilitating ways. This will mean that you will need to make changes in your life and have support around you, but it should not stop you from having a life. However, there needs to be acceptance and acknowledgement that some change is required, then to ensure a process is in place to help manage the symptoms of the hidden disability.

Many people believe that you cannot have more than one disability at a time, but the truth is that of course you can! Disability does not have a set time or agenda for how and when it will affect an individual. It can be at birth, following an illness, trauma or even through a dormant gene being activated. You can't buy a disability and you certainly can't give it back. You have to learn to accept and find ways to manage it. This is where the support and help are most needed, so please do not live in silence and get the advice and guidance you need and then tell people. Those that don't understand are probably the people that will never understand and you don't need people like that in your inner circle.

There is a quote by actress Teri Garr that really feels right to share: *"When you hear the word 'disabled,' people immediately think about people who can't walk or talk or do everything that people take for granted. Now, I take nothing for granted. But I find the real disability is people who can't find joy in life and are bitter."*

Many people had no idea that I had a disability from birth and, let's be honest, even I was not truly aware of this myself until I became an adult as the word disability had not been mentioned. I had worked, danced, travelled, was a singer, actress, magistrate, and even set up my own business. I had not allowed my disabilities to define who I was but I was still nervous to share this with family, friends and my wider circle.

One of the hardest things to deal with when you have a disability, is having to deal with your mental health. We all have mental health but where we are on the mental health continuum will vary. With my disabilities, my mental health fluctuated. There were days that I could not even get out of bed, yet I would force myself to so that I could get on with the day, do my work and make sure that no one knew or found out. I am sure that when I did my social media 'lives' with my happy face and bubbly personality, everyone watching would have no idea of the level of pain I was in or how I was feeling.

For some reason, at that time I wanted it that way but slowly, over time, that thinking was changing. I started to share and be more open about the details of my disabilities when I started my own business. It started with my physical disability and then when I was diagnosed with FMS, I started to share the details of my hidden disability. A number of people messaged to thank me for sharing and also to let me know that I had given them the strength to share their own stories of disability and also the struggles as parents with a child who has a disability. When I asked them why they had not told anyone before, they all said they were afraid of being treated differently, that they would lose friends or their jobs, and that their families would be embarrassed by what society would say. I could relate to this on so many levels as I had also felt like them. I also felt quite angry for those parents who had a disabled child and could not get support from their families for fear of being judged, criticised or even ostracised.

Thinking about now and how I live my life, it's all on my terms. I tell people I have a disability and if they don't like it, that is their problem. If they don't understand, then I am happy to help them too but it is still their choice how they choose to be with me, and if it's negative then they do not need to be part of my life. I have managed processes in place to help me at home and in my work. I have a wonderful husband who understands my needs and is there for me. Our older dog Neo is like an assistance dog and knows when Mummy is not having a good day and our younger dog Ri watches at a distance. I have the most amazing support team who rally round when needed to help me, my husband and our two dogs. I feel very lucky and blessed that although there are difficult days, I am still able to lead a successful life following my dreams and my passions, having a positive impact on others and inspiring them to lead a life of their choice and not what is expected of them. My disability makes me stronger and wiser, to be able to cope with whatever life throws at me and the ability to help others.

As Stephen Hawking said: *"My advice to other disabled people would be, concentrate on things your disability doesn't prevent you doing well and don't regret the things it interferes with."*

So, who am I now? I am an award-winning celebrant, toastmaster, public speaking expert, magistrate, singer, actress... I support charities that help disadvantaged children, I am a wife, mother of two children of the four-legged kind who love to say woof and, I have disabilities...

Dedicated to all the people who wake up each day with a disability and still lead a fulfilling life.

New Woman 16

Jaswinder Challi

Transitioning New Woman

"Knowledge has a Power,
that enables you to grow and flow."
Jaswinder Kaur Challi Sahiba-Nur

Introduction

In this story, you can see the unfolding of strength, endurance, resilience and power, from places of transition, feeling all is lost, a hopelessness and isolation. It can enable those going through something of a similar nature to learn that there is purpose in adversity, pain and change.

Phase 1 – A Woman of the Past

I was born in India and brought up in the UK, in an era pre-internet. A young girl of second-generation Asians and dual culture, English at school and Indian at home. Conditioned by a British lifestyle and influenced by Asian morals. I actually loved both cultures and loved my parents too.

I enjoyed going to school; in some ways it was a form of escapism, and in others it was like a social outlet. I could be with my friends and we would laugh and share conversations, especially with my Indian friends as we were all in the same boat regarding what was going on around us. It was at school that I could enjoy activities and play. It was at school I found my mind was stretched intellectually in a way that I could resonate.

However, life was not easy growing up and as my parents were both working, there was always a lot of work to do at home. I learnt very early on to become a doer and a carer for others, especially after we lost my baby brother. I feared my parents too would die and I did not want any harm to come to them. So in all the 'doing', I forgot that I was a little girl growing up and becoming a woman.

I remember the time of puberty; my friends and I were all scared of what was happening to us. It was something we felt ashamed of and guilty instead of this transition being embraced and celebrated in the way that I would have wanted to. I can't really blame the parents or mothers because they were all busy working and trying to make ends meet. They were surviving in ways that they could and the majority had more than four children which would have been a handful for anyone to cope on top of working in factories.

So as I transitioned into a woman, I could not really relate to make-up, fashion, nor did I know how to do any of it. Some of the girls were getting into it, as some were lucky to have older sisters, sisters-in-law, or young aunties that were there to help and support. I didn't have any of that. I was the eldest girl and my poor mum was always at work.

To be quite honest, I wanted to study. My mind was always on learning and I wanted to do some kind of academic study. My brother was really encouraged to study; we had the same teachers and they would say to me, "I hope you're going to do as well as him." If only! He was encouraged and I was not! However, he was a big influence in my life in wanting to do well; it was almost like I was able to model him. He always had interesting books around that I was able to read, and he was encouraging, so when the teachers were saying that, I was actually becoming motivated to be that. There was a yearning, a hunger, a longing and a love of reading and learning.

Sadly, this all came to an abrupt end when I was told that I had to get married and was not allowed to pursue further education. I was heartbroken and had to adhere to the norms of the culture of that time.

My marriage was also short-lived, ended abruptly and when I was able to recover, I trained as a secretary and worked at the council for many years, which I thoroughly enjoyed for a long time. Towards the end, I was getting bored and wanted someone new, a new learning, but could not figure out what. However, wanting a change, did bring forth my second marriage, but not quite how I had anticipated! This too ended abruptly.

I remember, in my marriages, other women laughed at me because I just did not know fashion; yes, I dressed well and clean, but not necessarily colour co-ordinated or in the latest fashion trend. I seemed to always be the one that ended up doing all the household chores, making sure the cooking was done, the house was clean and everyone was looked after.

I often admired women looking so glamorous and beautiful, all made up looking like works of art. How I wish I could do that, look like that, I would think to myself. Not that I had the money to try it either, not even in my marriages.

Transitioning Phase 2 – A New Cycle

After a mystical experience at the lowest point in my life, the revelation changed things forever. A door that I never even imagined opened up and led me into the passage of time that was going to be about knowledge and learning. This is something that was not previously available to me in the way that I wanted it to be. All of a sudden, I was now learning psychotherapy, how and why we do things the way we do. The revelations were just opening up in front of me like the pages of a book turning over and over with so much knowledge and insight.

Abuse, patterns , stress, depression, victim; you name it, I was learning it. The more I learned, the hungrier, I became, I was becoming empowered! I was awakening, I was opening up, I was being fed with so much knowledge. It didn't just stop with psychology as I was also awakening to a spiritual knowledge and began to connect with the spirit world on a much deeper level than I had before.

Astrology also became a big part of my learning, as some of the challenges I was going through were explained through my birth chart which gave me a sense of peace and understanding. It helped me to make sense of my life on a soul level of my life lessons. It was giving me strength in the weakness I was feeling, it was keeping me up when I was falling, and it was opening the path of spirituality combined with the psychology.

I went through my first Saturn Return; this is a concept in astrology that there is an understanding of growth to a much higher level of maturity and responsibility. It is the lord of Karma, we get our karmic lessons that take us to that maturity.

Whilst Saturn was giving me my karmic lessons, Pluto was bringing endings and transformation to so many things. Many things had left my life physically and I was taking off layers. If I had any sense of wanting to adorn and beautify myself on the physical level, it was gone, totally gone. I ended up a very simple 'Plain Jane' and somehow it didn't matter to me what I had become and that I looked like a pauper because I was in alignment of what Pluto energy was doing to me and what it was allowing me to become. However, the cycle endings of Pluto are not without its dark side and grief is the impact of one of them in an enormous way, for loss puts one into bereavement and as I had a lot of loss, there was a lot of grieving to do.

Understanding my birth chart was a huge turning point in knowledge and awareness, not just about my life but the world in general and the Soul's Journey within that. The insights were allowing me to become the woman I was meant to grow into.

Becoming a woman also gave me a huge opportunity at this time as I began to utilise much of what I was studying and put it into practice. I was lucky to get a funded post as a counsellor at a Women's Centre and that was also the making of me. I had clients from the whole of the Asian continent, South Asia, Thailand, China, Vietnam, as well as some Irish and Caribbean women. Being with them and listening to their life stories and struggles was such an honour, and despite some of the language difficulties, we managed and worked through things. What was interesting was that I could see a part of me in each one of these women and the issues they were going through. From homelessness, abuse, poverty, mental health, confidence and family issues, whatever it was that they brought to the sessions, I was able to identify with and resonate it with my own life.

Whilst doing all this work, I was able to embark on a hypnotherapy training course which again opened another door of opportunity. During this training, I was able to finally understand that I could work on my issue of selective mutism – a psychological result of having my voice silenced though my childhood and abusive arranged marriage – and begin to use my voice. So once I opened that door, not only did I begin to work on my voice, but I started on another pathway to teaching!

My dreams were now becoming realities. I was directing students in counselling and psychotherapy courses and now I was the one teaching them all about issues and patterns in psychotherapy, but that is not the end of it! I was offered another opportunity and that was to teach the hypnotherapy as well! Wow, the universe was on my side and all the struggles and hardships were being rewarded.

Through my years of hypnotherapy teaching, I learned so much about the subconscious and beyond. I learned how to reprogram my thoughts and how to teach my students techniques that would help not only them but their clients and others around them. The hard work here and years of continued service was recognised and I was awarded a Fellowship, which I received with much gratitude.

Transitioning Phase 3 – Another Cycle

I reflect back on the journey so far as I begin to enter another cycle of my life. With my hand on my heart, I give thanks to the universe for the previous cycle of me where I achieved so much and learned so much, even when I became a single parent. So just as this is phasing out and I transition into the new one, my son leaves home, which obviously is the healthy thing for a child to flee the nest.

As I lovingly allow him to do that, the grief of this huge ending grips me and I sit in solitude. I listen to the universe, I listen to my intuition as I reflect, and the pandemic of the Covid-19 hits. I think of my grief and see more grief waiting ahead of me as it won't be long before my parents depart my life and this world. The tears well up inside of me, the flood that I experienced at the beginning of my life, and the second cycle hits me once more. The changes, the endings, the beginnings...

My son consoles me in my deep grief. "Mum, this is time for you. This is your chance to fulfil your unfulfilled dreams, write your book, travel, even do some dating!"

My son is an old soul. As I look at him, I can see why his friends all turn to him; my family, his family on his dad's side, everyone values his wisdom and advice. He is a visionary and words from him flow at the right moment. "Yes, you're right," I told him as his words took me back to my childhood when sometimes I had wished I could just be on my own completely to do some of the things I wanted to do; now that time has come as one those things is writing.

Just as I began to transition into this cycle, I co-authored my first book called *Our Infinite Power to Heal*, along with 101 others, and what an elevating experience this was. The second co-author opportunity was out of the blue just as my son had left home and it allowed me to put my focus into a creative source. This led to three more co-author opportunities one after the other. So as I put my focus on writing, I allow myself to feel a sense of healing of all the things I've been through.

My son's encouragement to do some dating has led me to work with a coach on my inner feminine aspects to allow the beauty and love to return in a renewed sense. This is now looking at the outer more physical things that I had put on hold whilst I was busy pursuing the more spiritual and psychological aspects.

I'm not alone in the struggle of doing things for oneself as I know many women find it easier to do things for everyone else rather than themselves, and I definitely have been one of those women. So as I sit at my table alone, playing with my food, I have to find ways that are loving for me and cooking that meal as if I'm on a date with myself. I've spent almost a year now in developing this love for myself at meal times and it's getting better as now I'm exploring recipes and dishes to be more adventurous rather than what's convenient.

I look in the mirror and sometimes, I like what I see and other times I will find fault, so I'm working on those bits that I find fault, such as my greying hair, my pot belly, my chubby cheeks, or just an overall dislike. I turn them into positive focus, so I can appreciate and value myself and my womanhood of who I am. All the nurturing I've done for others, I'm learning to nurture myself with meeting my needs.

In my own space, on my own, I see things of the past that hold memories and I've held onto these for so long, so now it's time to release these things and let them go. It's a slow process as sentiments and memories have strong attachments and you have to be ready to make that release, or at least that's the way for me.

I let go, I release, I move on to new horizons, new ways, new chapters and a new life. I now work with my second Saturn Return that takes me into the next level of maturity – as you sow, so shall you reap.

As I reflect on my 30-year cycle, what started in March 1991 from much pain and to March 2021 where I feel such healing and vibrancy, I think of all the work I've done with women in the field of therapy, coaching, helping, mentoring, supporting and befriending, with much dedication and commitment. Today, 7th March 2021, I receive an acknowledgement of recognition by the Women's World Record, International Women Achievers Award, nominated by the lovely Ritu Sharma. Receiving this for International Women's Day is like a huge treasure from the universe saying, "You deserve this, well done!"

Some Final Thoughts...

I was lucky that part of my life journey was to come to live in England where I could have these opportunities and change my life and grow as a woman into who I wanted to become. Part of the reason I want to say this is because over the last decade as I visited India more and more, I became very conscious of the divide amongst caste systems and that I come from a community that is of a low caste and very oppressed. Historically, they were denied education and many other rights, so it could be that I was strongly compelled to study and learn so that I was not held back by the ideologies of society and culture. I would like to think that I could be an example to women of the lower castes and classes who think that some things are beyond their reach. I certainly thought that at times and maybe if I were still in India, I might be having those thoughts as some of my relatives who are still stuck in the systems.

Caste or no caste, I want every woman to believe in possibilities and opportunities. I want every woman to feel that they have the rights and chances without inferiority or suppression.

Dedications

First and foremost to myself and my younger self who was and is still known as Saro and Jaswinder.

I love you for who you are; I know it has been tough at times and you've always made it through. I'm so pleased that now you are embracing yourself as a woman.

Secondly, to my mother, Bachni; my sisters, Sukhi, Bally, Ra; and my grandmothers, Jai and Shanti.

To my nieces: Sonia, Aisha, Sonam, Soma, Jyoti, Jaspreet, Sonika. All my sisters-in-law.

To my cousins: Amar, Satya, Raji, Kinde, Paushpa, Rajan, Bandia, Paupa, Biro, Kamo, Shindo.

Thank you all for being in my life and giving me your input for my growth, through good or bad; it has been welcomed and honoured.

Thirdly, to all my friends and to you, dear reader, and all the other woman on our planet. Never deny the woman you are; you are beautiful and wonderful.

Much love to you all, Jaswinder.

New Woman 17

Yvette Pearce

The Knowing Soul

"I am fearfully and wonderfully made,
marvellous are your works,
and that my soul knows full well, I give thanks."
Psalm 139, the Bible

You are Unique.

I know you are reading this because your soul, the inner most part of you, is craving to fulfil wonderful adventures from all that was placed within you, including all your experiences in your life, both positive and negative. When you inhabit a place of disconnect from the creator of your soul, your posture on the inside is crouching down and curled up waiting to expand and excel.

To know who you are, you must know and understand your life's purpose. Nurturing your inner being is as important as taking care of your physical being. Wrapped up in the soul are your feelings, emotions and desires. The soul is where you experience transformation and renewal. Herein is where the real you resides.

Growing up, I used to hear that your soul must always be prepared to die. This limiting belief stopped me from caring, from being anything even that which was external, necessary or useful to my life. What was the point? I was being let down by adults, but now I understand that their souls were as lost as mine, I can now accept my past.

Creating and producing another soul into the world, led me to search for what my soul desired. I embraced forgiveness, which felt like a loved one returning from a faraway unchartered journey. I share with you in hindsight, about what you 'shouldda' done. I have been, and still am doing my own work. I have learnt that there is so much more to you than you show the world. I spent many years knowing that there was more to me than I was experiencing, but when you're nurtured in certain cultures and homes, you tend to learn your place, the one that adults have slotted you into.

Some learn to shine because they are allowed to, told to or assisted to. Not always the best position to be in because you have no idea whether you're coming or going. If you were compliant, you became the martyr; you did as you were told and were safe enough for a while. If you were defiant, you ran the risk of being used as the scapegoat or the whipping post, but you'd already given up on ever connecting with your soul's true being. You learnt to just settle. You played down who you are for so many years that you forget to remember. By the time you're 'awakened', 30, 40 or so years have passed, and now you finally know what you want to do with your life. Don't get me wrong, you may have been living and doing your duty, making your life work, but were you truly living your life's purpose and was your soul able to sing, click or connect?

Having experienced so many defining moments in my own life, it's only fair to briefly share some of them with you, so you know that I am still crafting the New Woman that I am becoming. My life has taken the path that I now guide other women along from breakthrough to being; to becoming their own New Woman.

The first defining moment was when I tried to end my life at 12 years old. Yes, life was so painful and unhappy at home and within our close-knit community, that I preferred not to be here anymore; well, not be in the life I was living. I wanted to go back to heaven and come back again into a family that actually wanted me. I wanted to be born again – they talked about it at church all the time, so why not me? I wanted to belong to another family that would love me and care for me. One that was calm, quiet and happy and had everything for a good life. Not one where there were constant beatings, cursing, violence, crying, pain and never enough of anything. I wanted to come back to a mummy and daddy that were ready and prepared for me. It could even be a white family. I wasn't fussed. Anything would be better than where I was.

As you can see, I survived my suicide attempt at age 12, but I had some deep questions for God, and maybe for myself, such as:

Why am I still here?

Why didn't you want me back?

What do I do now?

But the most painful question of all that I asked myself, was what would have happened to my baby sister and brothers if I had gone? That was the day that I decided that suicide was not the way out for me. I had three little people and an adult that were depending on me and I had to be here to take care of them. Being the eldest of four children, this became my 'why'. Why I was still here, and therefore dictated how I manoeuvred myself throughout my childhood and teenage years. I created a brick wall around my heart, a fortress that only four other people were allowed in. This is how I spent most of my life, keeping people out that wanted any part of me.

We each must find our reasons why we choose life. Why we rise daily and ritualistically do what must be done.

Rinse and repeat, until we realise that life is worth living and our soul can begin to feel again, or maybe for the first time that you can remember.

I started hearing voices and also answered them. I began seeing things that hadn't happened as yet. Quite frightening at first, but I learnt to live with it in silence. The church, family and neighbours were already saying my mum was plagued by demons or she was just plain mad. Sometimes I would be caught talking to myself and be laughed at by the other children. So I became quiet. To this day, I love silence and my own thoughts.

Life was to continue like this for many years. I wasn't a mute, but I learnt to be silent around adults and more so around children that were prone to repeating childhood chatter to the adults for attention, consequently getting those of us who were more vocal into trouble. I would get beatings for something someone else said or did, because I just chose not to answer or defend myself; it was easier. You were beaten into agreement with the lie, so you just simply learnt to accept the lie as your truth, so the beating would be a short sprint instead of a marathon.

My invisibility allowed me into spaces that most children were shooed away from, because I was always attached to my mother's apron strings. My self-enforced silence and statuesque demeanour gave me access to adult-only spaces where I heard so much but repeated nothing… until now. I had my own way of coping with all that I heard. I would sit and suck my thumb as if it was actually giving me substance, which is probably why they addressed me as 'dumb pikni'.

Have you ever heard the statement 'more is caught than taught'? As a child, I caught all that what I felt or thought was of no significance. I also caught that my life was of little value to the adults around me unless I was fetching or carrying for them. There were so many ugly words said around me that I caught that feelings were never useful to be shown. I caught that any expression, verbal or non-verbal, was best left where it was, deep inside my already wounded soul, for now. We pick up so much from well-meaning adults, our community and media.

My father seemed like a charming, sweet, jovial, handsome, well-dressed man around town. But behind closed doors, he was the most manipulating, abusive, controlling, destructive individual I knew. He had a level of cruelty and callousness, so I quickly adjusted and learnt to accept him for what he was: someone to be kept out of my heart space. His moods dictated our very breathing as children. When he was around, we could only have a good day when he felt like it. If he had a good run on the horses, he would come home, smiling, jolly and ready to play. He was engaging, funny and chatty; he would make the evening special. Admittedly, those days were few and far between.

I had no idea what triggered him; it could be anything, it was never always the same thing. My father's level of brutality was relentless, especially towards my mum. On rare occasions, he would collect us from school, drive us around for a little while, then bring us home just past the appropriate time. As we approached the front door, we could hear mum sobbing and begging God to bring us home safely. In his 'frankly my dear, I couldn't give a damn' kind of way, he would walk through the door smiling. If she complained, he would call her mad, tell her she's losing her mind because she didn't remember. He would often yell at her, "You should be in St Margaret's!" – a local mental hospital. He even threatened to take her there on many occasions; in fact he did once, but that was never repeated.

He would move things and tell her it was never there. He would bring things in the house and she would ask him where they were from and then the nasty vile words would just spill out of him, followed by the beatings. He would use anything he could find: a belt, a shoe, a chair. We were never allowed to comfort her when he was around. We did once and got beaten just as she did, so we waited until he was out of the house to soothe and comfort her. This was our ritual.

The most frustrating days for my father were the days that he was not able to break Mum down. He could not shred her emotions into tiny little pieces and leave her begging to be left alone or simply to be set free. She was taking some serious medication for another nervous breakdown, I was telling her what to do and what not to do, and she started standing up to him in small ways. If there was something he brought into the house and it didn't belong there, she would throw it out, and when he asked for it, she would say she hadn't seen it. He would curse her out under his breath. He couldn't handle her telling him what to do, or even if she raised her voice. At those times, I wished she would walk away or fight him, but she didn't. He would cry and apologise and say that he would change. She, of course, would always forgive him, but Dad never did change, not for her. She left him and went back many times.

Today, Mum would say it was fasting, praying, the church, talking to God and reading the word of God that got her through those times. I'm not saying it didn't, because today I'm deeply spiritual, but sometimes I feel she's forgotten how we children played our part in keeping us all safe. Although they had four little people that belonged to them and depended on them, both Mum and Dad were wrapped up in their own little separate worlds. Nothing really existed outside of my mother's God, church and her Bible. For my father, his god was music, gambling, the pub and alcohol. There is not enough time to mention the other women – I would be here all day.

I watch my mother today like I watch many people within my world, as they walk through life with shattered souls and broken hearts and deep emotional wounds. Your soul responds to whatever you feed it. Accepting that you are uniquely created, is the first step in embracing your soul, and acknowledging that there is a purpose to your existence.

I realised that I had stepped into the roles of parent, protector, advisor, scapegoat and sometimes joker within the family. For some young children, growing up in homes with many societal issues, such as drugs, domestic violence, alcohol, and abuse, you learn to adopt a way of being. A way of existing that is protective of yourself and those you love dearly. You can't afford to live recklessly, explore or live life with child-like curiosity or playfulness.

Primary school life was tense. There was no time for friendships or connections after school. I couldn't afford to get into trouble or have the teacher keep me back after class for whatever reason. I had to ensure that I collected my siblings, and we were home at the right time, or it would end in Mum having a meltdown. It was important for each of us as children to play our part and care for and protect the one adult that was there every day. We couldn't risk anyone finding out exactly how our home was run and what was going on behind closed doors. Many of the nurturing, caring, supporting skills that we developed as children, I can see being utilised in all areas of our lives today. We don't always get it right, but we try. We are able to negotiate, discuss, calm situations down, bring an element of order when chaos is about to kick off, help people find their voice and speak their truth.

Talking about truth, a sad but defining moment was that I found it difficult to be alone with my innocent, sweet mocha-skin baby daughter. It was nothing to do with her; she was amazing. I believed that I was void of the tools, skills or the ability to grow and develop this bundle of innocence and joy into an amazing woman. I was a teenage mum with my own baggage of emotional pain from my childhood, strapped to my back like a Radley rucksack. I was married (still am) to the most amazing guy, I was active in my local church and a stay-at-home mum, and struggled showing up as me. I was a living lie!

I was dutiful towards my daughter. I made sure she was educated, disciplined, fed, clothed, kept safe, made sure she smelt great and was presentable to the world. If I learnt anything from Mum, it was how to show up looking like a film star while her soul was perishing.

Yet every time my daughter's eyes caught mine, I felt like a piece of me was being sucked in by her. My chest ached, the sharp stabbing pain quickly rose and created a blockage in my throat which led to an explosive loud heavy thud in my head, followed by uncontrollable tears. This happened on several occasions, so eventually I visited the doctor, was strung up to machines to check me over, only to find there was nothing physically wrong with me. He asked questions such as if I was stressed or worrying about anything. My health visitor, Nurse Butler, was great; she would say, "You're a new mum, it takes a little time".

Some might call it fate, but I call it God showing me how and where to step into the next level of becoming the unique soul, mother, woman that is present today. It was the early eighties, and my sister registered on a nursery nursing course at the local college. She brought home three books that to this day I have on my shelf. One was a child development book, the other was about play and the third was about a boy whose parents were his persecutors. It was the beginning of my soul's healing journey.

Over the years, I have experienced many defining moments through actions I took via employment, training, ceased opportunities and deep soul work, that I continue to do today. I have worked with a number of children with behavioural issues in many local schools across the West Midlands. I developed a system that works on their emotional soul state. Most of them experienced a breakdown before they got a breakthrough. I discovered that the children I worked with were drowning in their adults' stories. I saw so much of myself in them, that I knew the steps to take to help them.

As an Early Years Consultant on a trailblazer Sure Start government funded programme, I have trained and facilitated on seven parenting programmes, but each one seemed to be missing something. Therefore, I created a parent coaching programme that proved valuable and successful for the parents. During that time, I also became a life coach and applied my newly gained skills in developing Unique Coaching 4 You with a number of umbrella projects attached.

I have and still am help women to heal their souls' emotional scars, and place them on the road to be their unique self, live their unique life and to stand up as a leader wherever they are in life.

You are an amazing creation of God.

This is not the end of my journey, but I pray that I have served my children and others well enough by showing them that the most important thing in life is to follow your soul's leading with the spirit's guidance. I urge you to know this; everything that comes into your life, you must question how is this serving my soul's purpose? Trust me, you will get an answer. Never throw out everything or say anything was a waste of time. No, look for the golden nuggets and breadcrumbs that will steer your soul, because the soul knows full well what it has to do.

Here are a few things for you to focus on:

You will know your living your purpose when that purpose honours your soul.

Whatever your beliefs, you cannot separate soul from spirituality.

Your soul is moulded by everything that comes into your life, seen and unseen, past, present and future.

Ego can destroy your soul's future. Don't let it!

Stop looking outside of yourself; everything you need is right there under your nose.

Your soul takes on its own unique character – let it be free.

New Woman 18

Sophie Kemoko

Mission Grace

"This is your new land and I will open the doors to inspire you with your story."

My story begins as a little girl born in France, where I lived with my family. In 1986, the Republic of the Congo (also called Congo-Brazzaville) was calling all Congolese journalists to come back and as my father was a journalist, he decided to return and took his family with him. I was six years old at the time. My father was quite high up in the journalist hierarchy, and my mother was a school office administrator; they were able to give us children a brilliant childhood.

As children, we were able to do so many things together. We went on holidays, planned trips, visited the zoo, explored jungle-like areas with our father, drove from city to city to see family, swam in river with friends, and much more.

One memory that I will remember and cherish forever was my grandparent's 60th wedding anniversary in 1989. We travelled up to my mother's village, which was around a four-hour drive and when we got there, there was such a huge crowd of people: uncles, aunts, cousins and all the people from the village. The party got going and ended two days later. My grandparents owned a farm, so there was always so much stuff for us children to do: feed the animals, play in the river, and hang out with all the cousins. And the fellow villagers who were at the party told us funny stories and scary stories; I have great memories of everyone telling stories around the campfire at night.

We lived very happily and we didn't want for anything. Our parents ensured we had the same level of comfort that we would have had in Europe – as well as being a salaried employee, my father was also a businessman, and my mother was an entrepreneur as well as being a school secretary. During my childhood, we lived in a huge house on a farm that my father owned where we raised pigeons, guinea pigs, hens that laid eggs for us every morning, and sheep, and we had acres of land. One of the best bits of living on a farm was that my father allowed us to share in his experience of working on the farm. For example, one day a goat gave birth and my father helped her, offering us an unforgettable performance of being a veterinary surgeon, helping out every time she got into difficulties and then giving the kid to the mum. We had chickens that gave us fresh eggs every morning and my dad would go to the market to deliver eggs to the merchants. I remember that every time there was the feast of Eid, Muslims from around the area would come to my dad to buy goats to eat for their feast, and it always made me cry to see our animals leave. I was so attached to them – we all were – as they were all part of our daily life.

Our world resembled the Garden of Eden, with all our animals and our beautiful land. We were very happy to be surrounded by all these animals. They gave us so much joy. And I'm so grateful that we also got the chance to learn how to cultivate vegetables and fruit. At weekends or during the holidays, my father would take us to help pick the food and also enjoy some fishing!

We had beautiful flower gardens, and lush fruit and vegetable gardens, which allowed us to eat organic food every day. However, what we couldn't eat, were our animals! We would rather not eat the animals we killed at home, so my dad would fill the freezer with meat and fish from the supermarket!

My parents made a lot of money with the business which brought a bit of jealousy in the neighbourhood where we lived.

I remember one evening when we were getting ready for bed, my father felt the animals were getting agitated, screaming for help. However, it was ignored and we went to bed. What we didn't realise is that evening, a huge python had 'visited', one so big that it had terrorised all our animals. It had sought out its prey and attacked. My father heard some noises so he went to investigate and discovered the python was not able to move anymore because it had swallowed an entire lamb, whole! All of us children were mesmerised by this bizarre sight!

My father went closer to get a good look at the snake and we got scared and rushed back inside the house. My father quickly went to look for one of our neighbours, who was a hunter so had a shotgun. They came and killed the python. Early the next morning, the hunter and other neighbours came to share the snake to eat. They cut it into pieces and each one of them had their share. That morning there was an article about the story in the paper, a story that even now, decades later, still gives me goosebumps!

I would go on long holidays, either to my paternal grandparents who lived in a town called Dolisie, or to my maternal grandparents who lived in a village called Mindouli. I love the fact that I was able to get to know them so well and was able to spend quality time with them. My paternal grandfather was a great businessman with a successful bar called the Blue Pavilion where we would see 'live' drunk men tripping and falling over each other. Couples would come to party and have a good time. During the holidays, I would help the employees to clean up, wipe down the tables, put away the chairs, and wait for the customers to arrive from noon onwards.

At this time, my grandmother was busy. She would get up very early in the morning at dawn and go to the fields to water and plant and would then come home in the early afternoon to look after my grandfather. My paternal grandfather had two wives; he was a polygamist and lived on an estate with my aunts and uncles.

One morning when I was 14 years old, my grandmother woke up my cousin and I around 5am to go with her to pick vegetables. This was our first experience of selling my grandmother's vegetables at the local market so we were really excited! We had to walk far to get to the field and after digging up the vegetables, cleaning them and tying them up, my cousin and I then sold them at the market. We spent the whole day laughing with the other market traders and the customers who complimented us for coming to sell our grandmother's vegetables. Everything went well, and we were always happy with our sales. Our grandmother always gave us a bonus in addition to our 'wage' and this made us very happy – it made us feel valued. We sold the vegetables at market during the long holidays, which in the Congo last two months. These were unforgettable moments and always a lesson in life.

All this encouraged me and my brothers because when we went back to our parents after the holidays, we always had stories to tell, things that motivated and inspired us, giving us the inspiration and mindset that we had to succeed and work hard at school. Our parents would take us back to France during the holidays every couple of years to enjoy the summer in France, often travelling from one city to another to visit family and friends. We would go to the zoo or to the coast for a change of scene. It was a great feeling, because when we returned to the Congo we always had amazing stories to tell of our adventures over the summer.

In June 1996, my big sister Benedicte moved to Benin (Cotonou) to continue her studies, which created a great emptiness in the house, because she and I had been partners in crime. But, in turn, it brought me closer to my brothers with whom I spent more time.

We were a Catholic family, so I went to catechism every year where I received all my sacraments and from the age of 14, I joined the church choir, which allowed us to go out and visit other churches and also to spend time with the nuns in the convents who taught us to pray. I loved this time of sharing, and had dreams of becoming a nun, living in a convent and devoting myself to prayer; the peaceful life nuns lead absolutely fascinated me. The nuns taught us how to sew, and especially to make things with wool such as dolls' dresses, table mats and even little jumpers for babies, as well as scarves. We had sessions every Saturdays where a nun would come and teach us to develop our talents and our awareness. I loved my childhood and treasured this wonderful moments.

However, in June 1997, everything changed. My parents decided it was prudent to send my brothers on holiday to my older brother Modeste, who lived in a safer area. While waiting to see what would happen, as we had heard worrying news that young men were being murdered in the town, we learnt that the police presence was being stepped up in the neighbourhood. Parents began to be afraid, and advised all children to go straight home after school.

One Saturday morning, thank God, one of our neighbours came to see my parents and told us that we should get ready to leave our house and the neighbourhood, because the militia were shooting their opponents and everyone was fleeing. My mother kept her cool and reassured my sister Rolix and I that everything would be fine and that we would go away for a few days. We decided to lock ourselves up in the house as we were so frightened, spending the day and evening feeling like prisoners in our own home with no way of getting anywhere.

The following day, another neighbour came and asked us why we were still here. He told us it was time to leave the neighbourhood right now, as the soldiers and militia men were forcibly entering houses, looting properties and killing anyone who stood in their way, including children. Blood flowed everywhere and it was like a scene in a war film, but it was real. We had to flee the house there and then, leaving with a few essentials.

My parents reassured us that we were just going to go to a friend's house a few kilometres away, but we could not take the car (my father had a beautiful Mercedes) so we had to walk. We were so frightened. The neighbourhood was emptying fast; everyone fleeing and taking refuge. We heard gunshots, which became louder and deafened us. We could hear bullets raining down on the roofs. It was terrifying. We walked 10 km to reach the house of my father's friend, with his wife and children, and took refuge in his house for a few days, waiting for things to calm down so that we could return home. However, one of his neighbours gave us the news that the situation was getting worse, that the militia were approaching, and that there were many dead on the side of the road. He told us that it was no longer safe to stay here, and that we should all leave immediately. It was total chaos and panic as we realised how serious the situation was, and that we would not be able to return home any time soon.

As we all convened in the living room of my father's friend that night to discuss where to go, the gunshots became more and more intense and loud. In fact, the opposing military were close by and the exchanges started with the government army, causing dozens of deaths during the night itself. In fact, whilst talking in the living room, a member of the neighbour's family was hit by a stray bullet which pierced the ceiling of the house. We knew this was a sign that we had to flee again.

At dawn, we took to the road again to get to my mother's village, and there it was. Chaos, blood everywhere, corpse of men, women and children lying on the side of the road. The crying, the trauma of seeing all these mutilated people who would never wake up again, was a terrible shook for us all, especially my sister and I. We began to question where we were going to live; in fact, even if we would live at all. As we walked all day, my feet became swollen and tiredness set in, on top of the stress and the fear. In addition, the vision and memory of all those corpses on the road was overwhelming and traumatic. We spent the night outdoors in a disused school. I was very afraid and felt sorry for my father, a strong man weighing at least 120 kg, who was starting to run out of steam and could not continue the journey to my mother's village.

It took us three days of walking under unrelenting sun to get to the village. We had left my father, who decided to travel to his father's village which was a little closer. He didn't want us to go there as he had never taken us there, and he felt that my mother's village would be safer, as it was close to the border with the Republic of Congo, allowing us the chance of safety as the future was so uncertain.

Arriving at my mother's village, we breathed a sigh of relief as we thought we had escaped from the military. A few weeks passed and then one morning we heard resounding bombardments in the village, as one of the military helicopters decided to come to bombard the village. Obviously, we could no longer stay with the family of my father's friend, so with other families that my mother had agreed to host on her father's estate, we all left the village to climb the high mountains to reach the summit and found ourselves on the border of the other Congo, the Republic of Congo. On the way, it took us three days, sleeping out in the open, in the middle of nowhere, in difficult conditions, to get to the mountain itself.

For me, this mountain experience nearly killed me as I had never climbed a mountain before. It took us a whole morning and, on the way with the sun beating down on us, the fatigue started to wear me down, and if it wasn't for my mother and uncles travelling with us,

I would have stayed there as I felt I could go no further. When we finally got to the top, I thanked God I was still alive and then I thought of my father who would never have made it to the top and this brought me to tears. Thoughts turned to my father, as we had received no news from him for several weeks, and the worry and stress set in every day and we prayed more than ever for the chance to meet again.

When we finally arrived at the border, we were looked after by HCR, a humanitarian charity, who placed us in refugee camps. As a French citizen, I was given the chance to be taken to the capital for eventual repatriation to France, and so left my mother and sister in the camp, as at that stage neither of them were French citizens.

Being in the capital Kinshasa, I would hear news about my parents from the charity, and was reassured that my mother and sister were in good hands. However, I was not so reassured of the fate of my father who, when we were finally reunited, told us how in the village he was kidnapped by opponents who accused him of working with the government, which was not true. My father was almost caught in the enemies' hands, but an angel saved his life, and my father thankfully survived.

After a few months spent in Kinshasa waiting for various repatriation procedures, and once they were certain that our old neighbourhood was safe and secure, my parents finally decide to return home and found absolute chaos. Everything in the house had been stolen – the car, the armchairs, clothes, kitchen utensils all gone – but the house itself was still sound so my parents decide to resume life little by little.

In 1999, my parents made the decision for my brothers and I to return to France, which was the beginning of our new life. I had to overcome all the bad memories and build a life leaving all the bad memories behind me. I made the decision to overcome the trauma and build a happy life and gave myself a promise that I would succeed.

When I returned to France, I immediately started a small job at McDonald's as a waitress, whilst at the same time continuing my BTS studies as an Administrative and Commercial Technician. After finishing my studies, I was hired by a big company, Bailly Déménagements, where I worked for almost 10 years. The man who became my husband arrived in France from South Africa in 2007 and we began the life as a couple. We decided to settle in England and were married in August 2008. I heard a voice ring out to tell me, "This is your new land and I will open the doors to inspire you with your story."

New Woman 19

Suman Manghra

The Power in Letting Go

"The universe does what it needs to do,
if you just let it."

I remember being that young girl who was promised so much, in exchange for giving up my free will and decision-making power. It felt like a bargain! I was willing to consider it; why not? If ultimately I was going to get "everything" I wanted, surely it was worthwhile to agree.

So, imagine this now; I'm sitting there, age 24, wondering where it all went wrong. How on earth did I miscalculate this so badly... I was supposed to be an A* student, with Maths being one of my particularly strong subjects! But this was a heavy miscalculation on my part and a huge error of judgement. I felt that I had been fed a bunch of lies, and man, was I disappointed! It just did not make sense – how I came to this point in my life, where everything felt like it was falling apart.

Having just completed my studies, after being advised that going to university guarantees you getting a dream job (lie), and then the person who promised they would marry me turned around and changed their mind (more lies)... (and fucking coward)... eventually I was made to believe my looks and my weight were the main reason for my downfall. Great stuff.

Bam! It finally hit me. The more I had looked up to kind, caring people in my life, thinking that when you do well for others, that 'well' will be done for you too... I felt that the opposite was actually true. I noticed all the snaky, untrustworthy, and manipulative people around me were the ones who were living at large, who had the whole world at their fingertips, progressing in life and winning. Not only that, but they were being supported by everyone around them to be this way! Boy, I was SO confused, not to mention annoyed! Urgh... I'm going back to my Maths again – this just didn't add up and did not make any sense to me. I had followed all the rules to the tee... everything I was ever told to do, yet I still managed to fail. FAIL.

I felt like a total and utter failure. I had failed at life. I spent most of my life being an academic, gaining grades, progressing through life, being made to feel if you're brainy and smart you can achieve whatever you want. I never really focused on my health and fitness much, as more validation was given to being mentally smart than anything else. Yet here I was, feeling like the biggest fool on the planet. Those A grades weren't there to help me. Those A-levels didn't help me. And even sitting there with not just a Bachelor's degree, but also a Master's degree, I had still failed! HOW?

For someone who rated themselves as being mentally strong, I sat there devastated, tears rolling down my face and heart broken to shreds, feeling totally and utterly lost and confused, with a complete lack of direction in my life. Not only was I out of a job, but I was also broken-hearted and actually broke with mountains of student debt, assuming that this would be my key to freedom. How wrong was I?

I sat there and analysed the whole situation (as I truly used to love overanalysing everything), and I came to a stark realisation. I had spent my life being like my father... Being kind and generous and overly giving to others. My dad was my hero, and still is. However, he set the standard very high. His saintly ways were just way too much to live up to. No one is born to be this divine. Yet again, I calculated how can somebody give and give and give, and be so offended to take from anyone else. Others literally just sat there, and they just would take and take and take and rarely give an ounce back. It really used to annoy me so much when I saw my dad being taken advantage of. I saw how much he did for others and I saw how little others did for him. I would witness him going out of his way to support others. Yet others would disrespect him within the click of a finger. This did not make sense to me and it hurt to watch this happen time and time again.

Often, I would ask my dad to get family members to help him back and he never ever wanted any help from anyone. Being a self-respecting man, he liked to be in control and in charge of everything. He generally did not like asking for help of any kind from anyone, which I later realised was just his pride and his ego ultimately getting in the way. For somebody who was so humble and labelled as being one of the humblest human beings that people had met, he did not know how to be humble when it came to asking for help. And I was exactly like him.

My dad's theory was that if someone asks for help from you, they could be approaching you from any form – such as godly form – and if God approaches you and asks you for something, you shouldn't say no, you should always give, always do, and always pay your karma forward so that good karma comes back to you. Good human beings do good deeds, don't they? Now I'm not saying this is wrong, or even bad to do. My big question was, "Well if other people could approach you in a godly form, can you not also yourself be a godly form when you approach others?" I also asked, "And if you are tallying up your good deeds, surely you should give an opportunity to others to also tally up their good deeds too?"

This is when I realised that there was a big crack in his logic where my dad was giving way too much and not receiving enough back. Rather than continue being offended for my dad, suddenly I realised my dad himself was part of the problem. **He had no boundaries.** He allowed people to walk all over him. Well if you're going to be a carpet and lie down, people are going to walk over you, aren't they? (Sorry, Dad, but it's true – I still love you for being you though, and am proud that you have FINALLY put up some boundaries now!)

For much of my life, especially as a young girl, I didn't always have the easiest relationship with my mum, but that is the norm for many teenage girls. Many times, she was quite blunt and bitter towards my dad over many trivial things. I often defended dad and said to myself, "Why do you always have to be this way with him? Cut him some slack, be nice to him." In her defence, she put up with a lot of crap from his family throughout most of their married life, so her resentments had built up over time. I promised myself I would never be anything like my mum.

However, the day I found out that my dad was the one allowing people to treat him the way he was being treated, a huge penny finally dropped for me which made me understand that I was also allowing people to take advantage of me too. I also understood it's good to be the way my mum was and so I incorporated her persona and started standing up for myself, speaking up for myself and creating boundaries.

In some ways, you can say that I did a full 180° turn from being a sweet, quiet and calm girl, to a loud, vivacious, abrupt and very bitchy lady. I became more like my mum than I had ever imagined, and she didn't like it one single bit (and I don't blame her). When she got a taste of her own medicine, she often criticised me; all I could respond was, "The apple doesn't fall far from the tree, does it?" My remarks offended her even more, which of course didn't really help me. Over a period of time, I came to appreciate that being a good balance of both my mum and my dad was the best way forward for me, but this took a while for me to come to terms with. (For the record, my mum was and is a badass, and I am super grateful for the amazing traits she passed down to me – thank you, Mum!)

You may be wondering what was it that I 'actually' did to change my life and how did my life even change. I'm happy to tell you that I am in a very good place right now and truly grateful for all lessons and experiences I ever faced. It was all down to one moment when I was 24. I switched the way I looked at things, and learned that re-framing a situation and changing how you perceive it in your mind, is key to changing how you feel about it. Furthermore, it's about changing how you respond, and therefore changing the results you see around you.

One advantage of doing a Psychology degree was that it helped me to understand the mind better and understand why people have certain behaviours, why they do what they do, why they have certain habits, and also what motivates them. On the same note though, I came to understand a little bit more about why people do not do certain things. What holds them back? Why do they not take the necessary steps and actions needed to move forwards?

Along this journey, I came across a coach in one of my seminars whilst doing my Masters in Work Psychology and Business at Aston University. This coach discussed a model called the GROW model which taught us how to set a goal, how to check the reality of our current situation, how to look at opportunities around us and then finally, to review our willingness to take the steps needed towards the set goal. I really love this model, especially the concept of tapping into and building someone's potential.

With my earliest work experiences, I recall whilst training learning about the individual skill sets of people. One remarkable young man really made an impact on me. This young man had been working in a call centre in customer service and advice for almost 10 years, yet he went on to tell me he had a degree in graphic design. I could not understand at all how a person with such a good degree and talent was sitting doing a 'phone job' so many years later.

Now don't get me wrong; I'm not looking down on his job whatsoever, as that line of work ended up becoming a large part of my own work experience for a good 10 years (isn't that ironic!). But I looked at this man and I just saw so much potential in him. I said to him, "Why did you not do a job that was in your field of expertise?" He told me straight that he had become complacent and he was comfortable in his job as he was working towards getting married and buying a house, so the regular income supported those choices he had made. I couldn't help feeling that he could have still gained that same income from doing a different job of his choice.

As I worked my way through several jobs over the years, I found that I was mostly over-educated and under-experienced for many of the roles I did. I started looking for better opportunities. The first step I took was taking up a life coaching course online. I absolutely loved everything I learned through this course but it was not cheap, and even though I had all the theory of business behind me through my previous studies, the practical part of doing business just went over my head. I felt alone and soon understood that working with people gave me more energy.

Part of the course requirements were to work with another coach as this provides the opportunity to learn from their coaching style too. By chance, through a friend I found out about another lady called Rose, who was also doing the exact same course as me. Fortunately, she agreed to become my coach, for which I will be forever grateful for.

Throughout the coaching sessions I had with her, I became more and more conscious that I carried a huge amount of guilt towards doing anything for myself. She asked me, "Why are you feeling so guilty?"

I replied, "I'm not guilty, I have nothing to be guilty about!"

As she opened up my mind further and further, it finally dawned on me that the feelings I used to feel, the sickness in my stomach, the tightness in my throat, the tension in my shoulders, were all an indication of my guilty feelings anytime I wanted to do something for myself. I was becoming more aware of the deep conditioning of my upbringing and my culture. It was inherent in me that I must always do for others and not for myself. I finally understood that I was a 'people pleaser.' In Oprah Winfrey's own words, I was suffering with the "disease to please".

Once this veil lifted from my mind, I became unstoppable. I started ignoring the curfews placed on me. I relieved the restrictions that I had been keeping myself within. I finally found the key and released myself from my own mental prison. My ambitions just tripled in size for everything I wanted to achieve for myself, rather than for my parents. They found it tricky to start with, but with time they were able to deal with it, and became very supportive of me. Their change of heart pleasantly took me by surprise too.

Even though I was happy doing and learning, I still did not feel successful. My coach recommended a book to me, *The Secret* by Rhonda Byrne. I was so intrigued. What is the secret? I needed to know what the answer was! I bought the DVD to begin with and then later I purchased the book. The book and movie blew my mind. The book teaches the principles of the Law of Attraction and how we can use our own vibrational power and flow energy to attract favourable people, circumstances, and resources into our lives. The book also taught me how I was one of the main reasons for the things that had not worked out in my life. This revelation was a real eye-opener.

I wanted to start sharing this with the whole world, hoping everybody would see what I could see, and begin to fix the world my way. Upon reflection, I could have handled this better. Sometimes we jump right in with enthusiasm but after some time realise in hindsight our original approach was a knee-jerk reaction; however, you live and you learn! Using the Law of Attraction principles, the first thing I wanted to put into practise was to attract my ideal job. I was at a stage in my life where I had been unemployed for three months and I applied for 10 to 15 jobs daily with no response. While I was receiving unemployment benefits, I had to provide evidence that I had attended interviews and applied for jobs. Every day, I chanted, "Please – I do not want a sales job, I will do any work, but I do not want to do outbound sales!" I received a phone call for a company who had seen my CV online and reached out to me for a job opportunity. I was so excited until they told me it was for an outbound sales role. I was gutted. I went along to the interview as it was worthwhile putting it on my job log. Sod's law, I ended up getting the job. I took it at the time, because as they say, beggars can't be choosers. Things happen for a reason, and it was during my time at this job where the Law of Attraction really started to make sense to me.

The subconscious mind does not process negative words, so when I used to say I do not want to have a sales job, the only thing the subconscious mind vibrated to the universe was "sales job" so, lo and behold, I attracted a sales job! To turn this around, the first thing I did was write down everything I appreciated about having that job, and as dire as that job was, there were some positives. I started incorporating the "attitude of gratitude." I appreciated the income the job gave me. I appreciated the friendships I was making at work. I appreciated being in employment versus being unemployed. I appreciated having something that was getting me out of the house and keeping my mind and skills engaged. I appreciated paying off my debt.

The next step was to list what I wanted in a job. Opposite, I listed all the things that I was unhappy about in my current job so it reflected what I wanted in my ideal job. I listed what type of work I wanted, the pay I wanted to receive, even the location of where I wanted to work and the type of organisation I wanted to work for. This time round with my renewed mindset, I only applied for one job, and though I didn't get the original job, they offered me another job instead. I was so shocked! This Law of Attraction actually works!

With renewed energy, I put in place the same strategy towards attracting my dream partner and even though I didn't attract him immediately, I did eventually find him, and seriously, he is the best man that I could have ever asked for! I am now on a mission to teach these principles to others and help them realise their own power, that they can really make a change in their life. It has been well over a decade now since I first learned of 'The Secret' and I apply this both in my life and my work on a daily basis. I went onto attracting many other things in my life from job opportunities, salary increases and various promotions. I also trained myself up in Neuro Linguistic Programming, Hypnotherapy and Time Line Therapy, where I am now also able to train others.

Eventually in 2020, I manifested yet another redundancy but this time round I was not sad about it, I celebrated! Up to this point, I had kept my coaching as a part-time business. I decided to go full-time with my business, and I have not looked back since. My biggest takeaway from my journey has been that it was one thing to take back the control I had lost in my life, but more importantly, I learnt to let go of that control again, once I was in alignment with my true path. The universe then, does what it needs to do, if you just let it.

New Woman 20

Saboohi Gill

Gain in Loss

"In pursuit of infinite joy,
We ride on the wings of thoughts.
To make these memories last forever,
Let's go to the ends of the ages.
The reins of time in my hands,
To chain down those fleeting moments."

In various stages of my life, I desired control over time, the ability to replay some moments, to relive certain memories, the times where I had no worries in the world and had felt the most secure, where my mother's calming presence and father's comforting embrace were around me. I also sought to release moments that had hurt so I would never encounter them again.

I was born in Lahore and grew up in many different places within Pakistan due to my father being an army officer. My parents told me when East and West Pakistan separated, my father was posted in Dhaka, present-day Bangladesh. In 1971, during the war, as a family we had a narrow escape as we were rescued by the army and sent back to Pakistan. Conversely, many army people became prisoners of war and were held back in East Pakistan for a while. Due to the traumatic events that took place in Bengal, my mother developed health issues.

My mother, Louisa Pervez, was a quiet yet confident individual who equipped me with life skills and passed on her beautiful values. She helped me with my studies up until high school and my love of reading was passed down from her. She expressed love through her gestures as she struggled to verbalise affection.

My father, G. D. Pervez, on the other hand, was very open in expressing his love. He would happily listen to my non-stop chat. Living in a male-dominated society, he was different than most men in his age group. He respected women, valued mine and my mother's opinions, and gave me equal opportunities to study and develop just like my three brothers.

I have lovely memories of my childhood when he was in the army. I remember on beautiful bright mornings, we would work out together. Some summer afternoons after his lunch break siesta, he would take me with him to the army base, where he would work in his office and his orderly would take me to the Captain's house, as his daughter was my best friend. I loved roaming on the barren hills behind my friend's house in Azad Kashmir and we had the most wonderful time.

I cherished the excitement when accompanying my father on fishing trips or hunting geese and deer. On our journeys together, we would speak about almost everything related to my little world. Still, story time was my favourite when I would lay on my bed or my father had me in his arms as he would tell me countless stories. I believed most of them were created through his imagination; they always had a good moral lesson at their root, and as I fell asleep the enchanting characters would remain in my mind.

I grew up with my three brothers: Shahid, Zahid and Nathan Pervez. However, in the last decade I lost two, Shahid and Nathan. The third, Zahid, I remain incredibly close to. Having three brothers around made me competitive; every game, from badminton to arm wrestling, was played with the resolve to win. We would also choose to watch TV or listen to the radio out of the allocated hours set by our parents, but I was a bad liar which always caused trouble, as I would start laughing when I had to tell a lie to my parents.

My father retired from the army when I was in Primary 3 and we moved from Azad Kashmir to Faisalabad. After five years of studies, my father became a homeopathic doctor and during that time, he started a carpet business which made a huge loss due to blindly trusting the wrong people. I observed my parents becoming anxious and that also led me to be concerned and insecure. Another collapsed business proved that, although my father was a wonderful human being and my hero, he was not a good business man.

I finished my primary education in Faisalabad and my father decided to take the post of administration and account management in Shelokh Mission Hospital in Jalal-Pur-Jattan. During my father's army service, we had never stayed anywhere longer than two years. However, we lived in Faisalabad for seven years and I had the opportunity to make strong friendship bonds. Therefore, I felt more of a loss regarding that move. Nonetheless, I found brilliant friends in Jalal-Pur-Jattan and finished my high school education there.

Sadly, during that time, my eldest brother had started taking drugs and this caused our family a huge amount of tension and grief. During that time, I felt and shared the helplessness, dread and distress my parents experienced. My lovely parents, who had shown me the virtues of love, compassion and kindness, who, for me, were the tower of strength, began to crumble and that was terrifying to witness.

In 1988, I began my degree in Psychology and during this time I stayed in a girls' hostel in Sialkot which was run by a Scottish lady called Catherine Nicol. It was difficult to leave my parents and the comforts of my home behind but it gave me the opportunity to encounter the real world myself. Around that time, I was actively involved with a Christian students' organisation, Pakistan Fellowship of Evangelical Students (PFES), and I attended a conference where I had a chance to play ping-pong with Peter Gill, a well-dressed, handsome young man. According to Peter, he won the game and I won his heart! Peter, after his first degree, went to England for a two-year diploma course in Missiology and I went to Multan for my Bachelor of Education degree. In 1989 we became engaged and in 1990 I came to see Peter in England. I joined him for a semester which gave me the opportunity to meet his friends and afterwards I could truly call them our friends.

In 1991, we married in Pakistan. My father-in-law, Rev. George Gill, a Gujrat parish minister, and my mother-in-law Skina, an open theological seminary teacher, and two sisters-in-law, Doris and Rebecca, warmly welcomed me into the Gill clan. Peter and I went to Murree for our honeymoon and from the huge glass window of our room we could see the snow-covered mountain peaks of Kashmir. Murree and its surrounding areas were the most scenic places, with an abundance of plants and wildlife; I fell in love with the North of Pakistan.

As a couple, we moved to live in Lahore as Peter decided to work with an NGO. After our summer vacation, I wanted to find a teaching job, although to be near Peter during the summer, I had decided to work as a volunteer in said organisation. I intended to stay for a few months; I ended up staying for 11 years! I realised the work I was doing with children and women was making a difference in their lives. I had wanted to teach children for the same reason. In addition, working there I was also getting the opportunities to support women which I found very rewarding. Peter and I worked in different departments but we had lunch and tea breaks together, which was delightful.

In 1992 ,we had our first son Sharoon Gill, and holding him in my arms for the first time, I felt immeasurable delight and excitement. There was also a shadow of fear in how I would manage to take care of the most precious being in the world. Peter was hugely supportive so raising our firstborn was a pleasant experience.

Five years after working with the NGO, Peter was appointed as the first national director of the organisation and later on, I took the responsibility as a co-ordinator of women's work. I had his full support for my initiatives for women's work and we were passionate about uplifting our community and bringing change in individuals lives.

The more I became aware of the state of oppression, depression and suppression faced by women, my passion to empower them grew stronger. Listening to their stories gave me an in-depth awareness of their challenges. I was in awe of their capacity to cope and live with their adversities and admired how their challenges made them resilient and unique. I felt encouraged and determined to bring change in their lives through raising self-awareness, self-worth and self-care. I prepared and delivered a course so they could discover their talents, refine them and establish their worth. I also arranged seminars on health, hygiene, balanced food, finance management and parenting. The self-awareness and self-worth they gained raised confidence and this aided some women to resist domestic violence due to their new-found self-belief.

In 1997, we had our son Shahrukh Gill. Soon after his birth, holding him in my arms, I was filled with pure happiness and immense gratitude. Looking at each other seemed like a long conversation. I welcomed Shahrukh in this world and told him I loved him so much.

Shahrukh was only eight weeks old when I received a threatening call that Peter's life was in danger as a blasphemy case was recorded against him. Peter was in Murree for a conference. I was aware that Peter would never say or do anything to disrespect or hurt anyone's feelings but I was worried that, for money, someone could easily lie and blame him. I felt dread so deep in my bones and all I wished was to see Peter again. I informed Peter's parents, my brother Zahid and Peter's secretary, who was a lovely Canadian lady and a good friend, and we decided that I would take the children to Murree so we would be together as a family. My brother and Peter's father accompanied us on that nine hour journey.

I was so thrilled and pleased to see Peter; however, we needed a place to stay and hide. Due to fear for their own lives, our good friends and different organisations' leaders couldn't provide us a place to hide. Eventually, we found an empty young boys' hostel – the children had returned to their homes for summer vacation. I missed the comfort of my own home but I was pleased that we were together and safe.

After a month, we were informed that the threat had been just a prank, someone playing a sick joke. I don't think they could even imagine the intensity of terror and insecurity they caused for me. That was the start of a long trail of incidents. After a few months, we found a dead eagle in our porch and over the next two years, dead goats' heads were thrown in our front garden, and a few times someone sneaked into our front garden and made strange patterns with flour.

The realisation that someone was that close to us made me more uneasy regarding our safety and security. In particular cultures, a dead goat's head or a dead eagle is a threat or a curse for death, and receiving those threats frequently brought immense fear and insecurity. I became very cautious and kept our double doors, both the wooden and iron ones, locked all the time. After our long-trusted armed guard died, I struggled to trust the new ones. The children could only play in the garden with a few trusted people and while driving, I was worried that someone is following us.

One evening in front of our gate, some people opened fire with Kalashnikovs and it went on for some time. I turned all our lights off and drew all the curtains so we couldn't be seen from the outside. From that day onwards, I drew the curtains as soon as the lights were on in the house.

In 1999 we had our daughter, Miriam Gill. Holding her in my arms, I felt delighted and blessed, holding my only daughter. I also felt fearful, considering our circumstances, for her safety. All those times when I felt anxiety and uncertainty, I leaned on my faith. Of course, there were times when I felt afraid and shaken but my belief in God's protection over us kept me strong and, thus I managed my family and work responsibilities.

In January 2003, my mother died after a stroke. Experiencing the first death in the family was hard. I managed that loss better as I had my father there for me. However, he missed my mother so much that he died of a broken heart in June of that same year. Not having my father on my side was really hard, as all my life he had been my support and strength. I was heartbroken, but, to my surprise, I kept going on and stayed strong for my family and brothers. I always dreaded the concept of losing my parents, yet I was surprised at how well I coped with and managed my parents' deaths.

I received a lot of comfort and support from Peter, and the children were aware of my grief. Their countless hugs were comforting, especially when they told me, "Don't worry, we are here for you." I felt a huge responsibility towards my younger brothers and we tried to support each other. Particularly having my brother Zahid around was very comforting in those early days of bereavement, as he reminded me of my father through his love and care.

Threats against our family grew more frequent and stronger, so in August 2003, following the advice of the Minister of Minorities, we left our homeland and came to live in Scotland, two months after my father's death. A month after our arrival in Scotland, I felt the intensity of my grief and realised I could not postpone the bereavement process any longer. I was grieving for my parents, I was devastated for the loss of my family, my friends, my beautiful home, and the country where I had been born and brought up. Losing my support network at a time of crucial transitions was extremely tough.

For years I had experienced fear for my family's well-being and security, so the first few months in Scotland I felt the same. Glass windows without grilles bothered me. I was perfectly mindful that my fear in Scotland was unrealistic, yet my mind was so used to feeling endangered at all times that it took me a while to reconstruct my thoughts and address my fear.

A few weeks after our arrival in Scotland, Peter became a full-time student as we came on a student visa. I took a part-time job in a care home as the children were young and I wanted to be there for them after school. On weekends it was lovely to see friends, especially Rev. Margaret Nutter, who became a massive part of our family, and has continuously been there for us.

Peter and the children were my source of strength and comfort. I struggled to talk with them about my grief as I did not wish to burden them, but I had wanted to speak to someone regarding my pain and loss. My degrees were not recognised in Scotland and that contributed to my feelings of frustration. I felt my achievements so far in the life were in vain and starting from zero was exasperating. On the one hand, I started feeling safe but my insecurities about our future still remained the same. Every year when we renewed our visas, there was the uncertainty of them being validated.

I volunteered with The Well in Glasgow, working among the immigrants and Creative Community Craft Centre and joined an Asian women's group. I felt well accepted at all places and that helped me feel more settled. However, I also felt frustrated because the country where I was born and brought up, had failed to make me feel safe and I did not yet belong to the country where I felt accepted and safe. I knew my losses through death and our move to Scotland still required acceptance, but I was determined that I would instead replace my loss of old identity through establishing a new identity in Scotland.

When Peter finished his studies, I asked him if we could consider living here as I fell in love with Scotland and our children seemed well settled in their schools. Peter found a job with the Church of Scotland as a minister and we finally received our citizenship after seven years. However, I was aware that to get a job where I could feel satisfied and fulfilled, I needed to pursue further studies and some training. For the longest time, I sought to study theology so I decided to do an MA Honours in Theology and Religious Studies. I found it intriguing to learn about people's beliefs, how they impact their way of living and their interactions with others. I loved to understand how beliefs were reflected in traditions and cultural values.

Peter has always been actively involved in interfaith activities in Pakistan and created an interfaith group in Renfrewshire. Our experience with persecution encouraged me to support an essential interfaith dialogue because, in my view, acceptance and reverence of others' beliefs can reduce religious tensions. I believe we must accept and celebrate our differences, as they make us unique and this acceptance can encourage peace and harmony within our communities.

In 2015, I lost my youngest brother Nathan, who was murdered. In 2018, I lost my eldest brother Shahid, who just disappeared and was never found. I struggled to grieve their deaths and get any closure for a while. I began to understand that losing a loved one through natural causes is hard, yet still easier to deal with than a death through unnatural causes. Again, I managed this loss with the love and support of my family and friends. Though I did wonder how people with less or even no support networks were able to cope.

I then decided to pursue counselling as a career, hence I did a one-year COSCA Certificate course for Counselling Skills and a two-year Diploma course in Cognitive Behavioural Therapy and groupwork. For my placement, I chose Cruse Bereavement Care so I could provide help to bereaving people. My own experiences of dealing with grief aided my understanding of other people's grief and allowed me to support them in the darkest time of their lives. I feel privileged when I help people suffering from different mental health issues. However, I further feel honoured when I am able to support people experiencing complex grief, as I know how it feels to be in a state of grieving.

Looking back at my tumultuous yet beautiful life, I observe the many transitions I have encountered thus far. There were times when I resented certain changes. I wanted to reverse time or forget about what hurt. However, the passage of time taught me that external transitions brought a transformation within me. I let go of my desire to change time and learned to accept my losses and changes, understanding that the challenging times of my existence made me who I am. In fact, now I treasure those times, as they provided a wealth of experience and enabled me to grow in my understanding of life. I still miss the ones I loved that I lost through death and disappearance, yet instead of recalling my memories with pain, I remember with gratitude and an abundance of love.

My loss through death created an appreciation for living in the present, my loss of security allowed me to become a secure space for others, and my loss of identity motivated me to understand who I am and assist others in finding themselves. I have uncovered my inner strength, my determination to achieve my goals and my own capability to induce positive transformations in my life.

To Rev. Margaret Nutter,

My friend, my mentor, my mother and a wonderful grandmother to my children.

Thank you for being there for me; your love, care, guidance and encouragement means the world to me.

New Woman 21

Bal Heer

To Be or Not To Be?

"The greatest privilege you have is knowing you have a choice."

This is a story about choices, how I chose to re-familiarise myself with my inner strengths; how I chose to set the right example and face my fears, but most importantly, how I chose to live and to be.

The greatest privilege you have is knowing you have a choice. Granted, sometimes we make bad choices in life; however, these should be valuable lessons that we can learn so much from in time. It's important to understand that when we fail at something, it only teaches us how not to do something as we try again.

As a young woman at the age of 25, I found myself in an exceedingly difficult situation. I did not realise how I had got to such a scary point in my life. My marriage was suffering a breakdown, and I had just recently given birth to my little baby boy in December 2005. I, like many other women, was exposed to domestic violence, as well as being a direct subject of this too.

During my marriage, I was constantly insulted on many levels as my then-husband's only interest was to sell pirate copy DVDs for a living, whilst claiming state benefit for not being able to work. When he was not burning DVDs, he was playing video games. This money would then be gambled away with his gambling habits. When I asked for a little help around the house whilst I was heavily pregnant and even after giving birth, this would cause him to erupt and take advantage of my vulnerability of being pregnant or nursing my newborn son. Many a times, I heard, "Where's Daddy now?" or "What you going to do, call your dad?" as he knew this was not possible at the time.

He had smacked me in my face, tried strangling me, and many times made me think that I was the one that was in the wrong, trying to emotionally and psychologically destroy me. At one stage, I even attempted suicide.

Although I had accepted this unreasonable behaviour of my now ex-husband for some years, I guess you could say that it was a wake-up call once giving birth to my son. I was not prepared to expose my son to awful experiences that will never ever truly leave you.

I wanted my son to grow up to be a respectful, kind and honourable young man, and this was never going to happen with such a bad influence in his surroundings.

Although very afraid of what was about to come, I made the decision to end my marriage. I was very scared and all alone, and this was not an easy choice, but more a duty I had to my son. I guess you could say this was my first step in deciding to acknowledge some self-respect.

I knew that if my son had been exposed to this behaviour, there was no knowing how he would end up in his adulthood, and it was more a duty to surround him with a good example of what being a good, decent human being meant.

Some years had passed since my divorce and, well, I guess you could say I have had my fair share of turmoil and traumas. Life was bad, I mean REALLY bad; I had no money, debt just kept piling up and I had lost faith in family, friends, and in God. I would cry many evenings wondering why this was happening to me. I saw no way out, I felt alone and stuck in a terrible situation, taking care of a highly dependent child.

I became angry with God, questioning, "Why me? What have I ever done to deserve so much pain?" I felt that it was unjust and that my son was also being made to suffer. I totally lost faith.

Many days passed where I did not even have money to feed myself properly. Some days, it was just a cup of tea and biscuits, because every penny would go towards feeding my son and ensuring his needs were met first.

Wherever I would go and whoever's path I crossed, I would smile and put on an act of a happy woman with no worries in the world, but little did they know how HARD and challenging life really was.

In the first year of my break-up with my now ex-husband, he would still try and contact me, as well as some members of his family, telling me how sorry he was and that he would change etc., but these were empty promises that I was much too familiar with.

One day I found myself on my knees in my bedroom in the middle of the day, crying so much it was as though riverbanks had broken and tears just came flooding out. I felt helpless, defeated, deflated and such a failure to my son. I was ready to give up. I was contemplating going back to my ex-husband purely because I felt that I seriously could not cope any longer this way and had nothing to offer my son. This would be the equivalent of suicide!

I called my mother and told her, "I give up, I give up, Mum. I can't do this anymore; he wins!"

I guess this was my light bulb moment where I had to be reminded of who I was. Mum did an exceptionally good job of this; looking back, it was almost as though when a mother is giving her child a good telling off, it reminds you of your strength and courage and not to give in just yet. She went on to say, "Bal, get up, go and wash your face, and just remember who you are. You can do this, and I don't know anyone as strong as you." I suppose this is exactly what I needed to hear, as I was almost ready to give up and give in.

After following my mum's sound advice, I took some time to think and tried to gain some perspective.

This was the moment. "To be or not to be?" I chose to be!

At this point, I may not have had all the answers to hand but one thing I had decided for sure was that life was not going to beat me and that although life had been particularly challenging indeed, I was about to become life's challenge and not the other way round.

It was time to step up, and that started with changing my perspective on life along with some self-belief and reinstating my lost relationship with God. Rather than seeing him as the enemy, I started to look at him as my greatest supporter, and that the reason I was made to endure so much in my life was actually only to make me stronger. These struggles were my preparation to be able to look fear in the eyes the next time I was acquainted with it without a flinch. I had to remember that I was a force to be reckoned with.

You see, in my culture being from an Indian heritage, it is said that when you do not have the blessing of your birth father around you, God is your ultimate father. As a daughter of God and with His hand on your head, you will always be blessed, and He is the one that hears and answers your prayers.

Looking back on my life, I now see that I had been blessed with so much! I always had the courage, determination and resilience that I would need to make such a turnaround in my life. I just needed to remember it.

What we do not realise is that we all have this ability; however, so many of us fail to recognise this within us because we are clouded and cloaked by fear. Fear is the ultimate enemy; when we fear, we push away hope, and when there is no hope, there is nothing.

I recognised and understood that I was capable of change and that I was not going to allow life to remain the way it was then. I also knew and accepted that this change was not going to happen overnight, and neither was I going to see the fruits of this overnight either.

My transformation was about timing. With my son still incredibly young, my priority was always going to be him and until he was able to be a little more independent, I just had to accept that things would remain difficult until such time. In the meantime, I just kept hold of that thought in knowing things will change, that there is more to me and there is more to my life. This was what I genuinely believed and refused for anyone to tell me otherwise; nobody was going to shatter my self-belief.

Once my son was able to start nursery and was a little more independent, I knew it was now the time to get back into work. Although I was educated with much experience under my belt, the question employers seemed to have on their mind was, if I still had what they needed in me – I was a little rusty, as I had been out of work for at least five years.

I did not care about status, or the fact that I was once an officer for West Midlands Police – I just desperately needed an income. I took whatever opportunity came my way, even working some evening shifts at my local chippy.

Three years after my divorce, I was still very reluctant about having a relationship with anyone. However, I guess what is meant to be will be, and I met my now husband. I am now the proud mother of two sons. In the early years of my second marriage, times were still financially strained as my husband was struggling to find employment himself. It was a time where many companies were enforcing redundancies and the UK itself was going through a financial crash.

I found employment at an estate agents. My role was meant to be as a receptionist; however, they got more than they bargained for, as I was the receptionist, administrator, and bringing in new business, as well as taking care of existing clients – pretty much an all-rounder.

I had displayed the utmost respect and loyalty for my employers in the three years I had worked for them. However, the same was not forthcoming. My manager would talk down to me and never let me forget who's 'the boss'.

This was the second time in my life that I needed to call upon the courage and strength that I knew I possessed within and faced up to the fear of what would happen if I left my job, as it was the only income coming into the household at the time. Nonetheless, I would not allow fear to take away my self-respect once again, so I left on 9th June 2014.

It was another do-or-die moment and with some words of encouragement from my husband, I took a leap of faith once again and decided that I would do what I had been doing for the estate agents, only this time for myself. On 23rd June 2014, my company Regional Homes Ltd was formed.

My first couple of years, like for many newly formed companies, were challenging, but building trust takes time and I was prepared for this. I am now the proud owner and CEO of my multi-award-winning company Regional Homes Ltd, Est 2014. I launched my second branch in July 2019 and my company continues to grow strong, even with the devastating effects of a global pandemic; a truly challenging time for all, my company continues to display the same resilience that I have.

They say that when it comes to branding, your business should represent you and vice versa. Well, I guess when building my business and the ethos we stand by, and when giving the business a slogan "Knowing your home is in good hands" shows that the same strength, resilience and respect I hold for others is evident within my company too.

Today, I am blessed to say that I am the proud mother of two sons: my eldest now having just recently turned 15, and my youngest being 10 years of age. My sons are everything to me and more, as well as being recognised as respectable, kind and honourable young individuals. I see this as my true success and the fuel that burns the fire inside me.

Being passionate in wanting to set the right examples in life to my sons gave meaning to my life. I needed to show my sons that whatever happens in life, you always have a choice, in most cases the choice to face your fears, and if you choose to work hard and be patient, as the saying goes, hard work always pays off.

My journey may have been the same as many to start with; however, it was maintaining that resilient mindset, that can-do attitude (self-belief) and wanting to set the right examples to my children, that got me to where I am today. From unemployed, pregnant and being in an abusive marriage, to getting a divorce, evening shifts in a chip shop still suffering from financial distress with debt piling up, to finally creating the opportunity to work for myself in real estate.

It is said that if you cannot look after yourself, how can you look after another? This is what changed almost 15 years ago. I stopped allowing fear to take over my life and started to believe there was more to me and the life I was living, as well as refusing to live a life stuck on state benefits.

The moment I started to believe in myself and understood the importance of timing and how it plays a big part, the more confident I became that by looking after me, I could look after others, allowing me to enable change.

When choosing 'to be' (to live), it means you have chosen to put aside all the excuses fear whispers into your ears and clouds your vision. It means that no matter how challenging life may be, you choose not to give in or give up. It is during these times that you get to master your resilience with the constant practise in learning to do what is right for you, what feels good to you. Most importantly, you must never forget or lose sight of why you are taking this road. The journey you are on creates choices to enable great change in your life.

You are the decision maker for your life and can make choices; some easy, some more difficult than others, but you do have a choice. Do not allow others to make significant decisions in your life, for your life and to take control.

I chose 'to be', to live and not be taken in by fear, the fear of rejection, the fear of failure. The fear of losing me and everything I had to give back to life and my family was much greater.

Today, I still face many challenges on different levels but now I laugh at fear – fear cannot get the better of me as I am too experienced and wise as the result of difficulties I faced in life. Fear plays a big role in the choices I take and make, but it will never break me or get the better of me, as I control my choices and refuse to break because of fear. Instead, I create solutions to problems.

What will you do the next time fear starts calling? Will you allow it to cloud your judgement, your capabilities? Will you let others choose for you? Will you take control and become the captain of your ship, where you choose the direction, even if those winds seem strong and dangerous? Remember your will to succeed is even stronger when you choose.

If you fall and fail, you can either choose to give up and let fear get the best of you, or you can decide to overcome fear, persevering through your struggles and never giving in by displaying resilience, self-belief and remaining true to yourself.

The very essence of this was being reuniting with my birth father after 20 years of separation. His love and protection are a completion to me and I now feel this extraordinary constant surge of energy flowing through my veins. I feel unstoppable and untouchable, as if my armour has been returned to me.

To have the blessings and protection of our divine creator is already an enormous feeling of power, but to combine this with the blessings and protection from my birth father is like titanium – it is bulletproof.

All in all, we are faced with many challenges in life and questions to which the answers may seem difficult to find and not so apparent at first. However, there is only one question that you truly need to answer: To Be or Not to Be?

New Woman 22

Jemma Rosenthal

Dancing with a Voice

"Nothing is impossible when you have
Love in your heart."
Jemma Rosenthal

As a Woman,

I've shrunk myself…

Dampened and dismissed my innate strengths and beauty…

Belittled my talents and my voice…

As a woman,

I pretended to be someone I wasn't and I made myself fit a box I just didn't fit.

As a woman,

I tried to be… perfect…

But it was never enough.

I still didn't believe I was worthy of being even just a little bit acceptable…

"You're rubbish. You can't do this. Don't say that. You don't matter to them. Your opinion is not important."

Those were the voices that kept my spirit from soaring and my expression contracted and cautious… "Don't get it wrong!" I was warned.

Until, one day…not one day, like every day…

I started piece by piece and day by day, to see a different woman

To feel and most importantly be a different woman

A Woman with Strength

A Woman with Courage

A Woman Determined to be herself.

And in the face of criticism, judgement, and at times hatred…

As a woman, I am still enough

I'm here

And I matter.

And these are not just words we have heard a thousand times before, in motivational speeches. They are a demonstration of what is possible.

So I stand here today

And I claim my power.

Yes…

As a woman.

I am sat on a bus. There's a slight smell of fuel and puffing sounds as the bus begins to move. Resting on the slightly itchy cushioned chairs, I watch as we slowly make our way onto the busy road that lead us towards the town centre. I feel the movement underneath the floor of the lower deck, ba dum, ba dum, ba dum.

This part of town is derelict and fairly bleak, not like the gorgeous greenery of so many other parts of Sheffield, which is one of the greenest cities in Europe. There may have been a few patches of green grass along the side of the road, but today, I'm not seeing it. I look up at the grey sky and matching grey roads, and I take a heavy sign in my heart.

Sadness and disappointment fill me almost to the point of tears, but I've yet to find the surrender enough to cry or truly feel it. I've just been in a therapy session. To be exact, it was for anger management, though as my counsellor tells me, I've learnt to see it as integrated emotional management, as underneath our anger can be many emotions, such as grief, envy and shame. This session was the first of this new approach and I had yet to fully accept the power of acceptance. I was still in my shame. Annoyed, resentful and unforgiving. I thought

I'd overcome this, hours of meditation, practicing my positive affirmations and going to retreats. I thought I was better by now. This is hopeless. I hear a ringing and I reach into my bag and answer the phone.

"Hi Jemma, it's Zainab from Sisters With One Voice. Linda and I were wondering if you could do a dance at our launch event. Happening in March."

I hear the words in gratitude, but my mind now turns to a fog of panic and worry. "Yeah, of course, I can do a dance," I reply tentatively, and with my best strong voice I add, "Can I do a song as well?"

"Yes, anything you like," she says.

As I put the phone down, I feel a sinking in my stomach of worry and doubt, yet equally, a joy, elation and honour at having been asked to perform. Thoughts swirled around my mind. 'I'm barely even making it through the day. And now I going to stand up in front of a crowd and dance and sing for all of those amazing inspirational people? I don't even know what I'm going to do!'

Even as I'm thinking this, I feel the bus start to move more lightly, the sun shine seems to shine more brightly, and I find myself humming and tapping my foot on the back of the seat, to the slight rhythm of hopefulness and possibility.

Ever since I was a child, I loved to dance, I loved to sing, act and write stories. I was a creative child as one could ever be. It was my safe space, where I felt at home. I would gather around friends and family members to play and create together. Creating in the playground, in the garden, filming and creating TV and radio shows. I would often take the lead and organise performances, and perform them to the parents, a natural mentor and teacher. I never imagined that when I grew up and later became an actual paid performing arts teacher, I would be in such unrest inside my heart.

"Arms stretched, feet pointed, raise your head, remember to smile!"

Day after day, I'd do my steps. I'd look in the mirror as I took a few deep breaths, and grounded my feet to the floor. "Be in this moment," I reminded myself and straightened my ponytail, and continued to teach the steps, "... a five, six, seven, eight."

One time, I rushed to class, out of breath, with my eyes filled with tears. I decided not to hide them; perhaps I was too tired and just felt alone. With tears falling down my face like I'd just put my cheeks in a waterfall, expecting the teacher and children to dismiss me as weak and unprofessional, I found instead a deepening of the heart. Though it hasn't always been the case, this day, as I talked it through with the teacher, I was met with empathy and understanding. Feeling comforted, I pressed play and some uptempo street dance music blared, so I led the class of young, vibrant, eager dancers in a lively warm-up. "Knees up! Keep going, that's it, now star jumps!"

At the end of the class, a young girl approaches and asks, "Miss, have you ever had panic attacks? I have and I wondered if you had?"

My mind flashes back to London 2011, to show rehearsals at my performing arts college… step, step turn and leap and… heart racing, mind clouded, hand on heart, can't think, can't move, can't… breathe… must get the steps just right, sing those notes exactly the way they were meant to be sung, remember my lines perfectly. I must look and sound perfect and be noticed. I must not make a mistake. Did I say the right thing to that person? Maybe I upset them, ouch! Daggers in the heart… mind racing. Maybe I got something wrong… maybe who I am is wrong?

These daily mantras, the thoughts that cover up the spirit, hide the soul, and terrorise the frightened mind that just wants to be free to be to love, express itself and create.

Bending only slightly to meet her, I turn to the young child, look into her eyes with a gentle nod. "Yes, I have," I say. And though we talk no more on the subject, we smile with a mutual understanding.

It was in 2013, soon after finishing a three-year Performing Arts degree and getting my first job in a school's tour pantomime, that I first broke open. My first dark night of the soul, my breakdown to breakthrough, my spiritual reckoning, or whatever you wish to name it. I was sharing a flat with a friend in North London, and though I still immersed myself in my creativity, after graduation I often found myself wandering aimlessly around the streets, auditioning and working in jobs that didn't always feel comfortable.

In a matter of months my life completely changed. At first it was depression, emptiness, boredom, then the mind expanded, weeks of trippy dreamlike elation, dullness turned to bright colours wonder and awe. In a bizarre plot twist, crippling fear, paranoia and haunting angst. Unable to understand time, moments of my memory started disappearing. What in the strangeness was happening to me? Just to be sure I was okay, I decided to return to my hometown of Sheffield. I would not see our London flat again.

A few weeks home, and I am losing all sense of time, space and reality as I had previously known it to be. The experience of feeling I was time travelling backwards and forwards, my mind didn't function in a linear way anymore; shapes were larger, brighter more vivid and colourful. Chunks of time cut out completely. It was fairly surreal and bizarre but in places also kind of exhilarating! A high my mind had created completely without drugs. I even sang as I was carried off into the ambulance... With nurses by my side, I was fascinated by both the inside and outside of the vehicle and, as I was taken away, I did not know what would happen or where I was going.

As I arrived in a waiting area of A&E, I hear voices, shuffles and muffles. It seems as if I was in a belly of the underworld. I felt a call of ancestral healing. I made sounds and the loudest cries that have never escaped my being. Deep from the depths of my belly, I called out, "Ohhhh... Ohhh... Ahhhhh... Ohhhh...Ohhhoh..."

I'd never heard such sounds, equally beautiful as they were surprising. Even though I was clearly sounding out of the ordinary, I felt a sense of rightness deep inside. A connection to my own sound and power. My Voice Awakened. As I walked out of the waiting areas, looking at my small frame, a lady asked, flabbergasted, "Did those sounds come from her?"

The next morning, I awoke in a mental hospital, in a small single bed. I lay, my body frozen. I stared at the blank wall, no longer singing. I held the unfamiliar thin hospital sheets around my body. A far cry from the prestigious halls of my dance school training, the theatres, friends and London life. I was curious as I suddenly heard a woman's voice, an older lady. To this day, I have no idea who this woman was I was speaking to; in my rational, logical mind, I now expect it was one of the nurses. Or controversially, perhaps it was all made up, in my own mind. I never found out. But the voice answered me clear as day. To me, it was me. It was my older self. Older, wiser, funnier and surprisingly much more Yorkshire sounding! I was terrified to look around; I mean, would you be able to face your older self? I concluded that if I did, I may die from shock so I stayed looking away, comforted enough to hear her and to know she made it through okay. Though I could not make out her exact words, the message I received was clear: "You're going to make it through this. You're going to be okay! You will live a full, happy and wonderful life! You will dance, sing and act again and so much more. Have faith." I felt a sense of peace, knowing my future was safe. Phew. It was still, nevertheless, very shocking. I mean, who can hear the future? Who can time travel?

When I returned from hospital with a diagnosis of bipolar (aka manic depressive), it took a long time to feel myself again. I slept all of the time, and I started losing clumps of hair and ate a lot, due to the medication side effects. I started meeting up with old friends again. Some remarked on my change of personality, or rather my lack of personality, saying that I'd become a shell of myself. I started to receive treatment in the form of talking therapies and meet-ups, working as a dance teacher and gradually gained some sense of self again. I immersed myself in books, training courses and meditation. I sang and wrote my songs. I used my creative tools. I was on the road to full recovery, and after a few years, I felt I had reached a mountain top and arrived. The climb wasn't easy, but I'd done it. I had decided to retrain as a life coach and work towards achieving my performing dreams again.

Back on the bus, on that winter morning of early 2019, I was facing the reality that I had just come out of admitting myself to a crisis house and back into therapy. This time with different symptoms and a new diagnosis of Borderline Personality Disorder and with new ways of treatment to manage my anger bursts. (I later found out a more forgiving name used to describe BPD – Emotionally Sensitive. Many people with BPD are very highly aware and attuned to the senses and are treated well with Dialectical Behavioural Therapy (DBT).) Although I was still hopeful, I couldn't help wondering had I failed?

Had I not recovered enough? How was I going to put myself out there again for the performance? I held on to that sense of hopeful rhythm I'd felt in the tap of my toes on the bus. I was different now. I was a new woman. My creative spirit knew the truth. She knew I had the means within me to keep going. She knew that my soul wanted to shine. That my soul wanted to give and receive a magnitude of compassion and resilience. My soul knew that I had so much more to offer and that another bump in the road is not the end of the journey but a reminder to slow down, and stay awake.

So when I arrived home, I breathed, in and out, in and out, in and out. I sat in stillness and listened. A blanket wrapped around my legs and feet, warm mug in my hands. I suddenly hear the words, "As a Woman." They seemed to drop in from the sky, and down through the top of my head. A direct download. I rushed to grab a pen and my phone so I can record it down as I hear. I was given the instructions, I then start to see it – a dance. A flick of a skirt, a whoosh of the hair, a pause here, an arm, a swoosh there. I feel the sense of inner satisfaction as the moves continue to fill my body with delight and surprise… I laugh and giggle and pout my lips. I feel alive again. The movement was a call to play, to regain the creative flair within a woman's body and soul. Mmmm. Happy with what I had created so far, I wondered, what could be next?

I moved to the piano. I started to play a song I'd been working on, called *Extend Love*. The song is a rise up call, about getting on your dancing shoes and being who you are meant to be. "There's no time for excuses. Freedom calls you now to sing!" I knew the song meant what it said! And for freedom's sake, I must fulfil it!

For so many years, I had felt so stuck. I knew I had a voice and something to say, but I often held back, keeping quiet when I could have spoken up, or perhaps saying too much unnecessarily, not listening to my inner wisdom. I always believed. I knew I had something to offer the world. But there was the sense of protectiveness. I've heard that when something means the most to you, it can be the hardest to surrender, to letting things be as they are meant to be and let the wind take the lead. I never wanted the creations to be criticised, trampled on or hated in the world. I received so much healing from them and I wanted to keep this sense of presence in tact. I loved them and held them tight, so dearly, so much that I almost suffocated them to death.

I was determined these ones would make it out there. Along with the dance and poem and another song called *Afraid of Love*, I was ready for this to be a catalyst for growth and change. I relayed my fears of nerves to the ladies at SWOV and they assured me that this would be a very supportive crowd. A loving environment for me to fully express my true self and art. This comforted my fears. As I contemplated what the song *Extend Love* needed, I felt there was a bridge missing, and as I played and sang, a new bridge naturally sprung forth.

"Sometimes you feel like it's hard,
sometimes you feel like your broken apart.
But nothing is impossible,
when you have Love in your heart."

It was the perfect fit for the moment. I truly believe in my heart that all is possible with love. It gave me the exhilaration, strength and courage I needed to go forward. March arrived and walking into the room all done out with posh chairs and a projector for the speakers, I felt honoured to be included and a part of something that recognised women's strength. Getting ready to perform, sat in a chair, my make-up almost done, I felt a sense of hope and togetherness that each of the women would bring to the evening. There were entrepreneurs, dancers and so many inspirational people.

I walked onto the stage, present and grounded; ready and sure. Stillness. Then the movement came. Although the moves were choreographed, I let the moment take me, my hips swayed, my eyes sparkled, with the hints of playfulness, my arms and palms floating me into a state of bliss and freedom. And as I stood up on the chair just before the last words at the end of the performance, with my head held high, I faced the crowd. I felt as if an electric bolt of energy ran right through the floor underneath me and up to the heavens as a declaration.

I'm a woman. I'm here. I am an artist. I have something to say. I matter. And as I allowed this courage to flow through me, in turn, freeing other women to do the same. The room erupted into applause.

A Woman with Strength.

A Woman with Courage.

A Woman Determined to be herself.

And as I write these words, I encourage you to keep moving to the rhythm of your own dance, finding and using the power of your voice. Remember, no matter what you may have been through or may be going through, even in the depths of despair, you always have the creation and courage within you to shine.

Yes...

As a Woman.

I dedicate this chapter the women of SWOV (Sisters With One Voice), for believing in me and supporting me in finding and sharing my voice.

New Woman 23

Susanne Virtanen

Reinvent Yourself

"If there's no challenge,
there's no change."

Reinventing yourself is possibly the most exciting journey you can go on. It's a journey of challenge, learning and self-discovery. Interestingly, reinventing yourself isn't necessarily about adding or doing more; it's actually about becoming who you really are and have always been. It's about becoming aware, accepting and appreciative of your situation – and seeing your growth potential in full. Reinventing yourself is about exploring and adapting to the right strategies to achieve your vision – in your style.

I'd like to share my journey of transformation and how the challenges I've faced have helped me to redeem, rediscover and reinvent myself. There is a great saying: *"If there's no challenge, there's no change."* So, you will come to see that your challenges are actually your greatest source of growth and wisdom.

When I first heard that 'you can be, do or have whatever you want', I doubted whether that could happen to me. I have always had such big ambitions and dreams – I often felt that I needed to do my bit to make the world a better place. These grand ambitions to change the world were very different from the people I often spent my time with, so I didn't tend to think or talk about them very much.

Growing up in a quiet village while dreaming of the 'bigger and better', I can admit that in my late teens I'd had enough of the village life. I decided to go on a journey, consisting of studying and working abroad, and within a five-year period I lived in five different countries. I was studying hospitality management and working late nights in restaurants and hotels. Within a few years, I'd had nearly 30 jobs, always chasing the next best opportunity or small pay rise. In many ways this was a great adventure, but I can immediately admit that I was hooked on the process of 'starting over', because the "grass seems to always be greener on the other side". It seemed like I wanted to continuously challenge myself, and others for that matter, and nothing felt like it was enough.

Deep within, I've always been a challenger – the "why" person who's thirsty for knowledge. As a child growing up, I was prone to question and challenge authority, including my parents, teachers and even the governing bodies; later in life, this included my bosses too. You can imagine that didn't go down well. I would read and do more homework than necessary, so that I could ask questions of the teachers. Unsurprisingly, many didn't know how to explain the meaning of life or why we are being taught contradicting theories about the history, origins and purpose of humanity – things that have always fascinated me. Let's just say that from a young age, I was told to be quiet. Later in life while developing my speaking career, I realised this was a major emotional obstacle and inner conflict to overcome.

Spending a lot of time studying and making plans for the future, I became a very achievement-focused person, striving to be the best in class, or just in general striving to get big results. Although I was recognised for some of my achievements, somehow it never really mattered to me much, because the next goal was already in mind. I got my first job at the age of 14, and moved to my first apartment at the age of 17. I was developing an unshakable confidence and bossiness, and my identity became achievement dependent. I was the decision-maker and ambience creator, both in the good and the bad (that's all of us, by the way). Becoming bigger and better falsely defined my worth and state of mind – always wanting more can become a never-ending and unfulfilling cycle.

After finally progressing to better management positions within the hospitality industry, I realised how much I loved supporting others to keep growing and challenging themselves. Ironically, only after a year of graduating with a first-class degree, I decided to pursue a career in teaching. This started the biggest transformation of all, as I realised my greatest passion is helping others to learn, grow and achieve their potential. I simply love learning and encouraging others to keep learning too, and teaching was one of the best ways to channel my energy. Alongside my several training and teaching jobs, I studied coaching and change management which led me to becoming obsessed about personal development. When I had my first personal development coach challenge my procrastination and excuses of, "It's not yet the time to make it big", everything changed. Finally, someone saw through me – I had all the plans but wasn't taking the action required to reach my desires.

When studying change management – how to help people and businesses go through change strategically – the pivotal moment for me was learning about my personality. This was the first time I took a thorough personality assessment, leading me to identify my past and current behaviours with myself. My test result was the 'Debater', with a tendency to focus on acquiring knowledge, initiating innovation and challenging the system. What a match! This powerful revelation allowed me to see myself in a new light, and better yet, from a different perspective. This perspective didn't include self-sabotage, but rather it focused on guiding me to make the most of my personality, build on my strengths, manage my weaknesses, and leverage my growth potential. I didn't necessarily need to change myself completely, but rather just learn to channel my energy in a way that is beneficial and helps me and others reach their goals.

After becoming obsessed with personality and character analysis, the question of "Why is this happening to me?" finally had an answer – I MADE IT HAPPEN. I was finally informed, able and willing to take full responsibility for everything that has happened to me and what is yet to come.

My first life coach pointed out that I was living in a failure cycle. This cycle consists of four stages. The first stage is starting projects with excitement and enthusiasm. The second stage is procrastination: postponing the very thing you need to do in order to achieve your important goals. The third stage is making excuses: the endless loop of "I haven't got the money/time/energy/support…" The fourth and final stage is blame: blaming and pointing at others for your "unfortunate" circumstances. But when one of your fingers is pointing at someone else, three fingers are pointing at you! And those three fingers stand for three words: I AM RESPONSIBLE.

I realised I had just been starting one project after another, without really taking the right action to see me through. When I owned the statement of "I am responsible for everything that happens to me", I started taking a different kind of action. And if I want my life to be full of adventure and learning, then I need to shift my mindset and language to match that vision. I now say to myself: "My life is an exciting adventure because I've set it up that way." These words from my coach challenged me to finally go on the exciting yet uncertain journey of entrepreneurship. Let's just say that I've always known that I only want to be reporting to myself.

With many years in providing training for managers and teachers, my main focus has always been to inspire and support visionary and transformational leaders. Right from the start in my business, excitingly named DiscoverChange, I began embedding personality quizzes into my public talks and workshops in events, schools and organisations. Later on, I volunteered for a charity to do motivational talks at schools – sharing my experience and empowering others to live a life aligned with their true values. Volunteering on top of all my other business projects was sometimes questioned, but I stuck to it because I could see how many people simply needed to hear how important they are and that they TOO can be, do, and have whatever they want. Just got to go for it!

Just START and say "Yes!" to opportunities, even if you're not sure how it will go. That's the exciting part because life truly happens outside of your comfort zone. If you don't go through the learning and the challenges, it's not possible to achieve your true desires.

Through these talks, I was giving others the very piece of advice that I had needed to hear at some point in my life. No point in blaming others though; I was out of the failure cycle and I knew that others should get out of it too! But I also knew that I had to study and learn how to speak and facilitate better, so that I could make a bigger positive difference in people's lives. It's not about just getting people into the room, it's about maximising what you can achieve with them in a short period of time.

As a result of my continuous development, I could see the people I was teaching progressed quicker and better. Indeed, there's a direct link between your input and what you receive. I heard a great motivational speaker once say, "One conversation can change a life." When I discovered that speaking is something you can build a career out of, I knew I had to make it happen! It's not like I'll stop talking anytime soon, so I might as well get paid for it! But I learnt the key is to not just speak, but to speak well. I decided to do whatever it takes to learn how to motivate people in one of the toughest environments of all: a prison. After some months, I landed the job and I took every day as a huge opportunity to learn about the psychology of change and transformation. I also knew that with my somewhat rebellious attitude, I'd be able to deal with challenge and resistance – because I've experienced so much of it and now know how to apply simple yet powerful practices to create immediate change.

Teaching multiple subjects, such as English, IT and Business, in this unstable and even dangerous environment was life-changing, and my aim was to get my students to want to learn and ask for homework. After trying different ways of conducting myself, by the end of the second year there, I had a queue of students waiting for printouts. Sadly, management didn't like this action and I was no longer allowed to provide these resources, much of which included information about mental health and self-care. I began to wonder where resistance to change truly comes from...

As a teacher in this environment, the students tended to say, "All I need is the certificate from this class so that I can get a better job." Later on I realised, especially through my own and others' experiences, that you can have all the qualifications and degrees you want, but unless you know how to apply it in practice, the information isn't very valuable. There are people with no qualifications that are very successful in business. Why? Because they kept it simple and responded to customer demand strategically. Yes, learning is good; however, knowledge is not power. The **application of knowledge** is power.

As an entrepreneur, degrees hardly help to reach big financial successes. Financial success is driven by building sustainable systems and automated processes, so that selling and scaling is easy and efficient. It is a fact that many top business owners do not thrive because of academic achievements, but rather because of building an infrastructure and teams that enable them to continuously achieve greater levels of success. Business success is ultimately about giving other people what they want, because that's how you get what you want. So if your commitment is to help people and make a difference, there are plenty of opportunities that are ready and ripe for you right NOW. Often there's no need to go on another course or do years of business development. There's a need to learn to leverage your strengths and network and, most importantly, learn how to love selling your services and solutions. And when you build your dream business, this positive energy will just ooze from you!

I founded DiscoverChange with a mission to support transformational leaders, change-makers and businesses to grow, especially online. Starting out with coaching and giving talks wherever I could, I now have a team and infrastructure that enables us to pursue an exciting vision of creating positive transformation, even globally. We've supported many businesses to create automated marketing and sales systems as well as digital education platforms and resources that provide information and inspiration for their customers or staff. It gives me great pleasure to see others share their passion and specialism with others.

I'm glad to say that my values of innovation, personal development and collaboration are strongly embedded into our business operations. It came through really accepting and appreciating these values I've always carried, and I recommend you build your business or movement around your core values too. That's how you can be the most confident in what you do! Through my own journey and the countless courses and coaches I've been learning from, I have personally come to see that strategic use of technology is most definitely the gateway to reach and help more people, to share your message in the most efficient way. Imagine if you had your expertise or "teachings" shared in an online format that is available for the world around the clock. The impact could be life-changing!

There comes a time when it's essential to redeem and reinvent yourself. It's NOW possible – in fact, change can happen in seconds. In our early years (and later), we can be trapped in our situation, but as adults we have the power to change our circumstances. You have the power to create whatever you want. The only limitation is your own imagination; it's the thoughts that you keep repeating to yourself. These repeated thoughts become your beliefs. I used to say, "I can't be a speaker, who's going to want to listen to me?" an "No matter how hard I try, I never get what I want."

According to research, we have about 60,000 thoughts every day – this equals 60,000 opportunities to think of something in a certain way. That's 60,000 opportunities to give energy to something. You have the power to change those thoughts. You have the ability to catch yourself thinking negatively and convert that thought into an opportunity to learn and focus on solutions. Find something good about the situation. Often the best realisation is, "When you know what you don't want, you know what you do want." Adversity helps you to see what is really important to you; follow that intuition. Your thoughts create your reality and this profound knowledge means you can bring anything to life, so dare to dream! Accept your desires and goals and take action. And remember to have fun during your journey – you'll need to remind yourself of this often when on your path.

Your life is a sum total of the decisions you make. And indeed, every day you have thousands of opportunities to make different decisions and choices. Ask different questions, meet new people. Go out of your way to learn new relevant skills to reach your next level of success. Get out of your comfort zone and do the thing you've been thinking and talking about. You know exactly what I'm talking about – it's the thing you've been thinking about for a while. For example, I love my outdoor adventures, but I had always feared going into a cave. I kept talking about how I would never go into one. The more I talked about it, the more I realised "the cave was calling for me". So I went caving, because I don't like hearing myself make irrational excuses. Caving was one of the best experiences ever, the type that makes your adrenaline explode! Facing your fears helps you to see that there's actually nothing to worry about. So just do it!

It has taken me some time to realise that I needed to continuously stop adding things – instead, I needed to let go. Someone who knows me well kept reminding me that "Less is more, Susanne". I didn't like the comment at the time, because I didn't understand it. I had always thought that it's only action that can bring you results, to work long hours, to perfect everything. I'm sure you know people that work incredibly hard but haven't exactly got much to show for it. This is a result of outside conditioning. Working well rather than hard is the solution. There are many successful people in the world with exactly the same amount of time than you have – 24 hours in a day. So how come some achieve success and some don't? It depends on how and who you spend your time with. Reflect on who you choose to get influenced by. If there's a need for improvement, get education and inspiration from coaches, events, books and audio. There is a resource and an expert for every problem.

I'm thankful for every single experience I've had, including the tough ones as they helped me to see what I don't want and then carve the path I most enjoy. These experiences made me ask questions that led me to profound realisations and great progress, personally and professionally. The key moment was that I started asking myself different questions. I learnt from my coach that "The quality of your questions determines the quality of your life." So as the 'Debater' and seeker of knowledge, it was crucial I learnt to word and channel things correctly. No longer should I be asking, "Why is this always happening to me?" or "Why don't I ever get what I want?". Instead, we want to ask "What is good about this?", "What have I learnt?" or "What is the solution?"

If you think you're not ready or good enough to go after your true desires, you can rest assured that your strengths outweigh your weaknesses massively. The secret to success is to learn to appreciate and build on your strengths. This important realisation was another pivotal moment in my life – no longer should I try to do everything and anything by myself but rather build a team and ask for help. This goes against my natural instinct of "I'll deal with it myself," or "When I do it, it gets done right". If you ever think this way, I'm glad to tell you that your weakness is someone else's strength – even passion! What might take you weeks or months, might take only hours or days for someone else. Imagine what you could be doing with your time when you don't need to do the things you don't want to do.

It's important to recognise that the things that can sometimes be perceived as weaknesses, can actually be used as strengths. I'm known to be the "Now person" who goes a thousand miles an hour with the occasional impatience kicking in. So it's time to change any weakness to a strength, for example:

I am the Now person; therefore things get done now!

I am the challenger; therefore I seek profound knowledge and share it with others!

I am changing; therefore I can help others to change!

I speak and I am the voice for good, I am a leader!

I am the boss, because, well, somebody has to be!

Accept who you are and have always been, and start using it as your strength. Come up with your own positive and reassuring affirmations and speak them out loud every day. Yes, you can (and should) learn and develop new skills, but at the core you came here with a personality and mission that has great meaning for creation. Even our ancient highly-talented ancestors had created complex maps and concepts to provide guidance and empowerment to help people to reach their potential, specifically using their core strengths and values. This profound knowledge from thousands of years ago indicates how significant YOU are as an individual and creator, regardless of what any other person or system tries to say.

There will always be some who take advantage of people and systems, and bad experiences with these cause many to lose trust and hope. We might think "What's the point in even trying?" But just because someone has decided to do evil things, doesn't mean that there aren't good people or that you should stop pursuing your good deeds. Quite the opposite! The more "bad" you see, the more you know that there is a need for good. And you can bring that positive change about through positive interactions with yourself and others. It is said that "You are the change you wish to see in the world". So if you think someone should change or behave to a certain standard, ensure that you are leading by example. Actions speak louder than words!

We can break the chain of unconstructive behaviour that has been carried from one generation to the next. I learnt about escapism at an early age, and then I used to aimlessly change or escape my environment, wishing things would change. You can escape all you want, but the same problems will keep happening... because it's you. You can't escape from yourself. And it wasn't until I stopped changing my environment and focused on changing and improving myself when things really changed for me. I knew I had to change, not my personality, but rather the unconstructive behaviours that kept me away from progressing and evolving. Remember that all behaviour is learnt behaviour, therefore it can also be unlearned. You can break the chain that has been carried over time and time again. There are many traditions to cherish, but there are also histories to be questioned and behaviours to be changed.

So how exactly have I changed? I stopped running away, learning to be still and appreciative of the now. I stopped blaming the people close to me for what I hadn't achieved. It's not what happened, it's the meaning I give it that matters. I realise that everyone is on their own path, not here to meet my expectations or standards. I listen instead of wanting or waiting to express my opinion. Instead of random actions, I plan my days and future to be as effective as possible. I model people who have achieved what I want. I also allow and take time off because I know that the best ideas come when I'm relaxed. I understand the importance of gaining experiences, not possessions.

When we reflect on our lives and experiences without unnecessary self-sabotage, we can actually create quick positive change. All your experiences, the good and the bad, have brought you here today, stronger and wiser than ever before. No longer is the question "Why is this happening?" but rather "How can I make the most of this?" The last few years have shown us all that the environment is radically changing. While there can be concerns, worries and uncertainty, you have limitless potential to make a difference in your life and that of others. The world needs transformational role models and leaders who see the best in others, so that we can tackle the unnecessary negativity and lack of growth controlling the lives of so many.

Thank you for taking your time to read my journey. Writing this has made me reflect and realise how the opportunities I've wanted have always been there. Some of the things and projects I said "Yes" to may have felt like a lot to handle at the time, but it gave me the experience and knowledge I have today. That's the same for all of us – you have already achieved great things that you can be proud of and build on, much more than you even realise. Whatever you want already exists; it's just a matter of you being aware of what you want, accepting your vision, appreciating yourself and others, and adapting your daily thoughts and behaviours to reach your goals. Now is the time to reinvent yourself and to discover change! Go on a journey of true self-realisation because you were born to win – do it in your way!

New Woman 24

Maxine Palmer-Hunter

Letter to my Younger Self

"I am now willing to forgive myself...
for acting like nothing when the truth is
I am everything."
Iyanla Vanzant

Dear Beautiful,

Life will throw you many curveballs which will shake your foundation, your mind, your health and the people around you, until you think that you cannot bounce back ever again from that episode. That voice will have you questioning everything and doubting yourself, not forgetting the external voices in your head that further emphasis what you thought. While you were grazing through life, many ideas were being formed to bring your lessons and experiences that would shape you in ways that you never saw coming. Because you did not know how to navigate the emotions brought forth by these experiences, they became a mass of turmoil and chaos with a navigating warped sense of emotion that your mind could not even comprehend. **Be gentle with yourself.**

Let's look at some of your experiences which enveloped your life with trauma and chaos.

The early trauma of your childhood from birth were the first lessons of your journey. Being catapulted into a cold-feeling world further aided your distress in an environment with those around locked in their own descending battle, unable to see your vulnerability and pain. The horror of being taking advantage of silenced you and left you with no voice. You became trapped in your world of confusion, isolation and terror. The loneliness that emerged from your prison of emotions soon followed a path that would shape you for many years. This would force you to make adult decisions that now in hindsight were not always the correct ones. When no one looked deep into your eyes and saw your pain, your anguish deepened, you isolated yourself further immersing your mind in books and music. These were your early therapies of life; within your books, the word on the page would escape you to another place whilst the lyrics would fill you with warmth, and the beat of the sounds would soothe your soul, immersing you in temporary escapism. **Music is the beat to the soul.**

Your quietness became sullenness, as you withdrew into your world of chaotic emotions, still not understanding the events of your youth and for a time becoming increasingly angry with those around who failed to witness your decline and protect you from the pack. Never being told that you were beautiful, worthy, a princess, a queen, of value, or that you were loved or good enough, certainly impacted on your ***self-esteem***, ***self-worth*** and ***self-confidence*** which brought on many challenges as you entered adulthood. Your nature was one of nurturing, empathy and compassion with the ability to absorb others' emotions soon becoming your forte. Unfortunately, despite your good intentions, others would use it to their advantage and use you to comfort and support them, drawing on your reserves and leaving you empty and bereft. But what could you say, who was going to listen to you? Who was interested in your feelings? This left you ripe for being relentlessly being bullied. ***Your feelings mattered.***

You continued to be that girl who helped others, pushing your fears to the back, becoming voiceless with your needs and invisible with your real self. Food became an emotional crutch with the sensuality of the textures bringing you an element of comfort that was missing from your life. This in turn would bring another challenge your way. Never being a dainty child, the weight gain added further anxiety; you were the biggest child within the immediate and extended family, so you further withdrew, and it became a vicious cycle of eating and loving cake. Food loved you and you loved food. It made you feel needed, wanted and satisfied. There was something satisfying about that huge hot steaming plate of culinary delights ready to be devoured by you. Being brought up in a house where fresh, tantalising meals were cooked every day bar Friday was a real treat; processed or fast food was not the norm. However, as you approached your teens you felt unattractive and disappointed with yourself, because you were not as slim as other girls of your age nor as pretty as them. ***You were unique.***

You threw yourself into extra-curricular activities, becoming an active member of the netball, rounders and swimming teams; went to dance classes; played the guitar and recorder; enjoying the spirit of fitness, togetherness and winning. Your body soon became womanly curves, more than peers of your own age; a blessing but it left you even more vulnerable and open as you entered adulthood. Your curves brought another challenge. To stay with those curves, a spell of bulimia followed and another secret that nobody could know soon emerged itself. The vicious cycle did nothing for your self-esteem but quite the opposite, leaving you alone in despair, not knowing whom to trust, whom to talk to without judgement, or how to break the cycle of destruction. Feeling temporary satisfied in the moment was one of euphoria, like a drug .You took it, it felt good for a while, then it went, leaving you wanting more of the same feeling. That was you, constant mask on. That little girl did not feel that her feelings were important enough to speak up; instead you continued to hide behind your curves and wall of protection. This may have been good for you at the time but once again you led these feelings into adulthood, not with the bulimia but other things replacing it. Always looking for something to fill the void that you felt, "Why am I feeling so empty?" ***Your inner child needs had not been met.***

Attaching yourself to people to help them overcome their situation became the norm, sometimes neglecting your needs whilst you were wilting and dying inside. This was to be your life for years to come, to the detriment of your sanity. Some were appreciative of your help, others took from the vessel and poured until none was left and not refilled. It took you a long time to see this pattern. From the age of four, the earliest memory was of helping others; conditioned to think it was the norm, you continued a pattern of behaviour that would now be considered as an "enabler" in today's society.

One chapter of your life that you thought would bring great happiness was your move abroad and eventually becoming a teen bride. The reality is you were jumping from the fire into the frying pan but did not know yet. That summer romance after the pregnancy that was no longer, the memory of your attempted suicide when you were 13, the bullying, the trauma, all the sadness, disappointment and guilt, were now replaced by a breath of fresh air, with something exciting, with a rebellious and fun nature who also loved this vibrant being, who excited him. **This was you.**

The next six months were a beautiful mass of long conversations, receiving heartfelt love letters and the whispering words of wisdom. "Someone truly loves me." You decided to live with him; he was older, more experienced and you were fascinated, felt that you would be safe and protected. However, instead you were quickly plunged into a world that was not your own, filled with uncertainty, turmoil, a darkness of craziness, false promises with many lessons. Here you were with a man who told you he would give you the world, luring you with false promises. He was in love with the ideology of the "Black English Rose" and you loved his edgy, conscious protective approach. You were running away from the traumas of your life that embedded deep rooted secrets and invisibility.

When you look back, prior to you moving in with him, signs were there regarding his lifestyle but you chose to overlook them, as you felt that you had met your knight in shining armour. However, reality crept in by the second day. Your first experience of physical violence left you in shock. What was this?! The honeymoon period was rapidly over. Your thoughts were scattered. You loved him. You were too ashamed to tell your family, afraid that they would laugh at you. You could not tell your friends, afraid that they would judge you. The only glimmer of support was his mother, pulling you to one side and telling you to go back home, and this was only the second day. Telling you her son would never make you happy and you should walk away now. Did you listen?

You were concerned about what she said but the apologies and declaration of love soon followed suit and her words became adrift until they would haunt you years later. This became a pattern of the relationship, narcissism, physical abuse, emotional abuse, savage violence and manipulation, slowly stripping away the last bits of worth that you had. At times you would glimpse rare moments of joy and feelings of safety, but that would be switched in a heartbeat. Did you know any better at that time, that you could get out and still be fine? You were living your life on adrenaline. Only 18 years old, you felt a maturity beyond your years, brought on by your experiences, and you had left behind those old feelings to enter this new stage of your life. All things prior to this new chapter were becoming a distant memory and a chance to rebuild your life. What you did not realise was that all the repressed feelings from the past that were not dealt with at the time would come back to haunt you, and would block you from fully loving yourself and embracing the uniqueness of your being.

Getting married at 19, despite his behaviour, confused your emotions further, telling yourself, "He wants me", "He loves me", "His behaviour is temporary", "He protects me" – a warped sense of belonging. Did you know any better? No. You were never taught to value you. When you were a child, you were clean, well-fed, well-dressed, did not live in poverty, but no emotional warmth was forthcoming. Everything was practical and validations were not the norm. If you had, things would have perhaps been different. You tried to confide in some close confidants but the words became jumbled and the mask went on. Why? Protecting you, him and them.

After one night of mayhem too many, you found the strength to walk away with the little worth you had and the saving grace of a stranger, who would eventually turn into a snake. Whatever emotions that were there before had now become magnified with feelings of lightness, being in a bubble, unrealness and fog. It did not help that you had become homeless, sofa surfing, at times with strangers, in undesirable locations and placing your safety at risk. Some people sensed your vulnerability and used it to their own advantage but because you felt alone, you allowed them to further abuse your emotions. This period saw you scared, embarrassed, ashamed and sad. You felt that the life you lived had dealt you a rough card – when would you receive a break? You still could not tell your family or friends about what was going on and stayed locked in silence with your mask on. You became so unwell that you ended having an assessment at a psychiatrist hospital. The verdict? "You are bipolar." So quick to judge without fully looking at why you were experiencing these feelings and wanting to admit you and medicate with drugs.

That was not happening; you were scared, you were homeless, you were broke, your husband made sure that you would be left with nothing, and now he wanted your mind. As you stumbled through the wilderness in survival mode, a glimpse of feeling wanted emerged. For a brief moment, all that happened could be forgotten but yes, you were still homeless, broke and experiencing unhealthy emotions. You ended up back at the place you ran from, pregnant, broke and having your first breakdown. It was not bipolar that you were experiencing, but stress, panic attacks, depression and anxiety. It was another terrifying episode in your life that saw you helpless. ***How would you ever bounce back from this?*** *Your faith is strong.*

Experiencing many losses from an early age – as young as four years old – whether from life cycles or death, left you with a hole that further gaped open with each experience. One of the after effects of this were that you held onto people longer than you should, especially those who showed you signs, but you did not want to lose anymore. The problem was that the muteness that followed, allowing situations to manifest themselves into your soul, watering your personality. Your vulnerability was not transparent, only silently emerging whilst in the comfort of your own world. How would you ever bounce back from this? You **did** time and time again. **Your inner strength has got you. Always.**

Love from your Older Self
Xxx

I wanted to share with you, the reader, some of the traumas, obstacles and challenges that engulfed me from an early age and left me feeling fearful, weak, frustrated and a failure. I wished that I had been advised from an early age that all storms do not last forever. The reason is that many of us are not aligned with some of the emotions that we are experiencing until later on in life, so we have no coping strategies.

It was not until I was 44 years old that I really started to embrace me; my feelings, my looks, my body and my personality. I spent a long time analysing and looking into why certain things were around me, my responses, my behaviour and other's contribution to my state of mind. Once I started that journey, I was on my way to becoming the New Woman that I was always meant to be. It has taken me over 45 years to embrace this; the realisation that trauma throughout my life had bound me internally and externally. Unravelling often came with painful memories that needed to be explored and dealt with. For a long time, I felt invisible, unlovable, undeserving, and not feeling that I belonged anywhere. My resilience was not always strong and many times I felt weak trying to navigate myself back to normality. Creating boundaries lost me relationships, simply because I stopped being the enabler. Obstacles kept appearing from every corner and when I thought that I had dealt with one experience, another came on top of it. I would soothe it and plaster it without giving the old wound a chance to fully heal. Every time I felt invalidated, I would mask it and move on, forsaking my happiness. I felt guilty at times, burdened by shame and that my voice and feelings did not matter. This stemmed from being silent and becoming invisible with my emotions from a young age. Even though I am not religious, I am spiritual and would often question the higher power. Why was He giving me so many battles? Being weighed down by all this baggage blighted my life and impacted on a lot of decisions that I made, which at times would later emerge as incorrect ones.

Allowing myself to grieve for every loss in my life took time to embrace, to define the impact it had on me and fully embrace the emotions that came with it, and regardless of how uncomfortable it felt to revisit, I had to trust the process. By having faith, attending therapy, reading personal development books, using affirmations and meditating, I was able to start to see the fuzzy ball in my head becoming clearer.

The road has not been easy and at times has left me feeling suicidal when exploring the past; however, I always remember we are only here for a gifted time and we do not want to waste precious time. Becoming the New Woman, I had to embrace my whole being and fall in love with me. Not an easy thing to do when you have neglected yourself for a long time. Embracing myself, not in a conceited or boastful way, but with an expression of humble love, celebrating my flaws, imperfections and quirks without feeling silly, indulgent, guilty or disappointed. I never used to take many photographs of myself, but as the peel started to come off, I wanted to capture me and every part of my evolving during the process. I started accepting compliments, trusting the words of the sender and no longer feeling uncomfortable and embarrassed. I learnt that Self-Care equalled Self-Esteem, Self-Confidence and that Self-Love would be paramount to my recovery. To do this, I needed to become naked, transparent and open, and start to heal my inner child void that had not been fully nurtured. I had to remind myself to pay attention to my feelings and that some of my experiences were not my fault.

Every day is progress; that is what the New Woman does. She keeps going, no matter how deep she sinks or what adversities she may face. She will rise and rise again whilst feeling the fear. Inner blockages will try to crush her spirit, the critical voice will hinder her and fear will impact on her but as Susan Jeffers says, "Feel the fear and do it anyway."

The New Woman will rise up from that bed, rise up from the floor, rise up from uncertainty and will bounce back even when depression and anxiety try to imprison her, knowing eventually this too will pass and she will re-emerge.

The New Woman will:

Celebrate her existence, her world, her being

Find joy in all that she does

Create boundaries

Be resilient

Feel the fear and do it anyway

Forgive

Use affirmations to encourage herself

No longer hide behind the façade of confidence

Use her voice

Show her vulnerability

Love the woman that she has become

Rediscover a new passion

Realise that it will get better

Practice self-love and care

Grow and evolve with every experience

Heal

I AM THE NEW WOMAN

New Woman 25

Diksha Chakravarti

Time to Rise...

"It was time to rise..."

Dear Reader,

Imagine playing a game of tennis using the rules of cricket.

Imagine no one told you that you were using the wrong rules.

Imagine how you would feel when you realised you were in the wrong game... but there was no one to guide you to the right one...

Herein lies a tale of fear, violence and learned helplessness; of confusion, split loyalties and anger. It is a tale of dis-agency, broken dreams and shattered lives.

But wait, dear reader...

Before this bleak landscape compels you to shut the book and walk away, I want to tell you that it is also a tale of courage, resilience and perseverance; of introspection, tenacity and endurance and above all, spirituality. So please, do read on...

It wasn't unusual for me to come home from school to find my Da being punished. He would be made to stand in the heat of the hot equatorial sun whilst we ate lunch. This was a sickening experience for me. Father (Babuji) looked stern and angry, Ma looked helpless, brother (Da) just stood shamefaced and hungry, whilst I had to eat freshly cooked food.

Often at times, our family dog and I had to jump on Da to protect him from Babuji's beatings. Someone somewhere had accused Da of wrongful doing, which Babuji of course believed without question, so punished him... one day he was so violent, he broke Da's arm and locked him in his room without medical attention...

The tone of our days were set by Da's misdemeanours and Babuji's level of punishment for these: how I loved my Babuji yet hated him for his cruelty and how I loved my Da yet hated him for his misbehaviour... I do not recall many happy days.

My world was insular and lonely. Books led me into the lives of happy children in faraway lands who ate jam sandwiches in sunny meadows and solved mysteries. Film magazines swept me into the glamorous lives and beautiful homes of my favourite film stars, and romantic film songs had me imagining the happy ever after. I was extremely studious and was only happy when I was at the top of the class. Once when I dropped a couple of places and had to tell Babuji, I stood outside ashamed and fearful... I had to be the child who Babuji could be proud of. If I did well at school, Babuji could hold his head up high: it was about 'izzat' (honour) you see, dear reader. One had a responsibility to protect one's parents' 'izzat'.

Get up. Get through the day. Get back into bed. Repeat.

1972 brought the atrocities of President Idi Amin's army. He had whimsically decided to expel all Indians from Uganda because he wanted the country to be returned to the indigenous people. Our lives changed overnight. Fear gripped the community. In order to escape molestation, it became the norm to hide from passing army trucks carrying drunken soldiers. One day, returning home from my sewing class, I was walking through a deserted street when suddenly I heard the dreaded sound: the drone of an army truck. There was nowhere to hide so I quickly walked to the nearest door and began knocking. The truck drew level. Wolf whistles and obscenities. The truck slowed down… I couldn't hear because of the pounding of blood in my ears. I wasn't going to look behind. I kept knocking on the door… After what seemed like ages, the truck began to move away… I waited until I could hear it no more… then I slumped on the front step, shaking and panting. A large padlock hung on the door: there was nobody inside. I didn't tell Ma and Babuji about my ordeal but never went back to sewing class.

We had started to lock all doors and windows before sunset, to tightly draw all the curtains and only use table lamps so as not to attract the attention of any wandering soldiers. Theft, rape and murder of the hapless Indians were regular events. At dusk one day, as we played outside on the street, several army trucks drove into the school next door. Frightened, we scuttled into our homes. Ma made sure all the curtains were tightly closed and she even put a covering on the table lamp to dim its glow. All night long we heard gunshots; we didn't eat or sleep a wink, terrified the army might burst through our doors. Dawn saw the army trucks drive away, leaving behind two corpses under the very tree where my friends and I had been playing the evening before. We were now hostages to the terrors of the army.

Get up. Get through the day. Get back into bed. Repeat.

My family decided it was time for me to leave the country. That I was in my final year made no difference. Nobody asked me.

My departure day dawned. I lay on my bed looking up at the ceiling, in a state of numbness. We travelled to Entebbe Airport in a convoy – this had become the norm for Indians who were fleeing the country to avoid harassment by the army at checkpoints. Not that this stopped the army, but at least it gave the Indians a semblance of security.

When I arrived at the immigration hall all alone, clutching my passport aged 15, I had just said a hasty goodbye to my family... the arrangements had been made with such speed that I'd had no time to even consider the magnitude of this event. So here I was all alone, about to board a plane to go to India to stay with family I hardly knew and away from the family I had never been apart from.

In one corner of this very large, desolate, empty hall, sat a solo immigration officer, swinging back and forth on his chair. He cocked his finger and beckoned me over. I have very clear recollection of this moment, a moment of utter terror. There was no one else around. As I approached, he leered at me, held out his hand and shouted, "Passport!" Hands shaking, I handed my passport over; he checked it out, brought his face close to mine – I could smell alcohol on his breath – and asked why I was leaving the country. I recall taking a step back. I had been tutored to say that my grandma was sick. Still leering and leaning forward, he asked me when I would return. The parrot in me replied, "As soon as Grandma is better", to which he swung back, crossed his arms, smiled and shouted, "Good! I will marry you when you return!" to which I squeaked, "Sure!" He handed over my document, enjoying my terror. I turned around and walked away. Sweat was pouring down my back and armpits, soiling my brand new outfit. Honestly, dear reader, I could feel his eyes boring into my back. By the time my shaking legs and prayers carried me safely to a table, I heard voices, indicating other people were coming into this dungeon of terror...

More humiliation awaited us as we made our way to the waiting aircraft in the balmy Equatorial dusk. We were spat and laughed at by the African porters who were glad to see the back of these 'muindees' (Indians), their enslavers, who for aeons had forcibly stolen what was rightfully theirs. As I got to the bottom of the steps leading to the entrance of the aircraft, I thought I'd say one last goodbye to my family, so I turned to wave at them. I was greeted by blackness, with just the terminal lights... my family was nowhere to be seen. I was stung.

The flight to Mumbai was chaotic: I sat squeezed between two elderly gents, watching wide-eyed as the harassed stewardesses frantically tried to store the excessive luggage the distraught Indians had brought on board. The Indians' fear was palpable as they desperately tried to protect these meagre belongings. They were now refugees.

We landed in Mumbai at 5am in the morning. It was dark. No idea what to expect. I was met by a lovely stewardess who speedily cleared all the necessary procedures and escorted me and my brand new suitcase to a waiting bus. She told me to wait for other passengers. We would be transported to a hotel to await our connecting flight. The bus was dark… I sat clutching my shiny new handbag, waiting for these other passengers. Suddenly the driver jumped in, closed all the doors and we took off. Where were the other passengers??? Fear returned and gripped me. Tears welled up. Here I was all alone with a strange man, in a strange city, going to an unknown destination… and there was nothing I could do about it. I recall feeling sick… then I heard the driver speak: he was telling me that I was safe… tears of relief spilled over.

My life in India gave me some stability and routine but yet again, I didn't quite fit in. It was all very strange – the food, language, culture. My relatives welcomed me into their homes but for them I was this 15-year-old girl who had suddenly arrived, barely spoke their language, had no idea of how to wash clothes or make rotis. The girls in my high achieving school were unkind and as I had no social skills, I struggled to make friends… and they all spoke in code. I threw myself into books and carried on with my existence as a loner… until these nasty girls realised that I had an aptitude for physics; they then became my 'friends' so I could manipulate the results of their experiments, ensuring they passed their tests. Well, they do say there is more than one way to skin a cat, dear reader. I still felt an outsider. My parents joined me 10 months later. The stress of the exodus had left Babuji a broken man; his health kept deteriorating. We lived in one small flat, had little money and Babuji was in no fit state to earn a living.

Get up. Get through the day. Get back into bed. Repeat.

Two years after I arrived in India, the decision was taken for Babuji, Ma and I to leave and join Da, who had set up a good life in the UK. Yet again, just before my final school leaving exams, we upped and moved countries. Nobody asked me.

When we arrived in the UK, I was shocked at how big the airport was and how small the houses were! We were going to stay with my sister-in-law's (SIL's) family until we got our own place. They were kind people, who had rearranged their living accommodation to fit us in. At 17 years old, this should have been an adventure, but it wasn't. I continued to remain outside, looking in.

One Saturday afternoon, SIL and I returned to find an ambulance driving away. Ma and SIL's family stood ashen faced: Babuji had had a heart attack. At 6am the following morning, I found myself hurtling down the stairs as I heard Ma's scream from downstairs: Babuji had left us. Ma was a widow at 45. She was devastated and lost; she was either hysterical or utterly silent. Her life had revolved around looking after Babuji, who was a disabled man. Da focused entirely on Ma, and I was left to fend for myself. I didn't know what to do, or how I was supposed to feel. I felt nothing. Total shutdown. I wasn't allowed to attend Babuji's funeral because "girls don't attend funerals" had decreed a so-called elder. Nobody asked me.

Babuji's funeral was on 18th June 1974. We had landed at Heathrow on 18th May 1974.

The family dynamics changed. Da found himself the head of our family at 24. Whenever anyone disagreed with him, he shouted. His life had taught him the only way to get heard was through violence, so he resorted to verbal violence. My grief, shock and utter lack of belonging destabilised and made me angry. The atmosphere in our family brought back dark memories.

Get up. Get through the day. Get back into bed. Repeat.

Amidst all of this, I suddenly found myself having to make important decisions. The only decisions I had taken thus far were choosing my clothes and deciding what subject to revise. Now I was faced with having to find an institution to carry on with my education. No one helped. I walked into the nearest technical college and enrolled. I returned to my natural habitat where I was most comfortable and had some control: studying hard. I was relieved that finally I was en route to my ultimate destination: training as a doctor. This had been my childhood dream and the beacon that had carried me through past challenges.

Fate had other ideas... the day I went to submit my entrance application, I found out that due to the erratic nature of my schooling, I did not have the necessary entry requirements to apply.

Imagine playing a game of tennis using the rules of cricket.

Imagine no one told you that you were using the wrong rules.

Imagine how you would feel when you realised you were in the wrong game... but there was no one to guide you to the right one...

Totally distraught, utterly fed up and feeling reckless, I walked into the college library and opened the cabinet housing the university prospectuses. I pulled one out and flung it open. It fell open on the page that said "Psychology". The prospectus was that of the University of Newcastle. Decision made.

My life was now in a tail spin...

Two years later, I got married (PS marriage had never been on the cards for me). This good man had fallen in love with me at first sight and proposed to me on our first date. I had then run a mile. But within a year we were married. No, I hadn't finished my degree (it had ceased to matter by then), and no, he wasn't the man of my dreams. He was a fine, handsome man, with great credentials, the promise of a happy ever after loomed high. But I intuitively knew that he wasn't the man for me. I had succumbed because Da repeatedly reminded me that he couldn't be faulted as a match. With these words ringing in my ears, I went to meet my 'perfect' match one Sunday for lunch. As I closed the door behind me, I told Ma that if it was sunny by the time I arrived at his flat, I would accept his proposal.

The sun shone brightly that day.

We had two beautiful daughters, 10 years of a fairly decent marriage, and 10 years of misery and unhappiness. I did complete my degree, got myself a MSc and trained in chiropractic.

Our marriage did not stand a chance: he had an idyllic stable childhood, wanting for nothing. My childhood was traumatic and unhappy. He was 24 and I was 21:

we were idealist children pretending to be adults. Our expectations were ill-matched: he was on a fixed path, I was lost. I kept grasping for a lifeline, he was calmly sailing the ship of Life. He couldn't see the storm, I was in the eye of one. Not having had stability, any demonstration of a loving relationship and no central core values, instead having only seen violence, fear and subservience, it was not surprising that I fell into a co-dependent existence. The only emotion that kept bursting forth from within me, was anger. I recall how he would look perplexed when I got angry. I lacked communication skills, had no idea how to negotiate or compromise. Discussions turned into arguments.

By now, I felt like I was trapped in a padded room, screaming for attention. I was worn out trying to fit in, battling the demons within and trying to find myself in the quagmire of my mind. What little strength I had left began to ebb away. I began doubting my sanity as I was constantly being told all would be well if I changed. Daily battles threw me back into my childhood conditioning of learned helplessness... disconnected... disillusioned... depressed.

The divorce was an acrimonious matter. He was angry and became vengeful. I was stunned. I had naïvely expected it to be sorted in an amicable manner and couldn't understand how his anger towards me could blind him to the hell he was putting the children through. I expected some semblance of compassion after 20 years of a disastrous marriage. Yet again, my expectations did not match reality. I was clearly a slow learner.

Get up. Get through the day. Get back into bed. Repeat.

Matters were made worse for me because at the time that I was fighting the fire of my divorce, I was fighting the General Chiropractic Council as well. I have no idea how I continued to run my small business. My mental and physical health were seriously challenged. My depression got worse, I could barely get through the day, the children were traumatised. My husband busied himself with work and became a very wealthy man. I have no doubt that he was also deeply unhappy...

A fish only knows it lives in water when it is taken out of it.

Looking back, I can see how the traumatic experiences I experienced in childhood led me to disconnect from life. There were no healthy templates for me, so I disassociated off to the lands of fantasy: books, movies and romantic songs. The only area I had any agency in was my academic career, so I put all my efforts into this and clung tightly to it. Other than this one area, I essentially sleepwalked through life, learning little and developing no useful life skills. So, when the lone thing I had clung to for salvation was snatched away, I had nowhere to turn.

Anger and despair were all I felt... and I began taking impulsive decisions.

Each day came and went and I simply trundled along in whichever direction life took me.

I kept lurching from one disaster to another and wondering why nothing was working out...

Imagine playing a game of tennis using the rules of cricket.

Imagine no one told you that you were using the wrong rules.

Imagine how you would feel when you realised you were in the wrong game... but there was no one to guide you to the right one...

Despite being deeply unhappy, depressed and overwhelmed, I never considered ending my life. My beautiful children pulled me through. It seems, hidden deep inside of me, was a tiny seed of Strength that my children were nurturing and willing on; this sustained me throughout. I guess this is what gurus term Resilience.

I have been blessed with a natural Spirituality. Oh, there have been many times I have yelled at my Higher Power, but my trust has never wavered. Slowly, over several years, I began to cleanse; debridement is more appropriate because it was a painful process. As I learnt new skills, completed projects to fruition and began to get in touch with my Being, my confidence and my self-belief grew.

The realisation dawned that I had to stop rationalising my existence as a victim; stop looking outwards for help. I had to stop blaming those who had injured me; stop repeating past mistakes. I had to make amends and free my Heart from captivity.

It was time to take responsibility for my own life, change the narrative, stop the rot.

It was time to rise…

Imagine playing a game of tennis on a bright sunny day.

Imagine hitting the strokes with confidence.

Imagine winning the game all by yourself…

So, dear reader…

Get up. Get through the day. Get back into bed…

…is no longer on repeat.

New Woman 26

Delcie Hopley

How I Found My Light

*"It's never easy making changes,
but if you learn to be patient and loving with yourself,
you can create the life you want to live."*

This story begins in my childhood. It was a happy one. I have a younger brother, Jamie, whom I love dearly. I'm from a small town in the West Midlands; it was a lovely little town, a good place to bring up kids. Our house was along a little service road set back from a main road. Once you crossed the main road, you were on the canal and beyond that, the fields and woods of the coppice. As kids, that's where we spent most of our time with our dad and the greyhounds – long-legged, slender dogs built for speed.

As Mom worked in the evenings and Dad in the day, we were at the mercy of Dad in the evenings, which meant dogs. Having greyhounds takes up a large amount of your time; they have to be walked, trained, groomed, mucked out, raced, cared for. We loved it! We were always outdoors across the fields and canal walking or training them. Running through the long grass looking for the anthills, there was always a black anthill close to a red anthill. My brother and I would very carefully pick up a black ant and put it on the red anthill and vice versa. Poor ants, safe on their hill until one day they are scooped up into grimy hands and plonked right in the middle of enemy territory. We would play on Tarzan swings being careful not to drop into the nettle patch; when we did, we would burst out looking for dock leaves to take the sting away from the already swollen lumps. We knew the names of all the different trees and plants; Dad would test us as we made our way through the woods with dogs running around, chasing things we couldn't see.

Our parents were and still are loving, caring, nurturing. Always there, they make a great team. There was no shortage of love, we were a happy family. Coming from a large family, we had lots of aunties, uncles and cousins; family gatherings were big and always fun with lots of us kids running around playing while the adults caught up on the latest gossip. I grew up with the belief that life and relationships looked like this; happy parents, happy kids, everything rosy. I feel I've always been blessed with good people around me. I realise how lucky I am for my start in life and I'm grateful for it. My childhood was happy, healthy and carefree.

In 2004, I got married. I was 34. I had a good job and a good man, Dick. We didn't have kids, something we had both wholeheartedly agreed upon when we met nine years earlier. Life was fun; no kids meant we had money to spend. We worked hard and played hard – weekends were for getting together with great friends, partying, having fun, camping, weekends away, beaches, camp fires, holidays abroad. I was a party girl, still enjoying life just as I had started out. I was always smiling and quick to laugh; that carefree girl never left me, she shaped the young woman I became; loving, trusting, loyal, caring and always looking for the good in others. Growing up surrounded by dogs and being outdoors all of the time has taught me to love and respect animals, the earth, our planet; I care deeply for the environment. So to me, life was pretty good to be fair, I wasn't complaining.

Fast forward to September 2005, just before our first wedding anniversary, and my life and outlook had changed drastically. When I looked in the mirror, I no longer saw the carefree girl of my youth, seeing the wonder in the world around her. The green eyes that stared back at me had a hardness around the edges with the look of a wounded animal; haunted, full of pain and confusion. I wanted to close them so I didn't have to face my shattered world.

Looking back now, I can see reality was going to hit some day. Life was always going to rip those rose-tinted glasses right off my face. Making it to 35 before it happened is quite the achievement.

It all happened when Dick and I had been visiting my brother Jamie and his now-wife Jacki for the weekend. They live in Swansea and there were a few of us going to see the Super Furry Animals. "I'm really looking forward to this; it's the first time I've seen the Super Furries live!" I said to Dick, eager for the traffic on the M4 to lighten up so we could get there as soon as possible. "And I can't wait to see Jamie and Jacki!"

"Me too," said Dick. "I think we're going to have a great weekend and the sun's out too, bonus!" We both knew our weekends in Swansea were always fun with music, drinking and merriment with family and friends.

Our journey home was very differen. No smiles and chatting about the weekend's antics. Instead I was in shock, unable to process what my eyes had seen. That morning I had walked into the bedroom in Jacki and Jamie's house to find my husband Dick on top of my friend Lorraine. I stood there unable to utter even one word as my perfect world came crashing down around me.

Dick and I had met in the mid-nineties in Tenerife. At the age of 24, I decided I needed to experience life outside of my hometown so I figured I may as well head to the sun. I worked as an OPC, more commonly known as a Timeshare Tout. It was an eye-opener, I can tell you; I was so naïve, I learned a lot about life and people in my time there.

I had been on the Island for a few months and on a warm, overcast Sunday morning down on the beach walk in Puerto Colon, I stood with scratch card in hand, ready to pounce on a pale-looking couple. The lack of a tan means "fresh meat" – you had to be quick before anyone else got there first, it was dog eat dog. "Hey, guys, take a free scratch card – you might win a great prize," I said smiling as I offered the card. They weren't as fresh as they looked and almost ran to get out of my way. A thick skin was required for this job. I chuckled as I watched them dodge the countless other OPCs that had stationed themselves along the beach walk.

"I know that accent. Where are you from?" I turned around to see the short, skinny guy attached to the voice.

"Walsall," I replied.

"I'm from Cannock," he said.

"No way! I've had a few nights out in Cannock," thinking it's always nice to meet people from your neck of the woods.

He walked towards me. "My name's Dick, what's yours?"

"Daisy," I smiled.

That was it: we met, we went out, we talked, we got on, really well actually. Before long, we had fallen head over heels in love. Life was an adventure and we enjoyed every moment. There were BBQs on the beach, parties, trips into the mountains, and more. Dick loved telling stories from his childhood; I would listen, fascinated, hearing all the antics he got up to as a boy; he made it sound like so much fun. His upbringing was different to mine – he'd been brought up in the kids' home, as he called it.

I thought him so brave and resourceful; he'd had some really tough times and was still alive to tell the tale. If not for my rose-tinted glasses fixed firmly to my nose, I would have seen the cynicism and bitterness that lay beneath his carefully constructed 'happy chappy' persona. At this point my eyes were so filled with love, they saw only what I wanted to see.

We decided after a couple of years to head back to England to get "proper" jobs as we called it. From the beautiful beaches, sunsets and sea of the Canaries to the very middle of England, with no sea or beach in sight. That was okay; we set about building our life together – we bought a house and after nine years of being together, we got married, it was now or never.

Now, just a few short months after our wedding, life had finally caught up with me, ripped out my heart, shredded it in to the tiniest of pieces, threw it on the floor and stamped all over it. It broke my soul as well as my heart. We had always said we were meant to be together; we were soulmates and I believed it.

I remember, I had moved out of our home and we were talking on the phone. Most of our conversations at that time would end with me in tears, not getting any answers, nothing was taking my pain away. I didn't know what to do.

"Dick, do you have any idea what you've done? You've broken my heart; doesn't that mean anything to you?" I said, feeling the pain of my words.

"Dais, I can't do anything else, I've already told you it was nothing."

"It isn't nothing to me, Dick. It's a huge something."

"Look, Daisy, we're just going round in circles. I'm not here to put up with this," and with that, he hung up.

His dishonesty was driving me crazy. "You're a nutter, you are; stop going on about the same thing, it's not gonna change anything," he would say to me. He would make me feel guilty for being heartbroken and asking for the truth. I let him make me feel that way. I was confused, angry, hurt; it was like my world had completely shifted underneath my feet and displaced me. I didn't know where I was, this wasn't my world anymore, this was somebody else's and I didn't like it one bit. I was broken, broken for the first time, and I had no idea how to fix me. As they say, "The first cut is the deepest." I truly understood the meaning of that now.

He never once apologised or told me the truth. Any truths I did find out came from Lorraine's partner. They had talked, she had confessed to everything, or at least to a lot more than I ever got from Dick. It was hell; I hurt all over; physically, emotionally, mentally and spiritually. Just like anything that's broken, once repaired, it's never quite the same again, but I came out the other side stronger and certainly a lot wiser. My glasses were now clear as a bell.

We decided to give things another go and got back together in January 2006. By April, we had both sold everything we could, stored the rest, jacked in our jobs, rented out the house and hopped on a plane to Thailand. We spent the next five years scuba diving, becoming instructors in Thailand, then flew to Grand Cayman to work. It was a great life, always outside, in the water, in the pub; my perfect life.

I looked perfect on the outside, but on the inside I was dying. Every day of the five years that we were back together was agonising, I felt like my soul was being eaten away leaving nothing but an empty husk. When I looked at Dick, I saw him differently and I hated what I saw now – he literally made my top lip curl. I regretted my decision but I didn't know how to leave him, how to be on my own. I had always lived and been with other people, my family, friends. I was older now, but I didn't know how to be alone. I desperately wanted out, but I was trapped in a cage of my own making, my mind. My friends, Suzy Marfleet, Cathy Kimball and Laura Clark, were my rock and I am forever grateful.

Around 2010, I was at work when the phone rang, "We've got a new girl starting in the spa. Her name's Samantha Friendship. She's coming to you at The Reef first. Can you show her around?" said Marion, my boss.

"No problem, Marion. What time can I expect her?"

"I'm not sure. She's got a few things to do and then she's coming down to you."

"No problem," I answered.

By this time I had gone to work in the resort spa, as having done my courses back in England, I could work as a massage therapist. The money was better and you were in the air conditioning all day – very important in the summer months in the Caribbean, I can tell you. My friend Cathy always used to say in her best brashest American accent – just so you get an idea of how she sounded – "It's hotter than hell out there." Always earning a chuckle from me, she described it perfectly!

Sam turned out to be a dark-haired lady of about my age.

"Hi, I'm Sam," she introduced herself when she walked in the door.

"Hi Sam, I'm Daisy. Marion told me to expect you. It's nice to meet you."

We hit it off immediately and chatted about where we were from, where we'd been and what we'd done before this point in our lives, the usual thing.

"What treatments do you do?" I asked, an important question in a spa. What free treatments were you going to swap with the new therapist, one of the perks.

"I do massage, lymphatic drainage and reiki," she replied.

"Reiki, what's reiki?" I asked, that top lip of mine curling in wonder. "I've heard of it before now, but I have no idea what it is."

"It's healing with energy," explained Sam. I think she could tell by the additional curling of the lip that I was still puzzled. She chuckled and said, "The easiest way to understand is to try it."

"I'm in!" was my reply.

We arranged a quick 15 to 20 minute session the next morning. I remember laying on the treatment bed and didn't have a clue what to expect. Sam explained how the session would work, and said I might feel some tingling or sensations. I'm like, "Yeah, fab, let's do this!"

I lay back and let Sam start to work her magic. "If you want the energy to work on something specific for you, just ask it to," she said.

"Okay," I replied. Lying there with the music playing, candles lit, looking forward to my reiki, I had a little think about what I may ask it to do.

Sam started with her hands around my head. I felt pressure, warmth and sensations of movement. "Please, reiki, help me mend my broken heart," I said in my head.

As soon as this thought was in my head, I felt the energy rush down through my head into my chest, getting to what I know now as my heart chakra, which is right in the centre of your chest, between your boobs. I then felt it bashing at my heart chakra, like it was hitting up against a brick wall. It kept bashing until it broke through and continued down through the rest of my body.

In my head, I was thinking, "OMG! What on earth was that?" I was stunned. I'd never felt anything like it before. That moment opened up a whole new world to me, like a switch had been flicked inside of me. I knew without a shadow of a doubt that I had been waiting for this for a long time. I knew I wanted to learn what reiki was all about; I wanted to do this for myself and share it with others.

"That's it, you're done," Sam said.

I opened my eyes, turned over, looked straight at Sam and said, "You have to teach me this, I want to learn about reiki."

And so it began. Sam started to teach me about reiki, how to meditate. She taught me so much more, the many things she had learned in the twenty-something years she'd been doing it. We spent as much time as we could practicing reiki, meditation, chatting about all things spiritual – evenings, lunchtimes, any time. I drank it in, all of it, I couldn't get enough. I was like a child rapt with wonder; I would sit listening, mesmerised by this amazing world of energy. For the second time in my life, I fell head over heels in love, only this time it was reiki that had my heart. The feeling you get from it, the healing that it gives you, the warmth and the love that it wraps around you. As soon as I experienced the energy, I changed as a person, I was never the same again.

The time came for my attunement. The attunement is a ceremony where you are aligned with the reiki energy, so now when I channelled reiki it would be a more powerful, focused energy. It was a day of deeply spiritual practise, the whole experience was amazing. I was not prepared for what came after.

Receiving a reiki attunement is like a huge session of healing – changes take place as your old energies, emotions, thoughts and beliefs are stripped away. A lot of amazing things happened to me in the initial days after my attunement; for me, it was a deeply moving experience.

Not long afterwards, I started to notice I was feeling very lethargic. I didn't want to go to work or even see my friends, I just wanted to lie on the sofa all day. "Please, guys," I pleaded with my friends Suzy and Laura one day, "if you're going out and I say no, remind me that I've asked you to force me to go out." I looked at them with a serious look on my face. "I don't know what's wrong with me but I just don't seem to want to do anything," I said. "It's not like me at all!"

"Blimey, Dais," said Suzy, "you're right, it's not like you! Don't worry, we won't let you stay in."

"Yeah, Dais, we'll come and fetch you if we have to," agreed Laura.

"Cheers, guys! I have no idea what's going on, I feel wrong." We had a group hug, as good friends do, they always have your back; these ladies are the best.

I'd booked a week off work and I was lying on the sofa feeling really melancholy, I had lost my oomph, I had no get up and go. As I lay there blindly staring at the telly, my thoughts wondering, I asked myself the question, "What's going on with me, why am I feeling like this?"

Bam! Immediately it came back to me. "I'm depressed. "It literally hit me like a bolt of lightning and I knew it was the truth. I had asked a question and the universe had answered. Feeling braver and now curious, I asked the question, "Why am I depressed?"

Answer. "Because I have to leave Dick." As the realisation washed over me and settled in my gut, I felt the change and I knew my time was near. Instead of feeling fear at the thought of leaving, I felt strength and purpose. I knew with every fibre of my being this was the healing of reiki, this was the healing that I needed.

Within six weeks I had left Dick. This was in 2011. I packed my life into a few bags, took my dog Rosie, and flew back to England. I didn't know what I was going to do but I knew it was right for me. I knew I was going to be okay; I have the most amazing family and friends who have been with me, giving me more than they will ever know. Self-healing is a journey to the self – I have learned and still continue to learn so much about who I truly am.

I now have my own healing business called Love Reiki Healing & Meditation. I teach healing and meditation so I can help others heal and find their path to self. My journey has been uncomfortable and downright painful at times, but I have learned to love the discomfort and pain, for I know it means my expansion and growth. I appreciate it for what it is. It's never easy making changes, but if you learn to be patient and loving with yourself, you can create the life you want to live. The life that's perfect for you.

New Woman 27

Rajee S

Awakening your Inner Happiness

*"Transformation begins with an 'inspired action'
with all the knowledge and wisdom,
which Awakens your 'inner happiness.'"*

I vividly remember that day. I woke up with the sun's rays gently falling on me. I could feel that there was something intensely beautiful about that day. There was a feeling of absolute happiness. I observed things around me; the birds seemed to be happier in their chirping, the breeze carried a piece of different music, the colours seemed brighter, the sun was gentle, the atmosphere around was charged with a buzzing that emanated something truly wonderful. My life, as I had seen it, was now dazzling with a different hue. Life was blooming in all its visual splendour.

It was the same; for many years, I had been waking up to this same environment, running through the same emotions. But that day, I felt a surge in energy; a different me had emerged from the cocoon and started to feel connected with my inner happiness. It was as if the butterfly inside me had found freedom. All of this had changed simply because I believed in a new me and I felt different. A new me had emerged, an empowered me, a happy me, and I was engaged with the source of happiness, aligned with it, truly basking in its glory.

Maybe this is sounding too dreamy and distant to your reality.

Is your reality different? Are you still stuck in the same loop every day?

Do you feel that whatever you try, you seem to end up having fallen flat on your face?

Well then, let me tell you my story, and then you can decide for yourself.

I am an Engineering graduate working in the IT industry, and I had a life that was abundant in every aspect. I was in a position that was comforting, but there were times when I felt that there was something missing. It was a constant monologue that kept raging in my head. I kept hearing that inner voice telling me that a void existed, and the voice would simply not go away.

The power of this voice was too much to bear and I was suffering from severe neck pain. Visits to the doctor followed, with gulping down tablets, but the relief was only temporary. The neck pain would come back soon. I had been ignoring this for some time now, not really knowing that my body was telling me something, pushing me towards something.

It was as if by chance or divine design, that the book *The Secret* by Rhonda Byrne, fell into my lap and into my life. This book catapulted me into a different orbit and it is here that I learnt about the Law of Attraction – that you can change your life by changing your thoughts, and your thoughts then become your reality.

"Is this really possible," I said to myself, "that by changing my thoughts I can change my reality?"

This thought was riveted in my head and pulled me back to the book, and I read it many times in the weeks to come. I had many questions, very similar to the ones that you are having now. I battled with these questions and my rational mind still could not wrap its head around this idea, and it kept saying that this may not be possible. However, an inner voice pushed me to try it out for myself so this conflict was still prevalent in my heart. I decided to test it out for myself; I took it to my heart and said to myself, "This book will change my life!"

I started to apply the Law of Attraction techniques in my real life, practicing positive affirmations and intent in small things like securing a parking space without hassles, catching the green light during the rush hour traffic, and receiving phone call from friends, and these things actually happened – even though I tried it just for fun. I began to think that this idea, these thoughts of mine, could change the reality of things around me. I remember thinking out loud to myself after having caught that green light consistently and reaching home in record time, "If I can really focus my thoughts, concentrate on it and truly believe in things and pave the way for little things, why not apply the same magic to bigger things in life?"

With this thought, dear friends, I started another adventure that seemed to make me think that the knowledge of the Law of Attraction had come into my life at just the exact time I needed it. I began to attend several workshops and training course drawn by a desire that pushed me further into this belief that I was on the right path; the path which had been my true calling all along.

Almost as if the entire universe was listening to me, granting my wishes, many relevant books then came into my possession and the guidance of Gurus came into my life. The criss-cross of this learning fabric was weaving into an experience that empowered me. I felt new. I felt different!

It connected me to the 'True Happiness' and I gained knowledge of many other spiritual modalities and increased my knowledge about the patterns of the human mind, behaviours and hypnotherapy. All of this study helped me to understand about the working of the conscious and subconscious mind, belief systems and how to reprogram your mind to achieve success and much more.

This paved my ascension from a 'life of light' to a 'greater light' and enlightenment – a connection to true happiness. I learnt many things that opened my eyes to different dimensions of life.

With inspired action and determination, I worked within. I worked on my thoughts, their reactions, the emotions that coursed through me. After intense bouts of decluttering, healing, I was able to define a better me. Gradually, I was walking into a happy sphere of existence. My neck pain that had been a constant companion, was completely healed without the use of any tablets or meditation. Sometimes physical ailments are by-products of our thoughts.

This is how I changed my thoughts and changed my life, putting positive affirmations into action. In this journey of self-discovery, self-analysis, and healing, I found the true happiness; true bliss in being me!

It was as if I was reborn with new energy, a higher purpose. I kept seeing women who were stuck too, unable to find their inner calling, struggling to find their potential. This paved the way for me to spread the light, becoming a facilitator, a friend who could help them unburden their difficulties in life and find joy in their living.

I have had fascinating experiences in this journey so far. I am inspired to share a story of one of my closest friends who came to me, visibly worried.

"Rajee, I am very anxious and apprehensive. Help me with your guidance. I am not sure of how I will deal with motherhood. It is all new to me. "

I had known her for a very long time. She was longing to be a mother. Seeing her question herself in the second trimester was a worrying sign. As she was ready to receive my sessions, I told her, "You have wanted to be a mother for so long. Why do you think that you will be unable to handle motherhood and all the changes that come with it?" She confessed that she had been on the verge of mental exhaustion, and her thoughts were always focusing on what could go wrong.

I hugged her and told her, "I am your friend and as a life coach, I can help you tackle these negative thoughts. Change your thoughts and change your reality."

It is here that my experience as a coach came to the fore. Bearing in mind that everyone needs a unique, made-to-fit solution, I gave her a list of practices that combined the Law of Attraction, hypnotherapy and positive affirmations. I asked her to take up these practices that could eventually change her thoughts and tune into to a happier frequency. I told her, "I will give you a set of activities that I have thought of just for you. Do this daily, keep your hands on your stomach, feel that life inside you, and talk to it. Bless your child, affirm that your bonding with the child is fulfilling, filled with love and joy. Also be grateful to your body for bearing life, for bringing to you the joys of motherhood.

Every day tell yourself 'This day is good and I can deal with it effectively and everything that is new is a new experience,' and trust and believe that everything is working out well around you."

She called me months later with a happy glow on her face. She had followed and practiced these techniques regularly. She gushed that these guidelines had given her great strength and said, "Thank you, Rajee. I am bonding with my child so wonderfully." This is where I feel my joy and empowerment as a coach.

I hope I have given you an insight into my interesting life as a life coach and how I combine my expertise of the Law of Attraction, providing breakthroughs for different people and situations by guiding them to seek their own answers.

I am sure that by now, you are also reflecting on your thoughts. I would like to add that this journey of empowerment is not something that can be just done once to see immediate results. A seed has the potential to grow into a tree but you have to believe in its potential and nurture that seed by giving it love, air, water, and sunshine. Your thoughts will also need more positivity, gratitude, blessing, intention setting and focus on the emotion to be happy, similar to planting a seed. The seed of your thought grows roots and rises above the surface, all of which takes time and patience. The unwavering belief raises the tree and bears fruit, resulting in a life filled with an abundance of happiness.

For many of us, happiness is subject to external circumstances and we are seeking external validation from our environment – our happiness is bound to an event. Its occurrence can give us happiness that lasts for a few minutes, but the struggles keep coming, and reality overwhelms us.

Additional to external happiness, we must seek our inner source of happiness as well. We are to marvel at our existence, be fascinated by the world outside. Practice gratitude for the things that are bestowed to us already. It is here that one finds inner joy in accepting ourselves as who we are.

Our thoughts guide us.

Accept them, acknowledge them and forge ahead.

Positive thoughts are a bridge to a higher frequency and remember, "Only when the old is emptied, it makes space for the new". It is here that you need to practice mindfulness and let go of these thoughts that pull you down. It is okay to let your emotions out; cry them out, write them down on a sheet of paper, then give them a way out and tear it up, or punch a pillow. Release them from your mind, body and spirit in any way you feel comfortable.

You must understand that deep down, life is about change. This change is permanent. We go through several phases of life, shifting to newer versions of ourselves, from childhood to old age. It is good to embrace change and accept that. Tell yourself, "I am acquiring new experiences that are needed for the new me in my journey, keep me grounded and focused on the present."

Let us take a pause here.

What are you focusing on? Which of the thoughts are you choosing that will create your future? Do they need a change in alignment?

Ponder on these questions...

Just as when driving a car, where everything from the steering, the gear and wheels needs to be working in synchronisation and harmony, to achieve your desired goals and dreams, your thoughts, actions and emotions need to be aligned. Practising these tools, such as living in the present moment and focusing on your inner-self, will put you on this 'path of alignment'.

Your pilgrimage, your metamorphosis, and your inner shift is awaiting you. It is possible! In the quiet of the night and in the light of the morning, there are forces at play that are pushing you onwards to a path of your true calling.

I found my true calling; my inner voice had been pushing me all along. I had found something that had filled my void and made me a new woman. This new woman stands before you today, bubbling with joy and bursting with hope! A new dawn awaits you. This journey of self-discovery is a path that you need to undertake for yourself.

Every woman, including you, has dreamt of leading a life that is nothing short of being perfect. My childhood was just that; everything came to me on a platter. As children, we learn from the world in many ways. Our ways of learning depend on the environment in which we are brought up. You have heard of the word 'vibes.' Yes, the vibrational energy of the house adds to the overall learning of the children. I, for one, was exposed to spiritual practices at an early age, and the philosophies of prosperity were deeply imbibed in my daily activities. These helped me one day to bridge my learning of spirituality and prosperity teachings to others. It enabled me to take the baton forward and help others. I was always encouraged to try my hand at things that I was passionate about. I loved to learn. I learnt yoga, dance, stage performances and new life skills. This has given my life new dimensions, set a platform for what I do today.

As I reflect on my life, I am drawn to these repeating universal signs – to people whom I knew, friends and families kept telling me, "You are an inspiration." It took me some time to realise that they were referring to the energy and vibrations around me that were full of positivity and prosperity consciousness. I have stuck to my strong belief that "I can do it," and every action of mine has been done with the same will and determination.

Quite early on, even from my childhood, I have been telling myself that "I deserve the best," and this naturally has progressed to many wonderful things happening to me as a young woman, juggling various roles and responsibilities. I have braved many challenges, taken the brunt of hardships head-on, knowing fully well that I will get through this phase of life.

Every time I was faced with a challenge, I kept telling myself, "Rajee, this is an opportunity to grow, to learn." This has allowed me to connect to my inner wisdom, or my gut instinct, as many refer to it. This intuition has been the source of my guiding light.

I have made it my mission in life to empower and enable everyone who seeks to find true happiness. Over the years, my experience has grown, and this knowledge and deep insight that I have acquired has enabled me to connect with people from all walks of life. I have built a beautiful landscape of transformational tools and techniques that enable you to kick-start your journey and not have to start from scratch.

Now, let us consider your own self. Each of your journeys is unique and awakening your inner happiness and peace is always possible, even though you may have experienced darkness or difficult moments in your life. You deserve a life that is filled with joy and prosperity! All you need to do is to be open to receive it, and you will unlock a better version of yourself – it's possible. I am sure of it and I wish you to try it too.

The key to your metamorphosis, transformation and connection to the inner working of miracles, is your unwavering consistency. Change your thoughts, change your destiny and find that elixir of happiness and understand that it's a gradual process that leads to a path of purpose, full of clarity.

If ever you feel that you are lost, remember that your guidance are your thoughts. Seek the vibes behind your emotions. The best guide in times of confusion are your emotional wheels. They will help you re-align with the energy of the source. Find something that gives you joy; this will set you back on the right path again.

All women are blessed with creativity and just like I incorporate my dance with meditation music to align chakras, so you too can explore your creative expression through arts, music or writing that helps you connect with your inner happiness and well-being. These creative connections guide the 'inherent life force' to flow so abundantly within you.

Wake up each day telling yourself, "Today, I am experiencing life filled with love and peace; all things beautiful are coming my way and I deserve to find true happiness. I am attracting a beautiful and empowered future."

The Law of Attraction, or the Law of Deliberate Creation, tells us that our inner world reflects our outer reality. So, focus on your inner happiness that manifests as outer joy. Believe your dreams, persevere and even if at times it feels overwhelming, do not give up, do not let the negative emotions take root. Chant this in your head, write it down each day. Start your day with this positive vibration: "I can and I will."

Do things that bring you joy and calmness – feel the joy in every moment and enjoy those tranquil moments within you and the answers will come to you. The quietness of the mind gives your own answers and you will find a way to your home of happiness.

The new woman that I am today, the one who has been transformed from the old way of thinking and doing, has gone through a mindset shift – a shift in the planes of energy. I have healed and forged ahead towards the greater light. I feel empowered in bringing this joy and giving a mindset shift in the lives of many women, who in their daily lives are unable to find joy. My strength is further fuelled by serving others to embrace this journey and instilling in them the desire to receive their light and joy willingly, transporting themselves to a different living. If I can find this source of happiness, you can too.

Believe that every action of yours is bringing you closer to what you seek, and trust that your life will flow in a way that is in resonance with your thoughts and actions. You will find yourself doing things with a single-minded focus, enjoying everything in life, from little to bigger things that bring smiles your way. Live in the present and be grateful for everything that you have in life.

Transformation begins with an 'inspired action' with all the knowledge and wisdom, which Awakens your 'inner happiness.'

Find your joy, embark on your journey of transformation that allows you to make a difference to the world around you. Love, Light and Blessings to you all.

Dedication

To my Gurus, beloved family and friends, and to all women awaiting for change!

New Woman 28

Shazia Nawaz

When Two Worlds Collide

"Empowerment begins within
and is seen through your external presence."

From a young age, I sought a purpose but always fell into the trap of appeasement, conforming to cultural constructs of the South Asian community. I was in a constant mental and emotional turmoil as I was being raised and empowered to express and explore within British culture, yet to oppress and repress every form of expression by South Asian culture. Years of abuse and questioning directed me towards finding inner peace, a place where both my worlds, the British and the South Asian, were combined in harmony.

So, here I am, 36 years old, in the middle-end of a global pandemic, writing a condensed version of my journey to empowerment, through the thorns of oppressive, abusive and repressive commentary which now serve their purpose as reminders of what I do not want to be part of.

Growing up, I absolutely loathed being categorised, "I am me, that's all you need to know," would be my thought, never confident to express as a loud voice! I would rebel to be different, to take on a challenge. I wanted to break stereotypes and cultural walls made of pride cemented with fear.

My parents were the most loving parents and throughout my childhood, their personalities grounded me to be respectful and raised me as a strong woman, not to take abuse from anyone – nobody had that power over another. Unfortunately, my parents too fell into the trap of conformity to avoid disrespect. I had to dress a certain way and was not allowed to go to college because as a South Asian woman, I only needed to learn the role of a good wife.

I always had opinions, strong opinions at that! I thoroughly loved expressing through poetry and debating from all perspectives, which was not the norm in South Asian society. From a British cultural perspective, this was applauded; however, by the South Asian culture perspective, it was frowned upon. If you did, you were wrong, you were labelled the bad one.

Through my pain and rejection from the South Asian community, I was able to be empathetic and understand others. I felt I was gifted with this level of awareness from an early age. But when my two worlds would collide, it would bring an internal storm of frustration, emotional pain, which impacted on every aspect of life.

In primary school, my earliest memory of creative expression was when I wrote a poem which voiced what I did not have the courage to. I wrote:

When one lets down, they do not just let down.

They break down eternal trust and love, which cannot be bonded or replaced.

This was my first attempt at venting in a manner that expressed how I felt yet not hurt anyone, truly making beauty out of my pain. I was praised at school and encouraged to write more. It was very strange to be rewarded for something I could not even comprehend to do at home. I realised at this point that I could be myself when outside of my home so I began leading two very different lives.

My taste in music varied from regular popular music to rock, to foreign music that I could not translate. I felt the music, not just listened to it. I was constantly mocked for not understanding nor liking songs from Bollywood, South Asians' version of Hollywood. I listened to feel and to guide my inner self, and never found this solace in Bollywood music. I was told I was weird and called a "coconut", a racial slur meaning I was Asian on the outside but white on the inside. I felt like an outcast, constantly being rejected by own community just because my preferences not only in music but in creative expression like art, varied so much from traditional South Asian standards.

I remember at secondary school wanting to explore the creative arts and being called names such as a "hippy" and "weird" for loving and seeing beyond the physical representation of art. I loved creativity. Creativity and expression went hand in hand for me, through art and music. This gave me freedom in a world where my mind and thoughts could be free to express myself.

Curiosity did not kill me, but sure came close to many occasions because it became a thrill to be 'free' and not be found out. During my time at work before I had to get married (yes, I had no choice but to get married), I loved to experiment. I opened up to my manager and colleagues, forming a close bond, like a true family. They would help me learn about the world and were very respectful that it was my life, yet quite intrigued. I decided I wanted to get a piercing – before I knew it, I had 11!

I wore a headscarf but managed to dye my hair red! Unfortunately, the fun was cut short when I got married. I had hoped I would find my soulmate and live happily ever after. But life with the in-laws and husband was as if I had travelled centuries into the past, where oppression and obedience was normality and where love did not exist.

As a daughter in-law, I had a disciplined and structured routine to follow. Wake up when the mother-in-law woke, make breakfast and begin my duties to attend to her every command until she went to bed. Whilst complying to the in-laws, I also had to obey my husband and not ever make the mistake of considering myself as a person with individual aspirations and desires – silly British me!

My escape came when my father-in-law encouraged me to work to support my husband, so that he was not stretched to earn. My foolishness at the time saw this as freedom. But I overlooked the fact that I would still be required to attend to the South Asian conformities of a daughter-in-law and wife too. So, I continued mastering the skill of leading dual lives in two different worlds, so far apart that if I tried to describe would take a book in itself, with multiple volumes! So, let us not.

My marriage went from bad to worse. In 2008, my husband tried to strangle me whilst I held my eldest daughter. Over what, you ask? I spoke up to raise a concern whilst he was eating. It had angered him and his mother that I did not put my husband's food on the table for him. They did not care that I worked from 2pm to 10pm. They did not care that before I left for work, I cleaned the whole house, made my in-laws their lunch as well as made the dinner. But because my mother-in-law did not like her daughter having to make two chapattis for her brother when he had a wife, she made my husband make sure I was to know of her disapproval.

When I spoke to explain, he lost his temper. I managed to break from his hold by collapsing and then ran and locked myself with my daughter into the bathroom, from where I plucked up the courage to call the police. Although my husband confessed to the police, I was pressured by his family to drop the charges, or my daughter would suffer. In doing so, I thought things would ease and improve, but how wrong I was!

My mother-in-law continued her vile abuse towards me and treated my daughter as if she were a disgrace. She continued to belittle and humiliate me amongst the family, telling a story full of distorted truths to receive sympathy from others. She made my life hell, and my husband accepted this mistreatment as they both believed I was wrong for calling the police and needed punishing. My husband was made out to be the victim by his mother and the South Asian community. This is South Asian culture, to punish the women that try to seek help – domestic abuse, in every form. The British 'me' knew it was wrong and wanted out.

My father-in-law would speak to me privately, in avoidance of the verbal abuse he would receive from his wife; he just wanted an easy life and would speak the truth to give me strength to continue. I would continue, for him and for the sake of my daughter, who was my life, my joy. She was that bright spark that would light my darkest moments.

At various points in my life, the confliction of being trapped in two worlds would constantly break me and I would go through the process of repairing myself and building strength to continue fighting the constant battle, that only I knew about and had to do so in such a way to hide the truth, the true me. It was exhausting and demoralising, but I had become accustom to being self-sufficient.

The strength was being built within me since early 2012 when my twins were born. I realised then that no one is actually there for you; even whilst appeasing to cultural demands, no one will be there; you have to build the strength within yourself.

During my pregnancy, I would struggle to walk to take my eldest to school; a short walk that would usually take five minutes took me 15 exhausting minutes. But no one saw my struggles to offer help even though I would walk past my in-laws to get to my daughter's school. But I took it as a blessing that I was able to be strong and focused my energy, although very little, on my children.

I felt isolated and was not enjoying motherhood. I thought I was being selfish and was constantly being told by family that my life was over, and that I had to focus on my children, which did not help the way I felt. It hurt but I was determined to make my life enjoyable even with children. I started braving outings with the twins on the train alone, and slowly but surely shrugged off the "can't do it" attitude to "I am going to try anyway" attitude!

In addition to having twins, I also now had the experience of raising an autistic child. My son was diagnosed with multiple conditions along with autism in 2014. A huge challenge in itself but one that I found the most empowering in opening my own awareness and changing my approach to the world.

Autism is a world within a world. The two can work in harmony if there is respect and understanding of each world. There needs to be a willingness to understand and adjust to accommodate the challenges of the individual worlds. This awakening helped me merge my own two worlds; the British with the South Asian, by accepting I need to adapt to what I have. The only person I am responsible for and can change is myself! If the South Asian community does not agree, that is simply not my burden to hold. I must let this go and I did.

Unfortunately, in 2017, I again went through another storm which had been growing in the background. My father-in-law sadly passed away in June, followed by my grandmother in July. Come November 2017, my father left my mother after years of cheating and dragging my mother and family through the usual scandals you see on soap dramas. It was a truly heart-breaking year for me. My dad was my world; I could not comprehend as an adult him choosing another woman over us.

There were questions after questions in my head with no answers. What did I do? What did we do to deserve this? My life decisions were made by him, against my wishes but to appease the cultural conformities he bestowed upon us before marriage – all for what? I felt as if I had wasted my life because I battled two worlds, close to my heart, for nothing. I was broken. The only way to express was through poetry, to make something beautiful from something so awful. I wrote:

I am you.

You burn through my veins.

I am you.

Your desires fuel my pain and guide my destruction.

I am you.

My happiness was you.

My strength was you.

Dreams I sacrificed to live in appeasement,

To you, my world, my everything.

You are my weakness.

You are my pain.

You leave me trapped in a world created by you, left behind by you.

I am still you.

I accepted that I am my father's daughter; I live in a world that his decisions created for me. Although they caused me pain, I accepted from now I live by my decisions and he will still always be mine. In doing so, I accepted I am a British woman of South Asian decent and that is who I am, and happy to be. I accepted the old me and started developing the better me.

Once you are broken, that is when the authentic you will rise…

However, I had not fully addressed all my broken parts; a huge part of my life was still on the battlefield. My marriage.

The final moment of realisation hit me in 2020. A literal breaking point that physically had manifested from physical, mental and emotional abuse. I was so broken in lockdown due to a global pandemic, physically trapped with daily abuse whilst trying to juggle university and homeschooling three children, one with autism. To say it was extremely exhausting does not come close to what I felt.

I ended up in hospital; my heart was literally broken, and I could not breathe. It was at this point that the hospital consultant told me, from looking at the cuts on my arms from self-harming, that the stress was impacting my heart, and that I would not last two years if this continued at the current rate. I felt like my life flashed in front of my eyes, as well as my future of hoping to see my children graduate and grandchildren! I accepted that this was wrong and impacting on my purpose, which was my children. If I am so broken, how can I guide them through this wild world? The British authentic me arose to stand tall.

Enough was enough. I decided to stand alone and strong, without toxic relationships.

I was aware the South Asian community would talk but soon they would forget and talk about someone else and the wretched cycle of sleeping fools will continue. I asked myself, "Are you going to live your life and then die without ever enjoying yourself and experiencing freedom of happiness?" That is when I started to put mine and my children's happiness first, ensuring that they knew how to listen to their emotions and accept the thoughts, but trying to understand people's opinions was a hopeless venture.

The key is to have an awareness of being human. Although we are beings, rarely we are human. We are not robots to conform or to be programmed. We have the gift of expression. The gift of creativity, which is individual and unique to each and every one of us, should be applauded and strengthened.

My blessings, my process, my purpose, was realised after years of questioning, abuse and trauma. My hair was falling out due to mental health implications. So, I cut my hair short, a big no in the South Asian culture. My mother-in-law had a lot of opinions and expressed her opinions of my hair freely everywhere she went. But they are her opinions, and I did not let her intimidation change my preference.

I started to travel alone. I was always greeted with verbal abuse from my husband and his mother due to it not conforming to what South Asian women do. But I knew I was not doing any wrong so continued to be a happy, independent woman, an example for my children. I started to wear clothes I was comfortable in – again, non-traditional South Asian clothing for a woman was deemed inappropriate and judged as misbehaviour. But I was comfortable and that was all that mattered. I am British and this is my expression of culture and more importantly, my preference.

After over 15 years in regulatory Civil Service, I decided to change careers and industry altogether! I went to university at the age of 34 because I wanted to experience university life and wanted to learn. I was told when I was 18 I was too old to study – but now it was my time. My time to break the chains of conformity and break stereotypes. I wanted to help others. That is where I belong and strive, I blossom, which is why everything skin fascinates me.

The science of skin conditions at a cellular level, their pathology and aetiology, are my loves. I love investigating the contributing factors and accompanying clients on their skin journey, as well as for some the healing journey because of the healing it brings others.

I began multiple projects simultaneously, because I was aware of my abilities and capability. Granted, it was stressful, but I knew how much I could do. I had faith and understood my potential which is always key in understanding your capabilities and only you know how much you can take on, and when to say no, no more, or stop and rest.

I began consulting and coaching in 2018 and am proud to be a specialist in my fields. Yes, fields! Who said you have to have one speciality? I am a qualified Aesthetic Practitioner BA (Hons) and trainer. I am an expert within the skincare industry and advanced beauty treatments. I like to help clients in their own right to be empowered within their own skin. I also coach business owners.

Progressing personally and professionally is a beautiful, happier place to be.

My advice to women is to be true to yourself by listening to yourself. Listen to your heart, improve your health, your own happiness, your own healing. This will lead to your empowerment. Organise your thoughts and actions at a pace you can manage without compromising on your health. And do not forget to reward yourself.

Empowerment begins within and is seen through your external presence. But it is also felt! My coaching always takes a personal approach. The pace is never rushed, it is always within the scope of the client. Experience in both personal and professional realms has enabled me to take this tailored approach.

I am a proud expert in autism and challenging behaviours. I have become an even stronger mental health advocate. I see people not only for who they are or what they can be, regardless of what society they come from. If I did not believe this, I would still be chained and abused in a dark world, with no end.

My journey was and is still complex because different worlds are intertwined. But my worlds are now one.

I prioritise empowerment and happiness. My world is bright and light, full of happiness. I will only surround myself with positivity. It is very underestimated, but do not be ashamed to try and experience positivity and gratitude!

I hope I have managed to spark inspiration or even acceptance and ownership of your thoughts. Do not shy away in accepting the old to bring development of the empowered, stronger, healthier and a happier, new you.

New Woman 29

Raj Rana

Full Circle of Love

"No matter what life throws at us,
we can still get back on track of the journey of life."

I was only four when the first challenges in my life happened. I feel now, looking back, it was such a young age of pure innocence. Little did I know that laughter, love and smiles weren't the whole meaning of life. I was blessed with a mum and dad that only gave me enormous amounts of love and protection, and gave me an illusion that this was what this world was all about. I didn't know that something would happen that was going to change my whole perception in life.

I remember my mom asking me if I had hurt myself and peeled a scab on my eye. I just said, "No," and was confused – why would she ask? Then later after some time, she asked again. I just said, "Mom, I don't think so," but I became curious as to why Mom had asked me again.

One day my dad called me, whilst he was sitting with my mom and said, "It's getting more white," as he looked at my eyes. I still didn't understand and just wanted to carry on playing.

I think it's important for you to know, I am Indian with brown skin and as you have no doubt gathered, little white patches started to grow around my eyes. It started small, but as weeks, months and years went by, it grew and grew around both my eyes. I remember looking in a mirror and being scared of my reflection. That wasn't me. It couldn't be. I touched my skin around my eyes to see if it felt different but it didn't; my brown skin just started to turn white, and a bright white at that. It was so scary as every morning instead of running down to play with my siblings, I ran to the mirror and closed one eye, to see if the white patches were getting worse. I would then hold my other eyelid down to see what changes had happened there. It just looked like a painting that had gone wrong.

Is this even right that a pure, innocent child who wished no harm and only gave love, would now have her first worry? What would my brothers and sisters think? What would my parents think? What would my extended family and friends think? This wasn't now just a worry every morning, this became a constant stress for me. Even when I was playing with siblings, I would think, "Are they looking at my eyes?"

One day my parents took me to a skin specialist who told them that I had vitiligo and that there is no cure. The doctor said it might get worse or it might stay the same, but there was no medicine to fix this. I remember their faces as they look saddened by this news and helpless but assuring me that it was all okay. I came home and just carried on playing, but questions flooded my mind. Why am I different?

Mom used to comb my long hair, and one day she styled it differently. I never understood at that time, as my mom just said, "This suits you better". But really, she was trying to cover this disease from me. My vitiligo had spread to my scalp, so my head was white and now my hair also became white. I didn't know for months that this was now getting out of control. My mom styled my hair in such a way that all my black hair was disguising my white streaks.

It was at primary school when things started to get difficult. Some girls refused to play with me as I was different and I heard them calling me names such as "Panda," and the worst one was "white eyes". Initially, I would tell my dad and say, "Daddyji, someone called me 'white eyes'." I could tell he was hurt; even though I was one of seven children, I believe I was my dad's favourite. I have four sisters and two brothers and I am the middle child, yet my dad brought me a light blue bag with 'Daddy's little girl' on it.

I felt special, like the chosen one, and I had decided I would just do everything to impress my dad, as he made me feel safe. I remember once telling Dad about someone teasing me, and he would hide his pain by asking, "Why the long face?" He would always just say, "Be happy."

I asked my mom, "Why am I different?" as there were seven of us and none of my other siblings had this. She would just say, "You're special; you're beautiful inside and out." I would be told not to focus on the vitiligo but to focus on being a good person, and all would be well. They emphasised that everyone's different, but we are all special in our own way, and we should all love and respect each other. You can imagine the daily teasing hadn't stopped, but I just kept loving me and ignored what people said. As time passed, I would look in the mirror and not see my vitiligo, as I became stronger in loving myself for who I am.

Wow! The power of my parents, who taught me gratitude at such a young age, which empowered me to know my self-worth. From a child who felt scared of seeing herself in a mirror, to a child who saw past that and saw her self-worth. My parents taught me to love others. But before that, to love myself first.

I remember one of my sisters saying she didn't look pretty and I said to her, "Why would you even think that? As a person with a skin disease, I have grown to feel pretty and beautiful inside out, by loving and valuing myself and to nurture 'self-love'."

I remember hearing extended family discussing with my parents, "Who will marry her as she has vitiligo?"

My parents would say, "She will be fine. She's kind and loving; we will find someone." They never let me feel like I had a disadvantage in the arranged marriage aspect of my culture and used to make me feel beautiful.

Once I overheard an auntie saying, "I could arrange a marriage with this boy, but the parents have shared their concerns that they wouldn't want to risk this, as she may have a chance of passing this vitiligo to her kids." I will **never** forget my poor mom's face. I always felt that whatever people said, I would win my husband over with pure love, and love can conquer all these man-made differences.

I told my parents to show me some boys and that we would see if I felt happy with that person, and if they accepted me as I am. I had vitiligo make-up, which camouflaged the white skin if I wanted to wear it but when I saw these boys, I chose not to wear the make-up so that they could see the true me. My parents showed me three boys, all of whom questioned me about my skin problem and made me feel less of a person for having it. Then one day, my parents introduced me to the man who became my husband. I knew he was the one, as he made me feel comfortable in my own skin. I showed him my eyes and white hair. He said, "Look, this could happen to anyone. Anytime. All that matters to me is this; if you are kind-hearted and a loving wife, this vitiligo means nothing to me. You are beautiful."

Of course, at that time we didn't love each other. When we said yes to each other, this was an arranged marriage but I knew if we worked at this and put our heart and soul into it, it would work. My husband made me feel special and beautiful daily, as he complimented and valued me each day.

I'm not saying the arranged marriage was easy, and as in any marriage, there is a lot of compromise. I do know we both worked hard to make it work and love grew stronger by the day. My husband never made me feel less for having a skin problem, and really loved me for who I was on the inside too, as well as on the outside. I had found my best friend, soulmate and husband.

My husband wanted to renew our wedding vows, so that our three beautiful boys could witness our love for each other. So we bought my husband's suit, my wedding dress and pageboy outfits. The planning was all underway.

However, three months before this date, my whole life turned upside down. It became the worst point of my life, which darkened my reality to the pits of hell.

My husband passed away suddenly, and tragically he was abroad at the time and I called him just to see how he was. He didn't answer and then I called his family to find out what had happened, to be told that he had died. It felt like I just got swallowed in hell and couldn't get out. This loving family in the click of God's fingers had become broken. I went into a deep depression and detached from my boys, my mom, my siblings; I decided loving was too painful. I decided not to love anymore and became suicidal and daily tried to leave this world, as I believed I could get to my husband. Nothing else made sense at that time; just that I had to leave my kids to get to my husband.

Every day became a living nightmare. If I managed to sleep, I would dream, and my husband would be with me. I could smell him and even touch him and my dreams were so real. Soon as I opened my eyes, I understood my nightmares had started again.

I asked myself, "Why me?" What was the point of loving for it to be taken away? How was this fair? What did I do wrong to deserve this? Had I been cruel to someone? Nothing made sense – if we were one and if we were soulmates, why would God take him away? I would ask everyone so many questions to try and understand. I resented God for doing this to me. I resented my mom for making me a kind human being. I resented my children because I kept failing in suicide and didn't accomplish it because of them; I was torn. I would describe myself at that time as a 'walking zombie' – neither alive, neither dead.

My children suffered as my mental health deteriorated. They would daily worry their little heads that when they returned from school, would I still be alive? My boys were only thirteen, eight, and six years old. This carried on for two years of their precious childhood, which I admittedly had stolen from them with my screaming and crying. My mom and my siblings who were scared, asked themselves daily if I would survive another day.

This knock-on effect of 'giving up' passed down to my children, unfortunately. I nearly lost my kids too. I overheard my younger two boys discussing how they would set the house on fire, so we could all die and get to Daddy, and it would be the end of all the family's heartache and we could all be one again and be happy. I don't exactly understand what happened to me, but it is as if a light bulb, in my mind, was switched on. Luckily, my mind understood that I could lose my boys as well, if I didn't help myself. I knew this wasn't going to be easy, but within seconds I decided that I would be the change, to help my boys through this horrific grief.

My poor children had only cried once since their father's death, as all the focus was on me; I was so vulnerable.

Luckily for me, I had support from family and lots of love. My amazing mom, who has been my rock throughout, such a pure soul; I love you so much. My brother and his wife opened a business and made me a business partner to help me on my journey of recovery. They aided me with simple things like helping me to get dressed and comb my hair, to leave the house to get to work, and encouraged me to communicate with family and eventually, customers. All my family played a part somewhere or somehow to support my healing, which I will cherish forever. Still, even with all this support, I was still grieving hard.

Three years after my husband passed away, I was introduced to an opportunity by a family member, to whom I'm forever grateful, which in hindsight saved me and my boys. It allowed me to have mentors and to build my self-belief back again. Who would have thought that an industry of network marketing that had been around for decades, would suddenly play a great part in my and my children's well-being? I am a strong believer that we don't meet people by accident, and everyone whom we meet is meant to cross our paths for a reason.

Along with my mentors, I started working on myself and believing in myself again;it took time but I never gave up, because my boys became my reason, my 'why', as they had already suffered enough. My mentors gave me tools to better myself, and I started to heal gradually. This gave me a purpose to be a role model for my children, never to give up and even in the most difficult of times to get back up and keep soldiering on.

I am a big believer, no matter what life throws at us, we can still get back on track of the journey of life. It is important we surround ourselves with love and positivity to face all the challenges that are thrown at us from family and friends, to total strangers. We can together make life better for us to live in. I began to accept and love myself again, which enabled me to help my boys grow into positive, strong, loving men.

My mentor gave me skills which I use to this day, such as the power of gratitude and the power of serving others. This has become my daily habit and daily ritual. I believe self-love and unconditional love for others has become a magnet to the love of life. My biggest achievement is that I found my self-worth, even after going to hell and back, helping myself on the path of hope and light, and the love of gratitude. I have been able to help my boys, and now hundreds of people.

I have had so many learnings on this journey. I have been blessed to have been loved, and to give unconditional love. I had to lose what I loved the most, my husband, the essence of divine love. I now understand it was not mine to own, but mine to cherish.

I am a new woman today of total gratitude to love, rise and find a purpose in making a difference even to one person who reads this. My life has taken a full 360° turn, and I begin my day with feeling blessed and grateful to God for another day with loved ones.

My husband's memories will live on for us to celebrate and cherish. This is about my journey, a full circle of love, and the New Woman I have become today. Love never dies.

New Woman 30

Sandhya

Reborn

"I stopped thinking those horrible thoughts and started focusing on striving through everything."

I had just found out that I was getting divorced!

The news landed upon me as a cannonball. I was scared, broken, deceived, tearful, ripped apart – and these are only a few of the things I felt. I was a complete mess, to say the least.

The realisation that my husband had decided to leave me and our two children for his girlfriend, was too difficult to absorb.

I was 41 years old, with no job or source of income, two kids aged 11 and 8, no family around, no bank deposits, and now this!

I had no experience of working either. I did not even have a house in my name as I was always the homemaker and we had kept moving house every six to twelve months for his anaesthetist job in the NHS. This was a conscious choice that I had made, so our marriage did not get affected by distance. I moved every time he moved. I loved him very much and sacrificed everything for him, including leaving my family back in India and moving to the UK, travelling between different cities for his job. I took full responsibility for making sure he and our children were taken care of and looked after at all times, doing all the cleaning and cooking and being a supportive wife. I always felt my marriage would not last long if I did not move along.

He had no job stability and he visited Birmingham frequently to see his girlfriend of 10 years or more. Although I had an inkling that this was going on between the two of them, I was hoping that it was either my overthinking or that he was going through a phase and that it would be over soon. Whenever we spoke (argued) about this, he would constantly apologise and mostly deny any feelings for her. I totally believed that he was committed to his children, if anything. He was attached to his children and would not make a move that would hurt them. But I was totally wrong!

I was never going to be prepared for this day. It was a big shock.

His girlfriend happened to be my old friend from school back in India, and families being friends for long, made it so much more painful.

Back in 2005 when I was carrying our second child, I happened to run into my childhood friend from India at a temple in Watford; we started chatting and reconnected. Oblivious to what could happen, I invited her to my home where she started interacting with my husband over dinner. It all started when my husband offered to drop her back to the station on two such occasions. That meeting is where she stole my life.

After meeting her, my husband changed! He was distant, and there was a loss of interest, lack of love and affection; it was more of a maid/boss relationship than husband and wife. He became demanding, aggressive, just a different man altogether. He gave me a timetable of how to take care of him and what to serve him for meal times. Every detail was itemised: such as 5.30am wake up, then warm water and wheatgrass. Tea, breakfast and lunch to be plated with two chapattis, one cup of rice, curry, lentils, salad, buttermilk then evening tea, healthy dinner etc. Sadly in spite of all this, nothing satisfied him nor could he pass his exams. Every six to eight months, the children and I were forced to go to India so that he could get his privacy for his exam prep. Little did I realise that this so-called 'privacy' was a perfect opportunity for him to see for his girlfriend.

One day in 2013, I found out that my husband was in Birmingham with her and I decided to confront him. Upon his arrival, he started to pick on me: the kitchen was untidy, the plants were not looked after, food was not garnished enough, etc., etc. I knew he was trying to get into an argument so that he wouldn't have to speak to me at all. But I was adamant and had questions I so wanted to ask. I understood his intentions and quietly sat with my Lord in the prayer room but even that was not okay for him. He ended up grabbing my hair, smacking my face on the floor and sitting on top of me, slapping me repeatedly in a frenzy. He was angry! I still find it difficult to understand how he could have reacted like this while he was in the wrong, while he was cheating on me! I felt completely devastated, shocked, alone, scared, deeply hurt, in pain, with nothing making sense as the man who was once deeply in love with me was today hurting me in many ways.

The next big fall out happened later in the same year, in 2013, when he got his registrar training number after great trials and family support. He seemed to think it was the right time to leave his family, hence he used to come home in a different mood and have arguments, creating violence every weekend and completely spoil the atmosphere at home. I used to eagerly wait for a Friday evening to have a lovely family time, cooking his favourite dishes, cleaning the house and making his bed, but everything was ruined in no time, leaving me broken and depressed.

I was devastated!

When I felt I couldn't handle the situation myself, I used to approach the family, my mother-in-law being very close to me. We shared a great bond for years but things had changed ,and very late in the relationship I understood that his family were working for him and his happiness, and not for any betterment for our marriage or relationship. It was much more depressing when I saw how tactful the family was in consoling me but played a totally different game behind my back.

He started saying he wanted a peaceful life and couldn't handle the kids and their tantrums and I was ruining his tranquillity. He had clearly made up his mind but I still wasn't ready to see or believe what was coming through. As things were getting worse, my brother put a condition on my husband that he needed to leave his extramarital affair, else I would be divorcing him. However, I did not realise that this would backfire and become a golden opportunity for him!

In December 2013, I was informed by email that he was divorcing me.

This is when the emotional abuse flared up. It seemed that my husband and his girlfriend would not stop at anything until they had ruined my life. They just kept playing mind games with me which sent me into complete depression. I was put on antidepressants, while taking care of two growing children aged 11 and 8, with an ongoing, acrimonious divorce case in court.

I even had an episode prior to this where my husband invited me to speak to his girlfriend in a park with him to discuss and get my opinion on how it would work to have two women in his life! I was not able to understand how anyone can think like this! How a well-educated doctor, working in a Western country, claiming to be forward-thinking, can talk about keeping two women so that his needs are taken care of in a better way? Yet even his family felt I was not cooperating with him in this matter. At some point, I started questioning myself if I was wrong!

Finally, we physically parted when in late 2013 he decided to move to Sheffield to take up his new position and I decided to go to Birmingham to offer my children better educational opportunities. He was not keen on taking us with him anyway.

I was trying to convince myself that I made a better choice for the children with grammar school options, as my heart and brain were tuned differently. I had to insist that he looked for a house for us to rent, rather than leave the task to us. He unwillingly settled us in a good four-bedroom house moaning about spending £800 on rented property but slowly, he started removing his name from the council tax and bills. All of a sudden, he told me that he wouldn't be paying the council tax which was due and couldn't pay the rent and so it was my responsibility to take care of everything.

I was in a total chaos, with two children and no job and no finances. There were no savings as they were all in his name and under his control and had already been transferred to parents in India. I did not know how I would survive in this country with two young children so I emailed the Edgbaston Ward Councillor. Thankfully she responded back saying I need to get legal help while the divorce proceedings were on and also that she would write to the City Council waiving the council tax.

As the property was through an agency and private landlord, I was asked to move out as I had no money to pay the rent. I was told that I was squatting in the property and that the children and I would be evicted by 25th December 2014, the time when our next month's rent was due. This was such a merciless act and when I asked my husband, he mentioned he couldn't help us. I again called my mother-in-law to inform her and plead with her to do something about it. She did not help either but put the blame on me, saying that I wasn't taking any actions to stop him from doing this. When asked what could I even do when he was so violent, she said that I could have complained to the police about his nasty behaviour. I heard the family tell me this a couple of times but never imagined I would do this to the person whom I loved so deep.

He used to visit us every weekend. The conflict was there and was only growing bigger. He visited us the night before my son's 9th birthday. Suddenly he mentioned that he would stay that night. I did not really know about his intentions as all legal paperwork was lying in my bedroom and he slept with my boy in my bedroom. I did not want any sort of mess with my paperwork which is so crucial at that stage with the fear of homeless, bill payments, along with running the home, court proceedings and children's mental health and so on. I am not sure what was going on in my mind with mixed emotions; I wasn't able to think straight!

On my little one's birthday, when my boy was excited to go to StarCity with his dad to have great fun on his special day, I was trying to be mindful of how this man's behaviour was at home, when my daughter came up to me. She mentioned how when the three of them were playing upstairs, her father would put his hand over her mouth during siblings fighting which was probably the type of play and fun they were having, but I could not take it in the right manner and immediately called 999. I did not even provide my address but the police came in and he was totally shocked while taken into custody.

I reacted very wrongly at that moment and could not forgive myself and kept weeping the whole day constantly looking out of the window to look for him while he picked up his car from outside our house, trying to whisper that I was sorry. I kept ringing the police station to find out if he could be released, as I was not in a proper mental state. My friends and cousin's family came over to console me and children but that guilt of sending him to police station and spoiling my boy's birthday ate away at me. His family who kept blaming me for not doing this earlier, were now cursing me for what I did! Blaming and shaming became part and parcel of my life.

I did not understand what to do. I was in constant touch with my family from India, America and my in-laws too. I felt like going back to India to take a break and not wait here to receive the court papers, to which I was bound to respond back to.

But to my distress, our passports had been hidden! I was forced to stay here only to see the allegation for domestic violence put on me wherein I was the actual victim! My heart and mind were in a complete state of denial. But I was left with no choice.

On 26th December 2014, he told me that I had to pay the council tax from now.

The next day, I was informed by the estate agency that they would be evicting me from my rented property, unless I was ready to pay the rent. I had no money in my name! Nothing at all!

In a week's time, I was homeless and had no money on me. My cousin, who lives here in the UK, helped me by paying six months' rent in advance so that we could secure a private property to live in. I was not ready to go to sheltered accommodation with my young children.

It was too late when I realised that my husband had already transferred all his savings and assets abroad and made it seem like he was in vast debt in this country. He made up health issues to give an excuse for not being able to work, to claim that he couldn't afford to contribute towards his family's needs. He stooped down even lower. He transferred all his NHS pensions abroad. Though I fought my case under legal aid, I got nothing out of this 13-year marriage.

I found the court case itself was so draining, but he didn't stop until he made it a living hell for me. I suffered a panic attack at my first court hearing and they continued throughout the whole process. My children were still so young and needed my attention but the court paperwork, files and other work associated with it kept me away from them when they were reaching out for my attention. I used to feel so incredibly guilty that I was unable to spend time with them nor able to put my little one to bed when he used to wait for me all the time.

This was totally a new area for me. Every time I got to know about more transfers, more beneficiaries changed, and there were more lies; I couldn't help but fall back to the start and lose hope. My tears and my prayers never stopped. It was so hard to hide them from my children. I always felt bad for not handling myself well without disturbing them but I just could not help myself. Strong thoughts about ending my life popped up in my mind every now and then.

One day, my elder sister said to me, "Have you thought about the trauma and pain that your children would face? Is your pain more than that of your childrens?"

That was it! This became my power and strength to live. I had to turn things around for my children. I had to be there for them. I had to show them that one parent was going to always be there for them. I stopped thinking those horrible thoughts and started focusing on striving through everything. I started to go to counselling sessions and put myself on different courses to keep myself occupied and to get better.

After accepting the truth that life was going to be in darker shades with no finances, no job, no experience, with new friends in a new place, I had been looking for jobs vigorously but somehow my coach suggested that I should start a business. My immediate reply was, "No, I am not a business person at all!"

He then asked me, "What are you good at?" I answered that I could do Bollywood dancing and I was good at cooking South Indian dishes. I mentioned that I was looking for yoga classes for myself and the children to help me cope with the stress.

That was it! He immediately gave me the idea of starting Bollywood dance classes and yoga classes and having my stall with South Indian dishes at the class! He mentioned that they would help me start and provide help with paperwork and so on for the first two years.

I don't know what made me act on that but I started my own dance school, which my daughter named as India Island Academy. Along with a few friends and my children's support, I organised a two-day workshop with different activities in August 2016. To my delight, a good number of people attended on the second day.

Many people appreciated my initiative and some were utterly surprised to see me start such a school coming from nowhere. It was definitely a huge struggle but with God's blessings, my children's support and the community's encouragement, I worked even harder and created my own identity through the Academy.

India Island Academy (IIA) is a registered company, an institution, a paradise of Indian Arts. Our aim is to promote Indian culture to generations to come and our vision is to make it available and accessible worldwide. It features Indian Arts such as Bollywood, Bharatanatyam, Carnatic Vocals, yoga and meditation, chess, Vedic Maths, Shloka and Vedic classes, Bhagavad Gita, Hindi and Telugu language classes, arts and crafts, and much more. This was all set up to educate children with the rich heritage and culture of India and keep them connected to their roots. We hold these activities all under one roof, and this is a concept that is much appreciated by parents and all students as it saves so much time and travel.

IIA gives opportunities to women who are skilled in various fields. We provide a platform for such women to gain experience and take up their passion and follow their dreams, while earning a secondary income for the family. We support women, giving them work opportunities, identifying their skills, passion and expertise in different fields. Around 95% of our tutors, admin, marketing, IT and accounting staff are women and we are always proud to motivate and encourage them, while providing them this platform to gain experience.

IIA provides tutoring opportunities to young university students and helps them meet their vast expenses. The aim of IIA is to promote Indian culture in generations to come. Its ultimate vision is to make it available and accessible worldwide.

In 2016, we started with two activities and 12 children on board. Today, we have around 20 activities with 45 tutors and over 200 students on board! These are the fruits of all the hard work done by myself, my children and all my friends and the team who supported me greatly.

I felt I was left all alone in this foreign land but this foreign land has now become my home, with so many friends and well-wishers beside me. I truly believe that God will open up another door for us if He closes one but I feel He has opened up several doors for me, not just one!

I always felt God had made me the mediator to get this wonderful job done of serving the community and educating our young children so that they can carry this on to the next generation. I was also delighted that I gave my children a much bigger family now.

I always believe that together, we grow. When we work towards anything with purity and good intentions at heart, it yields great results. People can relate to my own example: I had no business knowledge but the success this Academy has gained is a true mystery.

I would encourage every woman to never give up in life. Whatever situation we face, there is always a positive side to see! Though it is hard and we struggle to see light, I plead with everyone to never give up in life. Look for one positive thing and stand strongly for it. Never lose hope, always have faith and trust in the Almighty. Things will fall into place sometime or the other.

We, women and mothers, have unknown strengths within, which we only realise in times of need and when certain situations arise. These situations make us stronger and stronger! Whatever challenges life has to throw at us, then let it! But, always remember, a woman has the power to change the world, not just herself!

Even if one woman gets inspired by my life story and message, I would feel happy and contended to have played a small part in changing her life and that of her family. This one lady may inspire a few more and become their strength and power to live while changing their lives for good.

New Woman 31

Jayasri Banala

Believe in a Master Plan

"I was dreaming for a fairy tale ending,
for us all a 'happily ever after'..."

I was extremely depressed as I had just moved from India to the UK, leaving my four-year-old daughter, Simi, behind. I brought just two suitcases and was questioning myself every second. "Why am I doing this?", "Am I doing the right thing?"

I am still searching for an answer...

I had married a successful business man, named Surender. The wedding was arranged in a grand manner with all elders, relatives and friends' blessings and best wishes. I had dreamed of a life as a queen and never having to work.

Despite being educated to a Master's degree level in Computer Sciences, I always wanted to be a homemaker and mother. I believed that a homemaker is the one who gives the best to society in the form of responsible children. It was my dream that women have the power to build a powerful society by producing dependable, kind children who have strong moral values and ethics.

Circumstances changed quickly; we were married, had our beautiful daughter Simi, and my husband and I made the decision to migrate to the UK, in the hope of better career opportunities for us and a secure future for our daughter. I had never dreamt that this is what I would have to do when I was younger.

So, I arrived at Heathrow airport, not exactly with a plan, but a dream.

I lived in a shared room in London, with two cousins who worked night shifts. The cousins slept during the day while I slept in the same room at night. I went to the high street from shop to shop submitting my CV to see if anyone would hire me. With my cousin's reference, I was able to find some work in a fast food restaurant in an amusement park which was a temporary position for the summer. After that, I worked as an assistant in a supermarket; again, this was temporary. I then became a carer, where I worked a crazy seven-day week.

However, my cousins did not approve of my being a carer. They considered this position as below me, as third grade work that illiterate people do in government hospitals in India. This was not considered a respectful job. What they did not understand was the job itself was also posing challenges for me on a daily basis.

Firstly, being displaced from culture and home, I was feeling culturally challenged. In addition, I had to travel to my clients' houses which were often far apart from each other. It was dark and I had to travel by bus – I found the bus system very confusing and difficult to understand. On one particular occasion, I got completely lost on a late winter evening and had to beg some kind strangers for a lift. That was an extremely difficult task for me to do!

Despite all these challenges, I knew I had to work as I had to look after myself here, pay rent for my room, and send money to India for my Simi's education and other expenses. Not having my daughter with me left a large scar on my heart.

There were many scars to be had. This was just the beginning, only I did not realise...

After a year, while continuing to be a carer, I managed to find myself a second income. I was able to leave the shared accommodation with my cousins, as I started looking after an off-licence for a kind, old man. He gave me a room to live in for free, along with food, in return for opening up and closing the shop at the right times. I would cook for him and fondly called him 'Raj Uncle'.

I was so alone in a strange country. I had no one to turn to in times of emotional despair. There were moments when all these responsibilities became too much for me to handle. But I was ready to go through all of that and more if need be for my daughter, for Simi. Little did I know that God was going to respond to 'and more' soon...

I wandered alone in many places searching for something without knowing what that 'something' was. While handling all the worldly aspects of life, I was also trying to find the purpose of the body that I was in. One day while walking and wandering along strange roads in London, my steps led me to a meditation centre. They taught 'The Raja Yoga', which I found very interesting. I started meditating and also attending their events. It gave me immense bliss and introduced me to my inner self. This became my survival kit for life.

After being in London for two years, I finally felt ready to bring my husband and daughter over. I was dreaming for a fairy tale ending, for us all a 'happily ever after'...

Upon my arrival back in India, I found that my father-in-law was terribly unwell and had become bedridden. This was heart-breaking to see and the decision that I had to make in that moment was challenging. My only reason for the visit was to fly back to London with Simi and my husband, which after much deliberation, we did.

Seven days after we got back to London, we received the devastating news that my father-in-law had passed away. As all our savings had been eaten up by the first flights, we could not afford to go back for his funeral. My husband was very upset about this but there was no way we could afford it.

'Raj Uncle', the kind-hearted old man, generously gave the three of us shelter in his house for a couple of weeks until we found a larger place to move into. Within a month, I found a room in a house, where we lived for nearly a year. I found an outstanding school nearby for Simi, my beautiful daughter, where she was very happy and made friends.

I continued to work as a carer, and also became a dinner lady in a school. With my family's increased expenses, it was becoming more and more difficult to make both ends meet. My husband was also looking for a job. So that the family could survive, I started bringing leftover food home at night from my job as a dinner lady. I did what any mother would do to keep my family alive and safe.

It took another six months before I found myself a job in a betting shop, allowing me to give up both my carer position and dinner lady job.

With a friend's reference, Surender managed to get a job in a petrol station but it was miles away from London. But he immediately moved in order to grab the opportunity. Simi and I joined him within a couple of months. Fortunately, I was able to keep my job in the betting office by applying for a transfer to another branch. It was a seamless transition and I was able to resume my job as a betting shop assistant as soon as we moved from London to the West Midlands.

I was so pleased that both Surender and I had jobs. And Simi had a place in a school which was very close to home. However, this state of happiness did not last long. Surender lost his job as the petrol station shut down. The responsibility had landed on my shoulders fully again. This was the point when destiny decided that I was to take the lead, not just on the maternal front, but also the emotional and financial perspectives for my family.

The next kind person sent to me from God was Salma. She was a child's parent at Simi's school, who was from the same place as me from back home. We became friends and shared our personal stories very closely. When Salma knew that I was highly qualified but was working in a betting shop, she suggested that I speak to her husband about finding out about opportunities in the IT field. I took Salma's suggestion on board and after speaking with her husband, took one of the courses he had suggested.

I knew that my daughter Simi was not happy. She had been displaced one more time from London and I could see the impact it had had on her. I would see her staring out of the window all alone, without any direction to her vision. This moved me and broke my heart. I found it so difficult to watch my child being so unhappy and not enjoying her life. I truly believed that my daughter's well-being was my ultimate goal in life, whether I could be with her or not. With a heavy heart, I made the painful decision to send her back to India so that she could have a good time with her cousins. This decision is not easy for any mother to make… neither was it for me.

Once Simi was back in India with family, I no longer had to 'be Mummy' so had some free time. I decided to sign up for an online IT course from the USA. The timings were odd due to the different time zones, so I had to wake up at 2:30am every morning for three months… but I managed to complete the course, then consequently, managed to get a job in IT! However, I kept my job at the betting shop job, just in case.

After eight months of living away from Simi, I now assumed that my life would be stable again and I could bring her back, which I did. Simi flew back alone from India and once again I managed to place her back into a good school. Life was not perfect yet – as a contractor in IT, I found myself jobless every now and then.

After a long spell without a job, I managed to find permanent work but it meant moving again. I wanted Simi and Surender to move with me. However, little did I expect that Surender wanted to build his career as a video editor and he had friends who could train him, so he did not want to move. As a result, I ended up travelling down to Brighton and renting a room there. I lived alone from Monday to Friday and travelled back home for the weekend. But I soon discovered this was not sustainable, as travelling to Brighton every week cost me far too much money. Ever the resourceful woman, I managed to arrange a car share with a stranger, who fortunately was an IT professional from Harborne and travelled to Brighton on Monday mornings. So at least I managed to save a little money.

I soon realised that the money I earned was not enough, as I had to pay rent and all of the bills where Surender and Simi lived, as well as paying rent for my room in Brighton, the car share expenses for Monday mornings and train travel expenses on Friday evenings. Again, I found myself having to move Simi and took her to Brighton with me, where we ended up living full-time. True to form, I found her yet another place in a decent school which also offered after-school care, which was vital as I was living like a single parent. Fortunately, Surender visited us at weekends where we could be a whole family once again.

A year down the line, I developed a lump on my neck. I was absolutely terrified. What would happen to Simi? I was living alone with Simi, and the doctors were desperately trying to diagnose what was wrong with me. I spent many nights crying, assuming that it was cancer. Fortunately, it turned out to be less life threatening, though still serious; I had TB. This meant that I had to take time off work so as to rest and recuperate.

During my recovery period, Surender took wonderful care of me and I regained my health within three months. However, I did not want to risk my long-term health anymore, so I handed in my resignation to my permanent work.

Soon after regaining my health, I was, of course, on the hunt for another job. This time I found temporary work for three months in the East Midlands. But yet again, this included travelling long distances. I carried on doing short temporary work with long periods of being out of work, meaning that I could never build up enough funds to save any money. Whatever I earned from temporary work, was quickly used up during my long breaks to find the next job.

Feeling lost in the mad race of humanity, after all the grave and difficult challenges I had experienced, I now began to question my very existence. I asked myself, "What is my purpose? Why am I here?" Remembering the meditation centre and the Raja Yoga, it sparked a new way of being for me. Finding my courage, I made a decision to explore the world of spirituality once more, hoping to find answers and moving closer to the very source of creation.

So…fastforwardtotoday! I am a well-known and popular individual in my community, a proactive participant and a volunteer for many events, programmes and ongoing Vedic classes, whether in my own temple, with other people and even on my own.

It is my passion to learn as much as possible about the Vedic culture, also known as Sanatan Dharma. I believe that Indian classes are where the rich Vedic heritage and culture should be taught. Instead of waiting for schools to take initiative or pass the blame on to anyone for not engaging in the practice, I took up the baton and began fighting the cause.

I wanted Simi to have some extracurricular activities to keep her busy as she was an only child and would be bored at home. So she joined me in Vedic class, Bharatanatyam (South Indian classical dance) in the Balaji temple, where I found my own interest in learning and imparting Vedic knowledge to the next generation. I then became a Vedic class teacher and taught in the temple for five years.

I then started organising other shloka classes to adults and children online, as well as visiting another nearby temple (Krishna temple) to offer my teachings there. I love keeping myself as busy as possible! And I believe that each and every individual has social responsibility and should offer some of their free time to provide a service to their immediate community.

My ultimate goal has always been the happiness of my daughter and no matter how busy I am, I will **always** make time for her. I took Simi and her friend to Butlin's holiday camp for a four-day holiday. It was at this time that I planned my YouTube channel. I stayed indoors and let Simi and her friend explore the holiday camp and have fun together. Having had a taste of some fun and time together, a friend of mine organised a trip to Portugal where Simi and I had the time of our lives!

As the Covid-19 pandemic hit, it did not stop me from continuing to extend my services and classes to my community, by teaching children and adults the Vedic shlokas (mantras and chants).

I have a strong faith, and believe that this has all come together as part of the Almighty's master plan. Had I not taken a leap of faith to migrate to the UK, with my two suitcases and a dream for my daughter, I wouldn't have had all these opportunities to grow spiritually and professionally.

New Woman 32

Monika Bammi

Importance of Being YOU

"I didn't see the problems as problems,
I saw them as challenges that I needed to
overcome to achieve the life I wanted."

My name is Monika Bammi and this is my story of how I went from living a sheltered life in India, to moving across the world with a husband I had only just met, and creating my own award-winning business in England.

My story begins at my grandmother's house.

There was a street psychic, reading palms and telling people about their future.

The psychic came into my grandmother's house and told my aunties what their future held and when it was my turn, he said, "You will go on an aeroplane, you will have two cars and you will have one son."

To me, this felt impossible! I was 19, focused on my education and enjoying life. The thought of marriage had never crossed my mind.

I had actually just finished my degree in BA (Hons) Arts and started to study fashion design.

I decided to ignore what the street psychic had said as there was no way I was leaving the country. I continued my everyday life.

The same day, I was walking home, which was four houses away from my grandmother's house. My aunty stopped me in the street and said, "Your uncle has friends over from the UK and they are looking for a girl for their son and he has suggested you."

I said, "What, are you kidding me? I am so young and still studying; why would I get married to someone from another country?"

Later that night, my dad spoke to me about it and asked if I would consider it. I replied to my dad, "There is no way I would marry anyone in another country, I'm just not interested." This conversation went on for days but in the end, I thought, "I will just go see this boy so that he can reject me then my dad won't think I disobeyed him and it will get him off my back."

I asked my friend to bring me the ugliest outfit she had, in the lightest colour (as light colours don't suit me).

Next, I went to see this boy, looking as bland as I could look. I was draped in a dull cream-coloured Indian suit, which is something I would NEVER usually wear! This was to appear less attractive and it would take the pressure off me saying no or rejecting him, as I didn't want to do that.

In Indian culture, both families must approve and give their blessings before their kids can get married, so both of our families met in the park.

The boy arrived on a rickshaw and I was instantly put off because a rickshaw was not an ideal form of transport to meet your future wife! Back then, it was all about reputation and showing how a boy could look after the girl.

I was asked to go for a walk with the boy and have a chat to see if we liked each other. Unwillingly, I went for the walk. We had a five-minute conversation and he asked if I would move to UK... I said "No." I thought if the clothes didn't do it, then this would, as I couldn't be clearer than that.

We came back from our quick stroll and went back to our own groups. I walked away from my family and I had my back to everyone, as I knew the boy was going to reject me and my dad was going to have a 'moment'. It was like both families were having a face off, deciding whether they approved of each other. I knew my dad would have a fit as soon as I got home, knowing I just told this boy, whom my family thinks is well suited to me, that I would not move to the UK to be with him. I was not going to be part of his 'Indian bride goes to the UK' game.

After a few minutes, my aunty came to me and said that my dad wanted to know why I had told the boy that I didn't want to leave, that he had asked why I would say that. I thought to myself, "Well, you knew that already, what a silly question to ask!"

My aunty asked me if I liked the boy. All she wanted was a yes or a no. I didn't know what to say as I had already made myself clear to my dad. Not forgetting I had made myself look as ugly as I could to the boy. "What more do you need of me?" I thought.

So I didn't say anything. After a few minutes when my aunty didn't get an answer from me, she went back to my dad and said, "Monika isn't saying anything."

I was waiting for the fireworks, a rejection and a bit of drama, but I could hear people laughing and they sounded happy. I turned around, hoping and expecting it to be over, but instead I saw them shaking hands.

And there you have it. I was engaged to a boy who I didn't know, who lived in the UK and I was about to get married in 10 days.

How did that happen? What did I miss and why did my grand scheme not work?

Apparently, my dad said to the boy's family that when a girl doesn't say anything, then that means it is a yes...

Why did I not say anything? I was known to be outspoken, assertive and confident. Why didn't I say anything when it mattered the most?

I was shocked; I didn't know what was going on. I didn't know what else to do to break off this arrangement. I was getting shipped over to another country, thousands of miles away from home, family and friends. Away from everything I knew, and into a whole new world.

Five days before the marriage, my dad asked me if I was okay with this and said I could break the marriage off if I wanted to. He must have realised how sad I was, but it felt a little too late.

I became annoyed and told him that I was not a puppet, I had feelings.

I knew that if I broken the engagement off at this stage, which I really wanted to do as this was my last chance to take back control of my life back, I would be blacklisted in India. To give you some context, when the marriage is cancelled, the girl is always blamed. Assumptions are made that there must have been something wrong with the girl for it not to go through, and there was no way I was having that written in my destiny.

So, I said to my dad, "I am going through with this, so start preparing."

And that is how my dad's decisions became mine. I owned it and I took responsibility and control, at least that is what I thought at that point.

I was married five days later and I made this life-altering decision which felt like it meant my days of being a young, bubbly, happy and independent girl, were over. I was uprooted from my family home and was sent away to a foreign land with a person who I had only known for five minutes.

I was now in the UK, married, yet feeling more alone than ever. I was missing my family, my home, my friends and of course, the flavourful food! What a culture shock was the bland English diet!

I went from being a care-free princess, where everything was done for me and I never had to lift a finger, to having every single responsibility under the sun. Back in India, we had housekeepers, people who made my food and my bed, and now I was the one who was expected to do everything for this man I had just met.

In India, I was brought up to believe that all that mattered, was sleeping, eating, and studying, until I grew older and was married to someone who was very wealthy, who could look after me, and I could keep my carefree characteristics. As you can tell, it did not turn out that way.

There were many nights where I would sit by myself and cry. I felt so alone. I thought that when you got married, you would never feel alone again. I was mostly upset, not because I was with someone who did not care, but because I was close to my family and could not really understand why they had married me off at such a young age, and across the ocean.

I was trying to get used to the new environment, a new family, new relationships and above all, my husband, whom I would be living with for the rest of my life. We had our differences as we were brought up differently and had vastly different ways of living.

I have always been confident and assertive and had certain principles and values I lived by. I was brought up by these values and I held them dear to my heart. I knew I could spend the rest of my life upset and feeling sorry for myself, or I could accept what life has given me, the good and the bad, and make the most of this new challenge. I knew that this sad person was not me, and I did not like whoever this person was. I knew I had to start making a difference in my thinking right then.

I decided to join my husband in his retail business; this allowed me to get out of the house more and out of my comfort zone. I was required to interact with people who spoke only English and it was a challenge but I knew if I overcame this, the possibilities would be endless.

I stayed at the business for three years, during which time I became pregnant and gave birth to my beautiful daughter. DAUGHTER! Not son! **Psychic, are you hearing this?!** Thank you for the wrong prediction anyway, because I always wanted a daughter.

I decided to further improve my English and I continued my studies. I knew this would open new doors for me.

I then learnt how to drive and took my test, failed, took my test, failed, took my test, PASSED. I was determined not to give up. My independence was in my hands and in my control and I was not about to let my future be decided for me any longer.

Knowing how to drive meant I could apply for a job in the housing sector, working as a support worker, supporting women suffering from domestic violence, which I did for one year. I then got a job as a housing support worker and then as a team manager, and did this for 17 years.

When I was in India, I had a very comfortable life and was sheltered from the harsh truths of the suffering people faced. Seeing women suffer domestic violence, homelessness, drug abuse, alcohol dependency, violence, and self-harm, and the pain and violence they went through, shook my soul to the core.

This job changed my life forever but not in bad way. This is when I knew what my purpose in life was. To help people who needed it the most; people who did not have my upbringing and people who, instead of being sheltered from the real world, were exposed to the brutality of it. I felt blessed to be able to help people turn their lives around. I felt their relief when they felt better. I felt proud when they overcame obstacles that once held them back. I did love my comfortable life in India, but what I was doing now, was more aligned to my soul.

Although I had found what my passion was, I knew it wasn't exactly what I was doing at the time. I felt there was more I could be doing and new skills I could bring the table, which my current job did not allow.

I knew it was time for me to hang up my corporate working shoes and resign. Probably a mid-life crisis, but who doesn't get them at some point?!

I took a break for a month and a half to recharge my batteries, recoup and refocus to see what I really wanted to do with my second innings.

During my time off, I had many thoughts about my previous jobs. I saw many staff members go on sick leave due to stress and anxiety, then they would return and go off sick again. This became a reoccurring pattern for many of them. I felt like I needed to do something to help hard-working people who were feeling the effects of stress and anxiety, but didn't know how to combat it.

I had always been interested in a holistic approach for health and emotional resilience and because of this I enrolled on a program of Spiritual Energy, known worldwide as Reiki and I became a Reiki Master. This was 24 years ago.

I then went on to complete a course in NLP (neuro-linguistic programming) and became a practitioner. I also went on to study for my Life Coaching exams (over 20 years ago) and finally I had all the relevant skills to start helping people.

Despite knowing nothing about business, I had the passion and drive to make it, no matter what. At this point, I decided to open my own practice and truly have creative freedom down whichever path I wanted to take it. I also did not want to be told what to do and when. I wanted to be my own boss; the only person I could always truly trust was myself. I finally created my own company, Divine Health & Wellbeing.

Starting my own business from scratch had its own pressures and stresses. I felt overwhelmed and at times, alone. Something I learned quickly, was that it all starts in the mind.

I gained many skills coming from an academic background, to a holistic and spiritual one. I learnt that you can always find a way out if you have enough desire. I helped myself through holistic approaches and I wanted to share that with others.

This is where the next chapter of my life began. I started with zero clients but lots of enthusiasm and the intention to help as many people as possible. I was on a mission to help others. Now, several years later, I have helped thousands of people, including business owners, CEOs, doctors, nurses, teachers, accountants, lawyers, councillors and many stay- at-home mums.

All the clients I have worked with have managed to get the results they were desperately searching for, including helping clients with their aches and pains, thyroid conditions, IBS, mental health conditions, and so much more.

They felt more connected with their partners and were able to switch off and manage their personal stress and anxiety issues in a way they would have never done before.

In 2020, Divine Health & Wellbeing was awarded the Holistic Health Specialist of the Year 2020 award. I was so happy! Something I created had been recognised and I was awarded for it! It was even more special, because it was based on feedback and reviews from my own clients.

Throughout all this, I have still worked full-time to provide my family with a dependable income. I have three intelligent, caring, and amazing daughters, (clearly took after their mother!). I have a supportive and caring husband, and I worked hard to keep a good balance of my work life and home life.

I was doing reasonably well in the business and then came the soul-destroying pandemic, Covid-19.

As my business was all face-to-face, lockdown measures meant we were back to zero clients. Another curveball life threw at me, yet I saw it as another challenge to face and something else to make me even stronger.

I noticed that acceptance helped me grow as well as being solution focused. I was able to acknowledge this as one of my strengths, a strength I knew would take me further and help me adapt to different surroundings.

I thought, "What can I do in this free time? How can I utilise this time and still help others?" Social media and doing things online was something I wanted to do but never had the courage to do so.

My desire was so strong to help others, I decided to face my fear of going in front of the camera and create an online course, with my husband, based on my clients' feedback called 'The Magic Toolkit to Free You From Stress and Anxiety'. It was an uphill battle for a long time but dedication, consistency, and above all, passion to make a difference, had pulled me through this, and voila! The course was born.

Guess what? We were given an award for being in the top 100 resilient, transformational and innovative businesses in the Leeds region.

This shows our sheer hard work and dedication in action.

More recently, we were also given the International Women's Day Award for Health and Wellbeing.

Three awards in eight months! I didn't even expect to get one. I never started this for the awards or recognition; I did this purely because I had the ability to help, and I decided to use it.

Whilst I was writing this story, I came to realise that when I was going through so much (not everything I went through is written here), I didn't feel the harshness of reality. It was because I believed in myself and always had an outcome or a goal in mind that I was working towards. I didn't see the problems as problems, I saw them as challenges that I needed to overcome to achieve the life I wanted.

I have no regret; every decision I have ever made has taught me what I know today and without each step in my life, I wouldn't be who I am today and I wouldn't have come to what I'm most passionate about. But even though I am lucky enough to say I have no regrets, I would like to remind anyone reading my story, that you must take control of your life and not wait for your life to control you. Your destiny is in your hands; you just have to persevere and remain focused.

My husband is my rock. My children are my inspiration and my in-laws are my home. I go to India once a year and I get to be the princess again, I get to feel the love I miss and because I work hard, I have the financial freedom I need to do that.

The girl who was once a princess is now a queen who stands in her true power.

When I talk about my life journey in detail to people, they are shocked as to what they hear and ask, "How do you manage? How have you come out stronger than before? And how are you so positive, no matter what is going on in your life?"

So my final message to you, beautiful people, is that whilst I have embraced the importance of me, I invite you to **Embrace the Importance of being YOU** and live a life of expansion, prosperity and alignment.

So, that's my story and to thank you for taking the time to hear it, I would like to give you two simple steps to take away with you today, steps to help you become a better version of YOU.

Step one: Develop self-respect and self-love because you are the most important person in the world.

Step two: Look at the issues/crisis at hand with a solution focused approach. This approach will then give you the confidence to make better decisions and choices.

And remember, no matter what life throws at you, you have the ability to handle it and turn it into whatever you want.

Never settle for less than you deserve.

New Woman 33

Ritu Sharma

I Am Home

"I found it within me!"

"I want to go home," my heart cried out to me.

"But where is home?" responded my mind in a fraction of a second.

And all the systems inside of me collapsed into a heap of ash.

This was my internal dialogue and my personal representation for the first 40 years of my life.

At 39, I was a highly educated, happy looking, five foot tall, professional woman. I'd had my experiences with 'life' and on the outside, people would say that I had successfully got my shit together. But internally, this is what I was asking myself on a regular basis and I was full of anxiety.

It's amazing that the strongest realisations happen when you least expect them, when you have let your barriers down and you actually feed yourself lies that all is well. That finally you have got all ends covered.

I think I was just at this point in my life.

That time a new learning had made itself visible. That everyone I thought I could count on had withdrawn all straws of support and was okay to let me crash, burn and die. There was no one I could turn to.

I wanted to rush back home. I wanted to hide. I wanted to go to my place of comfort. I wanted to go home! I had a house that I lived in, but home... no!

A year ago from that point, I had officially become homeless. I was a single mother struggling to make ends meet, looking successful on the outside but totally distraught on the inside. I had lived in a rented house for the last two years that had just got burgled. My children were extremely terrified and my six-year-old refused to even go back inside. That rented house was no home anyways!

It had been so difficult to find a place to live with my then eight- and four-year-old kids after walking away from my marital 'home'. This had happened unplanned as a result of a physical assault from my then-husband. This incident had snatched the only place that I had ever considered home at some point. Now, I was so unsafe and so unhappy that it didn't come anywhere close to being a safe space for me or my children.

Anyway, the house that got burgled was all that I had at that time. I had managed somehow to put my life together. And then the burglary! They took the last of the little I had at the time. After getting divorced, it left me with huge debts, no money and limited income, a great deal of emotional wreckage, and yet the realisation that I was homeless beat it all!

That night, I spent the night sleeping (more like crying) on the floor of my neighbour's living room. I felt as if the whole universe was working against me and was bent on breaking my will to carry on, snatching my hope away that it would all be well one day. Feeling homeless was not new to me, but physically being homeless was.

This took me back to the time when I was young, dependent on my parents, a student, not knowing what direction I was headed in. It's just hurt that I could remember.

I was 20 years old, riding my two-wheeler Kinetic Honda to university, and I had to park on a side road to allow myself some crying time. Tears were blurring my vision and I couldn't carry on any further. I was so angry, upset and frustrated. I was heading towards my lessons from home. Half an hour earlier, I had been labelled a 'problem child' because I was winning appreciations and awards for being the university's best actress! I had brought shame upon the family and they wished I never existed. This was actually said in very clear words to me. That day, I went to my lessons, laughed and joked with my friends, snapped at the janitor in a corridor and returned to my parents' house and continued to live there.

I was seriously suicidal at the age of 21 and did make an attempt but was saved. The universe did me a favour. It was not letting me go anywhere unless I had honoured and shouldered the work that was assigned to me. Obviously, I had no clue then and was a nervous wreck at the time.

I used to look back and try and understand why and how that happened. How on earth I ceased to believe that the house I lived in was not home to me?

The one answer that comes to me is that possibly it was so because of my non-existent relationship with my mother. If you cannot relate to your mum, who can you relate to? If your mother doesn't feel love for you, are you even allowed to think that you could ever be lovable? For many years, I could not bear the sound of all these songs sung in praise of greatness of a mother. Why was I denied that privilege of unconditional love?

Bless her soul! She could not love me as hers, and I understand it now as I have an idea of how our souls are meant to go through experiences that help us to develop ourselves better. It was unbearably painful at the time but I can look back today and be thankful to God for each and every experience He has blessed me with. My biological mother was a helpful person and kind to many. But I totally believe that her and I have no spiritual connection anywhere. However, she did me the biggest favour ever. She showed me how a mother should and should not be. She shaped me into the most loving and caring mother.

In all honesty, I was a stubborn one too. I believe that it's my father's gene. I had challenged the social boxes and frames that I did not fit into. Feeling unheard and not understood, I had embraced rebellion and cut myself off mentally from my family. I refused to submit to the expectations my surroundings had of me. Any figure of authority would not have liked this. Neither did my dad. He was a hard-working, responsible dad and wanted the best for me. Unfortunately, his best did not fit into my 'happy'.

At one point, at the age of 24, I was held hostage in my parents' house for nine long months, where I was not allowed to make or receive phone calls, go anywhere, or see anyone. The dispute was about me wanting to marry a particular man of my liking who my high-status family disapproved of.

One particular night changed everything forever during this period. That night, situations and circumstances indicated that possibly I could be the next tally on an honour killings list. I was terrified and couldn't sleep for the whole night. I tossed in my bed for half the night, and the other half I paced up and down in the lobby of the house. That night kind of snipped any threads of hope or love I thought I had attached to that house and its inhabitants. People with whom I should have felt safest with, had made me feel most unsafe. I did not die that night, but all my feelings of belonging did.

I got married and spent 11 years of my marriage with the man I believed was the love of my life. I poured my sweat and blood into making a home with him. I made his family mine. I adopted his dreams and made them mine. In a desperation of trying to create a happy home, I gave everything I had. I wanted a home at any cost, and I wanted it so bad.

What I was failing to realise was that there was no home anywhere in this world, unless I created one within me. I had to develop some self-acceptance and had to learn self-love. I had to learn to remind myself to un-bow my head and be who I was meant to be, shedding the shame and guilt I was carrying of not keeping the norm and being a 'good girl'! I moved 11 times in my first 12 years in the UK without objecting, nine times just silently, following my then-husband's wish. Looking for a home!

The inevitable happened and at the age of 36, I was seriously suicidal again. My marriage was breaking down and I was totally distraught. This time, I had to be responsible for my two children, aged four and eight at the time. The idea of my happiness was nowhere to be seen. I kept questioning God, "Why is this happening to me?" What I couldn't see for myself then was that everything was happening **for** me!

I wandered the streets of my town for hours every day for months like a mad woman, fighting my self-harming thoughts, hurting for my failure and feeling sorry for my babies. What had I done? How had I ended up there? Where do I go from here? The man with whom I had made my home with was not my safe home at all. And then, one day, in a dire need to protect myself and my children from any further exposure to ugly situations, I left that house with my kids and I went on to the next phase of my journey.

It is then I realised in a series of events that a human being is alone at the end of the day. We expect people to stand by us. We expect them to feel for us like we felt for them, to have our back. But what we forget is that they are them, not you! Just because you feel for them and would go far to help and protect them, they do not have to feel or act in the same manner. I learnt this big lesson in a series of rejections over the next couple of years. I felt let down and lost even further. I was yearning to relate and be home.

What happens when you hit rock bottom? What happens when you know this can't get any worse? When you are at the lowest of the low point? You realise that you cannot go any further down. I had hit rock bottom and had started to see how it was going to shape mine and my children's future. And I was not okay with it. I had to rise back up.

I was reaching my fortieth year. In that phase of my life, probably for the first time, I made a conscious choice. I was going to get a home for myself. I was going to choose love over everything else. I was going to let my hurts speak and be heard. I decided to not pretend to be happy any more. I chose to be happy instead. In that moment, I knew that this independence and fulfilment was going to come to me at a price yet again. And I was ready. I was ready to finally take responsibility for my life and pick a life of purpose. I was not going to let anyone tell me how a woman's life should be. I refused to be 'normal' and fit into boundaries and barriers. I decided to let myself shine in full vigour. I was going to finally belong. I was going to be home!

I started shedding skins that I had kept on for all these years; that of guilt and shame, that of embarrassed existence, that of unworthiness of love, that of being lost. I want to say here that the above did not happen in a day or two. It is a journey. Each realisation is valuable. Each step is a leap. Each experience is necessary.

I embarked on a journey of finally getting myself 'home'. At the age of 40, I finally bought a house that actually felt like my place. Every time I walked into my house, I felt a surge of pride, love and belonging. I was happy to see my children growing organically in absence of social and cultural pressures.

And then the best thing ever happened to me. I discovered the mantra of fulfilment. The ultimate secret of having a home for forever, of belonging, of being in a safe space always, and of growth and happiness. I found my home and it was not far at all!

I found it within me!

I have often looked back and analysed, or tried to analyse, how and why everything happened and a few things become quite visible.

The most important one is definitely the understanding that one's blood family is not always where one belongs. It is great if that happens. As humans, we are programmed to belong with our people, our families. And I believe that it must be such a great feeling. I yearned to be that one person too for years. To belong. The universe had different plans.

Each one of us is on our own journey of discovering why we are here in this world. And contributing to others' journeys as well. And with this huge understanding, I cannot help but be full of gratitude. Be hugely thankful to God for creating this life of struggles and pain that catalysed me to become who I am today and give me an understanding of fellow humans at so many levels.

My circumstances were unusual, where lessons of self-worth did not come from my parents. They were on their own journeys. They had their own battles to fight and I truly believe that they did the best they could. It took me 40 years to make peace with the hurt that came from this lack of self-love.

I am totally thankful to both my parents for doing all they did for me, especially my high-class education. Even their inability to love and understand me as a child and young adult, turned out to be a blessing.

My ex-husband played a major role in preparing me to take the next big step. I used to believe that I was the cursed one. That everyone else had a home and I did not. That he was the reason for my homelessness. But I couldn't have been far from the truth. Today, I am so thankful to him too.

My siblings for whom I pray on a regular basis now and had always loved dearly. Had they not rejected me at the right time, I would not know the greatness that lies within me. I would possibly never have been introduced to my ability to grow new roots. I would not even have been totally liberated!

Some of my friends dumped me at the most vulnerable phase of my life. They were the people who needed to go, so a space for new, true friends could be made. I am thankful for their decisions too.

On my way to make peace with my hurt, it dawned upon me that every other woman is facing a challenge in this world. I could now see that I was one of the few, most privileged ones who has the gift of education, a voice that can be used, and a wealth of experiences. I am thankful.

I decided to turn around the narrative and become 'home' to those who needed it.

My actions of giving back helped me grow new roots. I am now helping myself by helping women to see that they are not bags of unworthy, useless burdens that some person or situation has made them to believe. They all have within them what they need to shine and be happy. And that self-love is the key.

My organisation, Kaushalya UK, works on that principle solely.

I get praised and appreciated now for the work I do. The truth is that I am the one person who is benefitting the most from my work. My happiness comes from this. My roots are becoming stronger. I am growing myself.

My businesses are flourishing and every day I learn something new about myself. There are so many things that are revealed to me, things about me that I did not know I was capable of. I stop by my mirror sometimes and tell myself that I am worthy of all the love and happiness. That I belong!

Another biggest realisation I have had is that my home was not meant to be with others. It was not meant to be created out of the love of others for me, but my own love for me. The notion that I did not feel that I belonged anywhere was down to the fact that I did not belong with myself. I was so used to bending over backwards for others, to please them and see my worth, that I failed to realise that I had to be the first one to see it.

So far, it has been a beautiful journey, that of massive lessons and realisations. The best gift I received on the way is that I found my home. I found the key to the front door and I am at peace with myself. For the first time ever in my life, I am at peace. I feel that I am where I should be, surrounded by those I should be with, doing what I should be and loving myself the way I should be.

Today, I am home with myself and am immensely pleased that I possibly will be signposting many towards theirs...

…that 'I am home!'

I dedicate my journey and my chapter to my daughters, Sajal and Sehaj.

I feel honoured and grateful to have been chosen to be their mother.

Epilogue

The New Woman: Stories of Kintsugi Experiences has been a beautiful journey of learning and growth for all who have been associated with it.

This book is the first of a trilogy that Kaushalya UK plans to publish. There are so many incredible women with so many incredible, inspirational stories and we want to bring them all to those who can gather inspiration from them.

While working on this book, one belief that was affirmed and reaffirmed is each and every struggle, is a valuable lesson in disguise. If you continue to believe in yourself, you **will** conquer.

The Contributors of The New Woman

New Woman 1
Illa Khagram

Illa is a Certified Master Teacher, a Guan Yin Lineage holder, Tao Song Practitioner, Tao Calligraphy Master Practitioner, Tao Hands Practitioner, and a Love, Peace, Harmony Ambassador.

While spending time in Ashram, she advanced on a spiritual journey. She learnt meditation to heal pain and hurt. She has been personally mentored and guided by the *E-Myth* author, Michael E. Gerber, combining business with the spiritual aspect.

Illa specialises in peaceful evolutionary systems (PES) within families, finances and business. Her passion is to serve souls to bring Love, Peace, and Harmony in their lives and she is a devoted humanitarian, making a difference wherever she can.

www.illakhagram.com

www.facebook.com/radiantlotusinternational

Facebook group: Love, Peace, Harmony Movement UK

New Woman 2
Tiffany Henkel

Tiffany Henkel is an aspiring Content Creator, Coach, and Writer, set to explore her life's mission of broadening the perspective of self-love within a woman's life journey. This is her first published piece, and she continues to pursue the use of other platforms to share her knowledge and wisdom learned through her own journey. Currently, Tiffany is an accomplished technical project manager at a global healthcare IT corporation, a five-year goal she manifested. She is a source of positivity to her co-workers, friends, and family members. She lives in the Midwest of the United States with her cat named Kevin.

www.birthofakcbeauty.wordpress.com
Instagram: @birthofabeautykc
www.linkedin.com/TiffanyHenkel

New Woman 3
Andrea Malam

Andrea Malam-Alexander is an award-winning Charity and Volunteer Ambassador, Community Champion, Author, Speaker and Diversity Role Model who enjoys making an impact, inspiring and motivating others.

A Crown Medal recipient for exemplary service for her role in law enforcement towards protecting the public, Andrea has supported her work colleagues with diversity and Inclusion matters.

Andrea is the Founder Trustee of the charity Saving Dreams, helping to alleviate suffering alongside enabling children to escape poverty with education and support. The charity supports various projects, helping thousands of underprivileged children and their families worldwide.

Andrea was born in India to parents of British ancestry but then settled in London, in the UK.

www.savingdreams.org.uk
www.andreamalam.co.uk
www.linkedin.com/in/andrea-malam-alexander-b38aa313a

New Woman 4
Hafiza Khatun

Hafiza is a 45-year-old mother to three children, residing in Walsall. She is originally from Newcastle upon Tyne. Hafiza moved to Walsall in 1995 when she got married. She is currently working in admin in a local secondary school, which she loves. Hafiza's main struggle in life is her health – she has numerous conditions which she suffers from on a daily basis.

Her main aim in life is to help as many people as she can in any way possible. Through all her struggles, she has learned not to take anything for granted, taking each day at a time and appreciating every new day.

www.facebook.com/profile.php?id=100043697181537

New Woman 5
Jenni Harris

Jenni Harris is a Certified Trainer /Coach and franchise owner with Feel The Fear Academy. She also has an online jewellery business, Sparkle In Style.

Jenni has several years' experience in sales and marketing, and has been a top performer in direct sales. A published author, she contributed to her first book in 2020. Jenni is a former police sergeant, having served nearly 27 years with West Midlands Police. Her passion is helping women overcome their fears so that they can be the very best version of themselves.

Married nearly 24 years, being a mum of two is her greatest achievement. Jenni's goal is to help women learn to stop playing small so they can achieve their goals.

https://linktr.ee/JenniHarris

New Woman 6
Azmina Jiwa

Azmina Jiwa is a Personal Development Trainer, Coach, Mentor, an International Speaker, Neuro-Linguistic Practitioner and an author of *Freedom to Be ME*. Her new-found passion and purpose came at the age of 40, when she found the freedom to express her own unique authentic self.

As a Personal Freedom Champion, she empowers others to be fearless, visible and vibrant. She leads them to open doors with her signature programme, '5 Keys for Freedom to be YOU', so they can experience happiness, fulfilment and peace.

Azmina is a mother of two successful kids and grandmother of two darling grandkids. Originally from Uganda, of Indian origin, she now lives in Surrey, United Kingdom.

www.azminajiwa.com
www.linkedin.com/in/azmina-jiwa-6a15849/
Twitter: @freedom2b_me

New Woman 7
Donna Joseph

Donna Joseph is an Author and a Speaker with her own *Good Vibrations* radio show and *Searching for Truth* podcast. Being mixed race and adopted into a white family, Donna spent her childhood seeking to belong, which – through many twists and turns – led her down a powerful road of self-discovery and awakening. Donna now sees all her previous experiences as gifts and uses her story and passion to share these gifts with others.

Donna is also an NLP practitioner and mindfulness coach. She lives in Birmingham in the UK with her husband and son.

www.donnajoseph.co.uk
Twitter: @iamdonnajoseph
www.linkedin.com/in/donna-joseph-6a277a6/

New Woman 8
Mirabel Ngong

Mirabel Ngong is a public relations specialist and women's rights advocate. She believes in sustainable societies where men and women have access to quality education and mentoring to explore their full potential and actively contribute in sustainable development.

Mirabel wants to inspire young people, She wants young people to look at her and say, "Because of you, I did not give up."

Mirabel has seven years of work experience and skills in media communication, public speaking, writing, planning, facilitation, project management and online advocacy campaigns.

www.cepcameroon.org
www.linkedin.com/in/mirabel-ngong-20757590
www.facebook.com/ngongmirabel.nfihkel

New Woman 9
Maureen A Lewis

I was born in Walsall, UK, to Jamaican parents who came over from the Caribbean to the UK, as part of the Windrush generation. I have been married for over 35 years to a great leader and have four wonderful children.

I currently work for a local women's charity, a job which I love. Working within the voluntary sector has enabled me to find my passion for helping people less fortunate. My dream is to impact and make a difference to the lives of people. Empowering them to be the best version of themselves and fulfilling their God given purpose.

Instagram: @maudy_lou
Twitter @maudylou
https://www.walsallbsc.co.uk/about/meet-the-staff/

New Woman 10

Nina N

Nina is a stroke survivor, cancer survivor and a keen yogi. Having lost the ability to read following her stroke, she is now a qualified English teacher living in London. As an advocate of holistic health and a strong believer in equality, she has worked in refugee camps in the West Bank, Palestine, and continues to stand up for the injustice and plight of refugees.

Having escaped an abusive relationship and battled with self-worth, she shares her journey here for the first time; a story of strength, courage and resilience, and finally finding a voice.

https://www.facebook.com/nina.nuna.3998/

New Woman 11
Sangeeta Patel

Sangeeta Patel has been a nursery nurse within the health visiting arena in the National Health Service for the last 13 years. She specialises in Child Health Development and Wellbeing, supporting parents with health promotions and encouraging their child to develop.

She qualified at Walsall College of Technology and later completed a Family Link Worker course.

Sangeeta has been a carer most of her life and is very compassionate about charity work, bringing the community together and feeding the homeless.

She can quite easily engage herself in comedy shows from her living room literally LOL to take her away from stresses and strains…

www.facebook.com/sangeeta.patel.180

New Woman 12

Ruth Cyster-Stuettgen

Ruth Cyster-Stuettgen is a mum of three is from Melbourne, Australia. She's a Women's Business Breakthrough and Corporate Performance Coach, Speaker and Founder of Inspired Woman TV, and Lunch & Learn for Women in Business. She brings with her more than 30 years' experience in the policing, teaching, training and small business industry, and has founded several businesses in Europe and Australia.

Passionate about Women's Empowerment, Ruth published *From Misery to Mastery: Journey to Freedom and Empowerment*, helping women rebuild their lives after adversity. She spearheaded *The Book of Inspiration for Women by Women*, a coffee table book with daily inspiration by women and girls across the globe. Ruth is passionate about giving back to her community.

www.ruthstuettgen.com
www.linkedin.com/in/ruthstuettgen
Twitter: @ruthstuettgen

New Woman 13
Samantha Pearce

Samantha Pearce is a soon-to-be published singer-songwriter known as Kiani, along with her brand 'Inspired To Inspire' which focuses on community development projects and ways to engage with the community sharing experiences and knowledge. Samantha is also the Founder of an International Women's Day celebration 'I Am Woman', which launched in 2020, and Radio Host and Producer at Hope Radio FM.

Samantha and her mother, Yvette Pearce, who also features in this writing collective were both born and raised in Walsall. From a young age, Samantha knew she would grow up to have an impact in her community through the arts, which she indeed has.

In 2019, Samantha had a near-death experience that changed her life forever. That was the day she knew she was here for a purpose.

www.facebook.com/kianismusicworld

New Woman 14
Poonam Karwal

Poonam is an entrepreneur who started this positive journey with three aims in mind: to help herself; to help others; and to raise her children to the best of her ability. She has worked closely with hundreds of vulnerable people up and down the country striving to give those in need a better chance in life. Poonam believes that life is short, and every day should be lived to its max. She has always dreamt of writing and is now excited to put pen to paper and share her story; if it makes a difference to one person, then her goal will be achieved. God bless.

www.facebook.com/poonamdevi.karwal

New Woman 15
Sonal Dave

Sonal has led an exciting and eclectic career starting as a child performer with The English National Opera and Sadler's Wells. Now as a multi-passionate, she brings her passions together as an award-winning celebrant, toastmaster, public speaking expert, published author and magistrate.

Sonal has won the hearts of many, won awards and been featured in mainstream publications. Daring to follow her dreams at the age of 50, despite setbacks and health issues, through her passion for diversity and inclusion, Sonal set up her entrepreneurial business, inspiring others to break down barriers to follow their dreams and to find their voice.

www.sonaldave.com
www.linkedin.com/in/sonaldave68
Twitter: @sonaldave68

New Woman 16
Jaswinder Challi

Award-winning Jaswinder Challi is a Fellow Accredited Hypnotherapy Society Hypnotherapist, Psychotherapist, Yogi, Counsellor and Spiritual Energy Healing Practitioner. She is a teacher of Counselling and Hypnotherapy as well as yoga and meditation.

Jaswinder is the co-author of seven books and is pursuing a love of writing by submitting articles for the Hypnotherapy Society and blogs. She is looking forward to publishing her own book by the end of 2021. In March 2021, she received an international award for Education and Writing. She also received an award from Mahesh Yogi (ex-Beatle guru) for cultural integration.

Jaswinder has been on many radio programmes and TV shows; she even met Prince Charles as part of a community project and was interviewed by the BBC regarding his visit. She loves to spend time in nature and practicing mandala ceremonies.

www.jaz-nur.com
www.linkedin.com/jaswinderchalli
www.facebook.com/jaswinder.challi

New Woman 17
Yvette Pearce

Yvette Pearce - Emotional Breakthrough Life Strategist, founder of Unique Coaching for You - is a passionate leader who works with women to release the emotional blocks and break the emotional chains that keep them stuck in a pattern that no longer serves them.

Yvette confidently serves her clients through one-to-one coaching, healing and renewal retreats and story-telling.

She believes that the intuition and wisdom of women as leaders are the missing phenomena that can transform society; once our broken places are healed, we can make this world a unique place to be.

www.uniquecoaching4you.org

New Woman 18
Sophie Kemoko

Sophie Kemoko is entrepreneur, mentor, coach, speaker, beauty Consultant with Mary Kay cosmetics, and the owner of an Afro-Caribbean cosmetics shop. As a woman coach, she is successfully building a unit of empowering, successful, inspiring, uplifting women so they can live their life on their terms and achieve their dreams. She is married to one amazing husband, Bruno, with seven smart, beautiful children. She lives in Walsall, in the UK.

www.marykay.co.uk/skemoko
www.facebook.com/sophiekemoko

New Woman 19
Suman Manghra

As a Masters NLP Coach, with a Master's Degree in Work Psychology and Business, Suman teaches people mindset mastery and manifestation, supporting them with personal, professional and spiritual development. Her exclusive Manifestation Matrix gives people clarity on their goals and she carries out one-to-one healing work to help them remove mental and emotional blocks which may be in the way, helping them discover their "flow energy".

In addition to her training and coaching, Suman enjoys walks in the park with her dog Kiki, loves indulging in a good self-help book, and likes to binge on Netflix with her husband too!

www.facebook.com/ManifestationMaven
Twitter: @SumanManghra
www.linkedin.com/in/sumanmanghra

New Woman 20
Saboohi Gill

Saboohi is a Cognitive Behavioural Therapist who helps clients experiencing grief, trauma and other psychological issues. For years, she worked with women who have suffered abuse. Psychology and theology are Saboohi's passions and she has an MA Honours degree in Theology. Saboohi finds it intriguing to learn about people's beliefs, how it impacts their way of being and their interactions with others. Saboohi supports essential inter-faith dialogue; she believes accepting and respecting our differences can reduce religious and cultural tensions.

Saboohi has three children and a very supportive husband. She writes poetry and enjoys music, nature and food.

www.facebook.com/saboohi.gill
www.linkedin.com/in/saboohi-gill-1331041ab

New Woman 21
Bal Heer

Bal Heer is a multi-award winner of Best Independent Estate Agency 2020 & 2021, West Midlands and Real Estate Businesswoman of the Year 2020 & 2021, as well as being a successful entrepreneur, public speaker and proud mother to two sons. She is also the founder and CEO of Regional Homes Ltd, established in 2014.

Bal has taken her business from a serviced office above a restaurant in June 2014 to a prominent standalone high street location in Smethwick, Birmingham in March 2015 and has consequently expanded further with a second branch in Wolverhampton in 2019. Bal has cemented her reputation through her commitment to integrity, honesty, hard work and determination to succeed as a collective and as an individual.

Bal is identifiable by her transparency, her true to her word approach, sincerity and respect.

www.regionalhomesltd.com
www.linkedin.com/in/bal-heer-345a13140/

New Woman 22
Jemma Rosenthal

Jemma Rosenthal is a performer, artist and creative life coach. She is the founder of Creative Hearts, and co-host of *Find Tell Share*, the Storytellers Podcast. She is also a multi-passionate creative, actor, singer-songwriter, dancer-choreographer, speaker, poet, and now author. Jemma loves supporting others in coming home to their Creative Selves! Receiving the Blend Kitchens Entrepreneur of the year 2019 for Find Your Voice, Jemma holds a BA (Hons) in Professional Dance and Musical Theatre as well as a Level 5 Diploma in NLP Performance (Life) Coaching.

Brought up in Sheffield, in the UK, Jemma also enjoys meditation, art and creative cooking. She is grateful to be able to uplift people by using her voice and helping others to find their voice.

www.storiesinbusiness.org.uk/find-tell-share
Twitter: @jemmarosenthal
www.linkedin.com/in/jemma-rosenthal-b78ba4204

New Woman 23
Susanne Virtanen

Susanne Virtanen is the founder of DiscoverChange. Her mission is to create positive change in the world through supporting businesses and transformational leaders.

Susanne provides innovative business development and digital transformation solutions to businesses, teams, charities and universities. With an awarded management degree and qualifications in teaching, training and change management, she has always been passionate about enabling others to reach their full potential in business.

Susanne sees life as an exciting adventure, and building your dream business is possibly the most exciting and rewarding journey of all. To make this process highly efficient and enjoyable, she provides informative and comprehensive training workshops and business development and growth solutions, found in:

www.idiscoverchange.com

New Woman 24
Maxine Palmer-Hunter

Maxine Palmer-Hunter is an award-winning Educator, and Health and Social Care advocate who, for over 24 years, has been dedicated to the elimination of injustice, inequality and discrimination evident throughout her life and career for young people, women and men.

As a Counsellor and Mental Health practitioner, she has undergone mental plastic surgery to unpeel the protective mask she had worn in her past to protect her heart and sanity. Overcoming adversity, she now stands courageously in her strength, resilience and transparency aiming to offer insight, courage, empowerment and hope to others in overcoming trauma and healing from adversity.

Raise2020m@hotmail.com

New Woman 25
Diksha Chakravarti

Diksha has worked as an Integrated Pain, Stress & Anxiety Therapist for over 20 years. Because of Covid, she has decided to focus on helping women. She knows of women who have had mental health issues for this particular reason. She has helped more than 800 clients, regularly gives presentations on how to manage stress, is an avid blogger, and has published articles in *BackCare* and *Private Dentistry*. She is a regular guest on BBC Radio Berkshire.

Diksha's family were victims of Uganda's 1972 exodus so she has first-hand experience of becoming a refugee and having to negotiate changing cultural landscapes. She lives with her 93-year-old mother in Berkshire, UK, and has two wonderful daughters. Her favourite pastimes are climbing mountains, playing tennis and drawing horses.

www.linkedin.com/in/dikshachakravarti/
Twitter: @FixmeDiksha
www.fixme.org.uk

New Woman 26
Delcie Hopley

Delcie Hopley was born and raised in Brownhills, West Midlands, in the UK. She had a happy childhood and life was pretty good on the whole, then she had two life-changing experiences, the first triggered the second which started a whole journey of self-healing, learning and self-realisation. Her experiences have created her desire to help women everywhere to realise their true potential as they walk their path of enlightenment and flourish along the way. As a Reiki Master/ Teacher, Meditation Teacher and Healing Guide, Delcie is driven to help people heal on all levels and take back the power we are all born with. She is mother to her fur baby Rosie, and her love for nature means she spends as much time outdoors as she can, especially if it means she can get in the water, enjoying wakeboarding, scuba diving and snowboarding. She now lives in Walsall, UK.

Facebook Group: Love Reiki
www.linkedin.com/in/delcie-hopley-76824061
Instagram: @lovereiki33

New Woman 27
Rajee S

Rajee is an IT professional who got into most leading-edge spiritual practices as a life calling, and is driven by her passion to create self-development and self-healing spaces.

She is an expert life coach, assisting and empowering women across the globe to gain clarity, achieve goals and illuminate inner-happiness. She transforms them by tapping into their innate-potencies and abilities and to become the "Deliberate creator of their life experiences".

Rajee is an Internationally Certified Transformational Life Coach, Advanced Law of Attraction Facilitator and Hypnotherapist. She has also received an Inspiring Women Achievement Award.

www.inspireandtransform.com
www.facebook.com/rajeeslifecoach
Twitter: @RajeeSLifecoach

New Woman 28
Shazia Nawaz

Shazia Nawaz is a multi-professional; she is an Aesthetic Practitioner BA (Hons), experienced skin expert, beauty trainer, personal development coach and business development consultant, with over 15 years' experience in the UK Civil Service from regulatory bodies to the Ministry of Justice and the Ministry of Defence.

Through sharing her journey of pivotal moments in her life, Shazia aims to empower women to break stereotypes and chains of conformity that have been imposed and constructed by South Asian cultures.

Shazia is a resilient and proud mother of three, a 'twins mom' and 'Autism mom' and domestic abuse survivor. She hopes to set up her own charity helping South Asian women escape abuse, violence and oppression through safe housing, as well as empowering women to gain vital skills to become independent women whilst under her wings of support.

www.facebook.com/shazia.haqnawaz

New Woman 29
Raj Rana

Raj is a confidence coach, property investor and entrepreneur. She is part of a team who have helped over 10,000 people on their personal development as well as business development in seven countries.

She has also helped hundreds of people to grow in confidence by building them up, which has enabled them to stand on their own two feet.

Raj believes the importance of helping others is invaluable, and an opportunity which can only happen if we believe in ourselves first and know our self-worth.

www.facebook.com/rajeshrajni.rana

New Woman 30
Sandhya

Sandhya is a kind and loveable person, full of love and energy, always having a thirst to serve the community, especially children. She is passionate about promoting her country's rich heritage and culture. Her motive is to set a great career path for her two children and give them every happiness she can. She wants to reach to a position where she can do even more good to the younger generation and society. She is the Founder and Director of India Island Academy which promotes Indian Arts and wants her company to reach greater heights which would benefit more and more people and families. She wants to inspire and be a great support for women, especially single mums of Indian origin, who are struggling to cope with the demands and challenges of everyday life while living in the West. She is the winner of several awards: Best Telugu Mahila of the Year 2019, Sutra Excellence Award 2021 in the category of Education & Social Activities, and Shubhodayam Velugu Award 2021 for engaging the community during lockdown.

Facebook: Sandhya Aaytee, indiaislandacademy
Twitter: @indiaislandacademy
Instagram: @indiaislandacademy

New Woman 31
Jayasri Banala

I am Jayasri Banala Ganesh, known as Jaya. I am IT professional and I work full-time. I am also a mother to a gorgeous 17-year-old young lady and wife to a caring husband. I love myself as much as I love my family. I will do anything for their happiness and well-being. I am a qualified classical dancer...Bharatanatyam. My pastime is dancing.

I am very passionate of knowing the values of Sanatana Dharma that India speaks of. While walking on this path, I discovered that my passion is to teach the young generation Sanskrit shlokas. As I understand it, the utterances of Sanskrit words have immense and positive impact on your psychology and surroundings. I teach young children divine shlokas every Saturday and Sunday.

I sponsor an under-privileged girl student in India as well as a cow shed for annum in India as the cow is most sacred. I am active participant in community events and have raised money by participating in 10k runs in Birmingham.

New Woman 32
Monika Bammi

Monika Bammi is a Reiki Master, Wellbeing Coach and an NLP Practitioner. With 25 years' corporate experience, she recognised the need for a more holistic approach to managing daily stress. Monika is the founder of Divine Health & Wellbeing and was awarded The Holistic Specialist of the Year 2020 by Corporate Livewire Prestige Awards.

Through writing social media posts and courses, Monika has found a love of writing.

Monika's mission is to enable thousands of people to release their negative past, be in the moment and be excited about their future.

Monika is a mother of three beautiful daughters.

www.masterdivinehealth.com
www.linkedin.com/in/monikabammi/
Twitter: @BammiMonika

New Woman 33
Ritu Sharma

Ritu Sharma is a women empowerment ambassador and personal development trainer, professional speaker, educator and an author. She is a multi-award-winning women's coach and speaker and spreads the message of empowerment and upliftment for one and all. In addition, she is the author of *Rich Man's Poor Daughter*. She is the founder and CEO of Kaushalya UK, an organisation which is dedicated to empowering women.

Ritu Sharma's vision for future is that of woman leadership. She has personally taken this responsibility on herself and runs projects to create women leaders in their respective fields.

www.ritusharma.co.uk
www.linkedin.com/in/womenemp0wer
Twitter: @womenemp0wer